COLERIDGE

Critic of Society

Oxford University Press, Amen House, London E.C.4

GLASGOW   NEW YORK   TORONTO   MELBOURNE   WELLINGTON
BOMBAY   CALCUTTA   MADRAS   KARACHI   KUALA LUMPUR
CAPE TOWN   IBADAN   NAIROBI   ACCRA

COLERIDGE

Critic of Society

BY

JOHN COLMER

Senior Lecturer in English
University of Khartoum

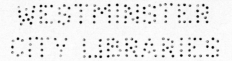
OXFORD
AT THE CLARENDON PRESS
1959

© *Oxford University Press* 1959

PRINTED IN GREAT BRITAIN

TO D.M.C.

PREFACE

I HOPE that this work will fill a gap in Coleridge studies and that it will reveal to the general reader an unexpected side of the poet's mind. It is based on the published political works; the original papers of Coleridge's journals, *The Watchman* and *The Friend*; the relevant files of the *Morning Post* and the *Courier*; and upon the manuscript Notebooks and other miscellaneous manuscript material in the British Museum and elsewhere.

I have dealt with the published works in strict chronological order so as to demonstrate the development of Coleridge's ideas—though indeed I am not primarily concerned with the evolution of his political theory as such—and because I felt that what the student and general reader needed was a straightforward account of each of the political works, the circumstances of its publication, and a discussion of the social and political criticism contained therein. Much of the published material is unfortunately inaccessible and is likely to remain so until new editions of the prose works and journalism appear, but I hope that the following pages will direct attention to the original works and will lead readers to wonder why they have not been reprinted. Selections have been made, for example, in *The Political Thought of Samuel Taylor Coleridge*, by R. J. White, who has also republished, though with some revisions and omissions, the two *Lay Sermons* in *Political Tracts of Wordsworth, Coleridge and Shelley*; but selections, particularly of Coleridge, are a poor substitute for the original.

This is the first study of Coleridge's political writings to make use of the vast amount of manuscript material that has recently been acquired by the British Museum. Frequently the Notebooks throw new light on the published works and they contain passages of penetrating social criticism that never found their way into print. The Notebooks demonstrate how much time Coleridge devoted to thoughts about society. He might have claimed, with far greater justice than Wordsworth, that 'he had given twelve hours thought to the condition and prospect of society for one to poetry'. And the Notebooks reveal a speculative daring, a spontaneity and forthrightness, which contrast strangely with the guarded, somewhat muffled pronouncements in many of his published works. They provide interesting evidence of his failure to establish a satisfactory relationship with a chosen public and to evolve an appropriate style and form of address for each; his continuous preoccupation with this problem; and of his constant but quite unnecessary fear that his words might breed sedition.

I am deeply indebted to all who have laboured in the field of Coleridge studies before me. But for the enthusiasm of Humphry House I should never have been led to explore Coleridge's political journalism; and I owe a special debt to Miss Kathleen Coburn for her encouragement at a critical moment in the genesis of this study and for allowing me to consult her typescript of two of the most illegible of the Notebooks, to consult other Notebooks before she took them to Toronto, and for permission to quote from the first volume of her edition of *The Notebooks*. I am also grateful to Professor J. Isaacs, Mrs. Barbara Hardy, and Professor J. W. Lever for reading an earlier draft of this study and for making important suggestions. Finally, without my wife's patient help and advice, this work would never have been completed.

J. A. C.

University of Khartoum
July 1958

ACKNOWLEDGEMENTS

THIS book is based on a thesis presented to the University of London in 1955 and accepted as satisfying the requirements for the Ph.D. degree.

A few paragraphs have already appeared in notes and articles in *English Studies in Africa*, *Modern Language Review*, and *Notes and Queries*, and I am grateful to the editors of these journals for allowing me to reproduce this material.

I wish to thank Mr. A. H. B. Coleridge for permission to quote from manuscript material of which he holds the copyright; the Bollingen Foundation, Miss Kathleen Coburn, and Messrs. Routledge & Kegan Paul Ltd. for permission to quote from the first volume of *The Notebooks of Samuel Taylor Coleridge*; Professor Earl Leslie Griggs and Messrs. Constable & Co. Ltd. for permission to quote from the *Unpublished Letters of Samuel Taylor Coleridge*; Professor Earl Leslie Griggs and the Delegates of the Clarendon Press for permission to quote from the first two volumes of the *Collected Letters of Samuel Taylor Coleridge*; and William Heinemann Ltd. for permission to quote from the *Letters of Samuel Taylor Coleridge*.

I also wish to thank the Librarian of the Birmingham Public Library for supplying me with information about *The Watchman*; the Librarian of the Bristol Public Library for answering my queries; and the staff of the Reading and Manuscript Rooms of the British Museum for their assistance. I owe a special debt to Mr. Michael Jolliffe, Librarian of the Newbold Library, University of Khartoum, for helping to overcome some of the many difficulties I have encountered in working in this field of study in a young African University. I am very grateful to my colleague, Mr. D. R. Ewen, for reading the proofs and for his advice on many matters.

I have also to acknowledge the receipt of a small grant towards the cost of microfilms and photostats from the University of Khartoum.

CONTENTS

LIST OF PRINCIPAL ABBREVIATIONS

THE following abbreviations are used for works to which reference is frequently made. Place of publication is London except where otherwise stated.

Allsop	*Letters, Conversations and Recollections of S. T. Coleridge*, [ed. T. Allsop,] 1836, 2 vols.
B.L.	*Biographia Literaria*, ed. J. Shawcross, Oxford, 1907, 2 vols.
Church and State	*On the Constitution of the Church and State, according to the Idea of Each*, ed. H. N. Coleridge, 3rd ed., 1839.
C.L.	*Collected Letters of Samuel Taylor Coleridge*, ed. E. L. Griggs, Oxford, 1956, 2 vols. published.
C. Life	*Samuel Taylor Coleridge. A Narrative of the Events of his Life*, by J. D. Campbell, 1894.
E.O.T.	*Essays on His Own Times, Forming a Second Series of The Friend*, by Samuel Taylor Coleridge, edited by his daughter, 1850, 3 vols.
F. (1809)	*The Friend*: A Literary, Moral, and Political Weekly Paper, Excluding Personal and Party Politics and the Events of the Day, Penrith, 1809–10. British Museum, Ashley 2845.
F. (1837)	*The Friend*: A Series of Essays to aid in the Formation of Fixed Principles in Politics, Morals and Religion, ed. H. N. Coleridge, 3rd ed., 1837, 3 vols.
F.	*The Friend*, Bohn's ed. 1865 and frequently reprinted.
L.	*Letters of Samuel Taylor Coleridge*, ed. E. H. Coleridge, 1895, 2 vols.
Lay Sermons	*Lay Sermons*. I. The Statesman's Manual. II. Blessed are ye that sow beside all Waters, ed. Derwent Coleridge, 3rd ed., 1852.
M.P.	*Morning Post*.
N.	*The Notebooks of Samuel Taylor Coleridge*, ed. K. Coburn, 1957, vol. 1 published.
P.J.	*Enquiry concerning Political Justice*, by W. Godwin, ed. F. E. L. Priestley, University of Toronto Press, 1946, 3 vols.
P.W.	*The Complete Poetical Works of Samuel Taylor Coleridge*, ed. E. H. Coleridge, Oxford, 1912, 2 vols.
P.W. (J.D.C.)	*The Poetical Works of Samuel Taylor Coleridge*, ed. with a biographical introduction by J. D. Campbell, 1893.
T.T.	*The Table Talk and Omniana of Samuel Taylor Coleridge*, with additional Table Talk from Allsop's 'Recollections', ed. T. Ashe, Bohn's edition, 1884.

U.L. *Unpublished Letters of Samuel Taylor Coleridge*, ed. E. L. Griggs, 1932, 2 vols.

W. *The Watchman*, Bristol, 1796. A complete set of the original papers that appeared from 1 March to 13 May 1796 is in the British Museum, Ashley 2842.

PERIODICALS

B.N.Y.P.L. *Bulletin of the New York Public Library.*

M.L.N. *Modern Language Notes.*

M.L.R. *Modern Language Review.*

N. & Q. *Notes and Queries.*

R.E.S. *Review of English Studies.*

P.M.L.A. *Publications of the Modern Language Association.*

T.L.S. *The Times Literary Supplement.*

NOTE ON THE TEXT

IN reproducing manuscript material, I have retained Coleridge's own spelling, punctuation, and occasional lapses, thus conforming with the practice of the editors of the *Collected Letters* and *The Notebooks*. For early Notebook entries I have printed the reading in the first volume of *The Notebooks* and supplied a reference to the serial number of the entry. For entries not covered by this volume I have referred direct to the manuscript Notebooks in the British Museum. Passages from the letters are consistently referred to by the page number in the book in which they were published. Only the first two volumes of the *Collected Letters* were available when this study was completed. Except for newly discovered articles, the text of Coleridge's contributions to the *Morning Post* and the *Courier* is based on *Essays on His Own Times*. References throughout are to the most accessible editions of Coleridge's work, early editions being cited only where there is a significant difference.

CHAPTER I

EARLY POLITICS

1. *Christ's Hospital and Cambridge*

COLERIDGE belonged to the generation of young men whose early lives were first irradiated and later clouded by the French Revolution. A new age seemed about to be born. It was a time, Wordsworth wrote, when 'the whole Earth, the beauty wore of promise', one when all ardent spirits,

> Were call'd upon to exercise their skill,
> Not in Utopia, subterraneous Fields,
> Or some secreted Island, Heaven knows where,
> But in the very world which is the world
> Of all of us, the place in which, in the end,
> We find our happiness, or not at all.[1]

Poets as dissimilar in age and temperament as Cowper, Burns, Blake, Southey, and Coleridge hailed with joy 'the morning rainbow of the French Revolution';[2] and at first Whig and Tory politicians alike joined in the general chorus of praise. The most striking effects of the revolutionary fervour were twofold. It gave impetus to the writing of books on political theory, the most influential of which were Burke's *Reflections on the French Revolution*, Tom Paine's *Rights of Man*, Mackintosh's *Vindiciae Gallicae*, and Godwin's *Political Justice*; and it revived interest in parliamentary reform, a subject that had ceased to exercise men's minds since the largely abortive activities of the Yorkshire Freeholders in 1780 and Pitt's failure to secure a moderate degree of reform two years later. Societies of two kinds were now formed: aristocratic societies like the Friends of the People, patronized by the leading Whig politicians, and the lower-class societies that spread rapidly through the kingdom, most of which were modelled on and affiliated to The London Corresponding Society. 'I was a sharer in the general vortex', Coleridge wrote of this tumultuous period, 'though my little world described the path of its revolution in an orbit of its own.'[3] The early path is difficult to reconstruct for neither Coleridge's letters nor the accounts of his contemporaries throw much

---

[1] *The Prelude*, 1805, x. 723–8.   [2] *B.L.* i. 123.   [3] *F.*, p. 140.

light on the period before he met Southey in the summer of 1794, and his retrospective accounts[1] of his political oratory and journalism in Bristol conflict with the evidence supplied by letters, notebooks, and published works, and were clearly coloured by the political views he had later come to adopt and by the need to defend himself from the frequently repeated charges of having been a Jacobin in his youth. He cannot, I think, be held guilty of deliberate misrepresentation, but his conduct on at least one occasion is difficult to defend or excuse. When he issued the rifacimento edition of *The Friend* in 1818, he added the *Introductory Address*, originally printed in Bristol in 1795, to the end of the political section, in order, he said, to prove that the charge that he had been a Jacobin in youth was unfounded. 'The only omissions regard the names of persons', he declared.[2] This was disingenuous, to say the least, as the omission of fairly long passages referring to Joseph Gerrald, Priestley, and Pitt altered the whole tone and spirit of the *Address*. He also omitted his comments on a passage from Brissot's *Travels in America*, since they committed him to a doctrine of economic equalitarianism that he no longer advocated. Clearly it is necessary to examine with the utmost care Coleridge's treatment of his own early years.

At Christ's Hospital Coleridge was flogged by Boyer because he 'sported infidel' after reading Voltaire's *Philosophical Dictionary*. *Cato's Letters* aroused in him a 'rage for metaphysics',[3] but no mention is made in either Coleridge's or Lamb's accounts of this period of a corresponding daring in political opinions. However, it seems likely that the reading of Voltaire and the Whig views of John Trenchard, the part author of *Cato's Letters*, influenced not only his religious but his political thought and predisposed him to welcome joyfully the fall of the *ancien régime*. To celebrate this event he wrote *An ode on the Destruction of the Bastile*, a poem that remained unpublished until 1834. It has little or no poetic merit. It was probably in origin an academic exercise and its rhetorical excesses make it difficult to be certain how much genuine

---

[1] See *B.L.*, chap. x; *F.*, pp. 140-3, 'Once a Jacobin Always a Jacobin'; *M.P.* 21 Oct. 1802; *E.O.T.* ii. 542-52.   [2] *F.*, p. 213.

[3] *C. Life*, p. 13; *C.L.* i. 78. *Cato's Letters* were written by John Trenchard (1662-1723) and Thomas Gordon (d. 1750). In origin they were letters contributed to the *Independent Whig* between 1720 and 1723. They were later printed in volume form and frequently reprinted. Trenchard was a Whig with popular sympathies but by no means a republican.

emotion that event aroused in the boy Coleridge. The last stanza ends on a note of triumphant expectation, that France's example will inspire the whole world with a love of liberty; and this note is given a distinctly patriotic colouring in the two final lines,

> And still, as erst, let favour'd Britain be
> First ever of the first and freest of the free!

At this early date to celebrate the victory of the revolutionary forces in France did not necessarily imply any lack of patriotism. The fall of the Bastille was actually set as a topic for poetic composition at Cambridge and at some of the schools. It was only after February 1793 when England and France were at war that the admirers of the Revolution became subject to a bitter inner conflict, one which many young men, including Wordsworth and Coleridge, resolved temporarily by 'expatriating' their hearts and welcoming 'the victories of the Frenchmen, as the victories of human nature'.[1]

At Cambridge his political interests were more fully engaged than at school. It is clear from C. V. Le Grice's account of the meetings that took place in Coleridge's rooms at Jesus College that he took an eager interest in the pamphlet warfare that was being waged between Burke and the advocates of the French Revolution. 'Ever and anon, a pamphlet issued from the pen of Burke. There was no need of having the book before us. Coleridge had read it in the morning, and in the evening he would repeat whole pages verbatim.'[2] No light is here thrown on his actual views; that they were radical and anti-Burke will soon be apparent. But the reading of Burke undoubtedly left its traces: on the style of early political works and on the thought of the later works. A letter written to Mary Evans on 7 February 1793 contains a reference to his political interests at this time. 'Have you read Mr Fox's letter to the Westminster Electors?' he inquired. 'It is quite the *political Go* at Cambridge, and has converted many souls to the Foxite Faith.'[3] The attraction of this pamphlet for the Cambridge undergraduates who had welcomed the French Revolution, lay in its demand that the Government should 'avert the calamities of war' by negotiating peace with France; and in its impassioned protest against any attempt at home to curtail freedom of opinion

---

[1] *W.*, p. 229. Cf. *The Prelude*, 1805, x. 757–80.
[2] *Gentleman's Magazine*, Dec. 1834.   [3] *C.L.* i. 51.

or expression. When in December 1792 the Ministry had informed the House that it was necessary to call out the Militia to quell the 'spirit of tumult and disorder' Fox had attacked its policy. He asserted that there existed a 'crisis more imminent and tremendous than any that the history of the country ever exhibited', namely 'whether we are to resign the exercise of our natural faculties to the Minister for the time being, or whether we shall maintain that in England no man is criminal, but by commission of overt acts'. He then proceeded to accuse the Minister of erecting 'every man, not only into an inquisitor, but into a spy, into an informer; to set father against father, brother against brother, neighbour against neighbour'.[1] The chief danger of such a policy, as Fox pointed out to the Westminster electors, was that 'we confound the mistaken speculatist with the desperate incendiary',[2] a phrase that throws a world of light on the peculiar predicament of men like William Frend, Godwin, and later of Coleridge himself.

Pitt's general policy of repression produced repercussions within the University of Cambridge during Coleridge's residence. In the winter of 1792 it is recorded that,

An attempt was made in the University and in the town to represent those who differed from Mr Pitt as enemies to the constitution. Associations were formed against Republicans and Levellers, the resolutions against them were expressed in very offensive language, and all those who declined signing them were stygmatised as enemies to their King. The Dissenters (as a body) were included in that number.[3]

Acts of hooliganism by the undergraduates directed at the dissenters were actually condoned by some senior members of the University. For example, an attack on dissenters that led to the reading of the Riot Act was described by one of the tutors of St. John's as a 'laudable ebullition of justifiable zeal'. In view of his dissenting sympathies and radical political opinions it was therefore only to be expected that the trial of William Frend, a fellow and tutor of Jesus, should have aroused excited interest among the undergraduates. In May 1793 he was brought before the Vice-Chancellor's Court for having published the pamphlet *Peace and*

[1] *The Speech of the Right Hon. Charles James Fox . . . at the Opening of Parliament, Dec. 13, 1792*, 5th ed. B.M. 8135. b.13(2).

[2] *A Letter from the Right Honourable Charles Fox, to the Worthy and Independent Electors of the City and Liberty of Westminster*, 1793, p. 14. B.M. 8135.b.13(4).

[3] H. Gunning, *Reminiscences of the University, Town and County of Cambridge from the year 1780*, 2 vols., 1854, pp. 277-8.

Union recommended to the Associated Bodies of Republicans and Anti-Republicans. The main substance of the charge brought against him was that he had offended against the statute *de concionibus* by expressing Unitarian views and by attacking the Established Church; but it must have been clear to all who attended the trial that what had given chief offence were the radical political opinions expressed in the pamphlet; and it was no less clear that the University authorities were determined to stamp out heretical religious and political views by making an example of Frend.[1]

Coleridge was one of those who attended the trial. He made a public demonstration of his sympathy for the accused and narrowly escaped being expelled from the court. The most vivid account of the incident is given by Coleridge's first biographer, Gillman.

> The trial was observed by Coleridge, to be going against Frend, when some observation or speech was made in his favour; a dying hope thrown out as it appeared to Coleridge who, in the midst of the Senate, whilst sitting on one of the benches, extended his hands and clapped them. The Proctor in a loud voice demanded who had committed this indecorum. Silence ensued. The Proctor in an elevated tone, said to a young man sitting near Coleridge, ''Twas you, sir!' The reply was as prompt as the accusation; for, immediately holding out the stump of his right arm, it appeared that he had lost his hand,—'I would, sir,' said he, 'that I had the power.'—That no innocent person should incur blame, Coleridge went directly afterwards to the Proctor, who told him that he saw him clap his hands, but fixed on this person who he knew had not the power. 'You have had,' said he, 'a narrow escape.'[2]

Although the various accounts given of Coleridge's intervention differ in detail, all agree on one main point, that he was bitterly opposed to the spirit that animated the Prosecutor in this case.[3] His action in the court undoubtedly marked him out as a Jacobin in the eyes of the University. That all who openly sympathized with Frend were regarded as Jacobins may be inferred from a letter written by the Vice-Chancellor to Wilberforce: 'I don't believe Pitt

---

[1] For example, it was said, 'That there is tendency in the said pamphlet to disturb the harmony of society', and the promoter, according to Gunning, 'laboured hard to prove that the pamphlet was a seditious one'. Op. cit. See also Howell, T. B. and T. J., *State Trials*, xxii. 575.

[2] J. Gillman, *The Life of Samuel Taylor Coleridge*, 1838, p. 55.

[3] Accounts are given in Gunning, pp. 299–301; D. Stuart, *Gentleman's Magazine*, Aug. 1838, p. 126; and in Gillman. According to Gunning and Stuart, Coleridge was willing to see the innocent man suffer as long as he himself escaped punishment.

was ever aware of how much consequence the expulsion of Frend was; it was the ruin of the Jacobinical party as a University Thing.'[1] But the expulsion of Frend did not bring to an end Coleridge's interest in his fate; two letters to George Dyer ask for news of his activities in London.[2] After the beginning of 1795, however, inquiries cease altogether. Although Coleridge's acquaintance with Frend was prematurely cut short, it was of considerable significance, since it undoubtedly affected the pattern of his political activities during the next few years. Coming up to Cambridge with a mind predisposed towards daring forms of speculation, he was naturally susceptible to the older man's influence, the nature of which was to direct Coleridge's religious thinking into Unitarian channels and to establish a connexion with the political radicalism that was often found in association with this form of dissent. Thus it was mainly into Unitarian circles that he was drawn when he left the University and joined Southey at Bristol; the audiences that came to hear the political sermons delivered there were in part drawn from that sect and so, too, were the subscribers to *The Watchman* in 1796. In addition, Frend's trial gave Coleridge first-hand experience of the danger involved in expressing liberal or radical opinions after England and France were at war.[3]

After the declaration of war it was no longer possible to look forward optimistically to the success of the reform movement in England. Because of their previous connexions with the French National Assembly, the English reform societies became objects of suspicion and mistrust. Those who had hoped that the example of the French Revolution would help to bring about a gradual amelioration of the evils of contemporary English society were now faced with three possible courses of action: they could throw in their lot with the English Jacobins and run the risk of being sentenced to a long period of transportation; they could abandon, temporarily at least, the cause of active reform; or they could seek to escape from the atmosphere of repression. They could hope to emigrate to America, for example, a country with which England was not at war, but which had a republican form of government and seemed to offer boundless possibilities for all who longed to

---

[1] Gunning, op. cit., p. 308. Gunning denied that there ever existed, 'or was supposed to exist, a Jacobin party in the University'.
[2] *U.L.* i. 31 and 34.
[3] Feb. 1793.

create a juster and more democratic society.[1] Coleridge chose the latter course.

The scheme to set up the ideal state of Pantisocracy[2] on the banks of the Susquehannah River was not as wild, as hare-brained, and impracticable as has sometimes been suggested. Coleridge told Gillman that the sound of the name had made him choose the Susquehannah,[3] but the publication of Joel Barlow's translation of J. P. Brissot's *Nouveau Voyage dans les Étas-Unis de l'Amérique Septentrionale* in 1792 had drawn particular attention to this area's rich resources and the relative ease with which a republic might be set up there, and Coleridge knew this work and quoted from it in the *Introductory Address* given at Bristol in 1795.[4] Many of the details in the Pantisocratic Plan that seem most ludicrous today were based on contemporary descriptions of conditions there. For example, Coleridge's expectation that it would be unnecessary for the members of the ideal colony to work more than two hours a day was probably based on Brissot's assurance that 'a man in that country works scarcely two hours a day'.[5] But it must be admitted that inexperience of the realities of domestic life made Coleridge unduly optimistic of the ease with which their difficulties would be surmounted. To Southey he wrote: 'Let the married Women do only what is absolutely convenient and customary for pregnant Women or nurses. Let the Husbands do *all* the Rest—and what will that be? Washing with a Machine and cleaning the House. One Hour's addition to our daily Labor—and *Pantisocracy* in its most perfect Sense is practicable.'[6] When due allowance has been made for the many absurdities of which Southey and Coleridge were guilty in drawing up their plans, Pantisocracy can be seen as an attempt to carry out a small-scale experiment in social and political organization starting from first principles and based on the most up-to-date information. What has often been forgotten, however, is that the decision to emigrate at all implied a complete rejection of the

[1] In June 1793, before he had met Coleridge, Poole wrote to Purkis: 'I am weary of European politicks; America seems the only asylum of peace and liberty—the only place where the dearest feelings of man are not insulted.' H. Sandford, *Thomas Poole and His Friends*, 1888, i. 77–78.

[2] A society in which all are equal in rank and social position; all are equal and all rule. J. Isaacs, 'Coleridge's Critical Terminology', *Essays and Studies*, xxi. 86–104.

[3] J. Gillman, *Life*, p. 69.　　　　　　　　　　　　　　　[4] *E.O.T.* i. 26.

[5] J. R. MacGillivray, 'The Pantisocratic Scheme and its Immediate Background', *Studies in English . . .*, Toronto, 1931; Sister Eugenia, 'Coleridge's Scheme of Pantisocracy and American Travel', *P.M.L.A.*, Dec. 1930, pp. 1069–84.　　[6] *C.L.* i. 114.

existing social system and a frank recognition that the climate of
political opinion was opposed to any radical change. Coleridge's
reaction to the acute problems that arose in England as the result
of the French Revolution and the subsequent declaration of war
against France, was to turn his back upon them in despair. He was
one of many with radical sympathies 'who by 1794 had full cause to
fear that the choice lay between freedom in America and compul-
sory emigration to Mr Pitt's ideal colony at Botany Bay'.[1]

Preoccupation with Pantisocracy certainly saved Coleridge from
'the pitfalls of sedition'.[2] It also made a positive contribution to
the development of his political ideas. To begin with it led him to
know what was 'right in the abstract, by a living feeling, by an
intuition of the uncorrupted Heart'.[3] To it, he confessed he owed
his 'clearest insight into the nature of individual man, and my most
comprehensive views of his social relations, of the true uses of
trade and commerce, and how far the wealth and relative power of
nations promote or impede their welfare and inherent strength'.[4]
From this experiment he learned the two lessons that he never
tired of trying to teach others: that no political system could
succeed that was not based on an understanding of the real nature
of individual man; and that trade and commerce were not ends in
themselves, but merely means to improving the quality of life for
the individual.

Southey and Coleridge did not continue their collaboration
amicably very long. The letters exchanged during the period from
September to the end of December 1794 are largely taken up with
a discussion of the difficulties arising from the plan; suspicions,
misunderstandings, and recriminations frequently occur. Coleridge was in London. There he met Godwin for the first time, and
Holcroft who came fresh from his acquittal at the trial of the
twelve members of the London Corresponding Society.[5] He
formed a connexion with Perry and Grey of the *Morning Chronicle*
and contributed *Sonnets on Eminent Characters* to their paper in
the December of that year and in the following January.[6] The
'Eminent Characters' series included Erskine (who had been

[1] MacGillivray, op. cit., p. 144.   [2] F., p. 141.
[3] C.L. ii. 1000.   [4] F., p. 141.
[5] Thomas Holcroft, 1745–1809, actor and dramatist, was a friend of Tom Paine
and of Godwin, and took an active part in the London Corresponding Society. For
Coleridge's contempt for his fierce dogmatism, atheism, and ignorance as a scholar
see letter to Southey, 17 Dec. 1794. C.L. i. 138–9.   [6] P.W. i. 79–89.

the counsel for the defence in the State trial of November 1794), Priestley, La Fayette, and Godwin. The sonnets were either tributes to the friends of freedom or attacks upon its enemies; the conflict being seen in terms of a heroic struggle; and it is no accident that all should resound with Miltonic echoes, since for Coleridge and others Milton had become a symbolic figure to represent the double opposition against the party of Church and King.[1] It may even have been the example of Milton, who gave up the middle years of his life to political controversy, as much as the influence of the radical agitators whom he had met in London, that led him to abandon for the time being all thoughts of ideal systems of government and to enter the political life of his own country. This he did by giving a series of topical lectures in Bristol during the course of 1795.

II. *The Bristol Lectures*

It is still uncertain how many lectures he actually gave. Cottle, to whom he had been introduced at this time, declared in his *Reminiscences* that three series of lectures were given: political lectures on contemporary problems; a course of six historical lectures given at the Assembly Coffee House, their title being 'A Comparative View of the English Rebellion and the French Revolution'; and a series of six lectures on 'Revealed Religion, its Corruptions, and its Political Views'.[2] In fact the six historical lectures were probably not given, although a broadsheet advertising them was published, a copy of which is in the Berg Collection, New York. The list of Southey's and Coleridge's borrowings from the Bristol Library does not provide evidence of preparation for this course, whereas it does for the lectures known to have been given; and in the middle of November Coleridge stated that he had given eleven lectures, a number impossible to equate with the full list given by Cottle.[3]

---

[1] H. House, *Coleridge. The Clark Lectures, 1951–2*, 1953, pp. 64–66. The Whig party naturally looked to the seventeenth century for historical analogies to the contemporary struggle. In Parliament and the law courts the speeches of the Foxite Whigs made the great seventeenth-century republican figures live again. See in particular Erskine's speeches on behalf of the defendants in the State trials.

[2] J. Cottle, *Reminiscences of Samuel Taylor Coleridge and Robert Southey*, 1848, pp. 15–19. Miss Coburn has discovered a transcript of the theological lectures and they are being edited.

[3] G. Whalley, 'Coleridge and Southey in Bristol', *R.E.S.*, Oct. 1950, pp. 324–40; also by the same author, 'The Bristol Borrowings of Southey and Coleridge', *The Library*, Sept. 1949, pp. 114–31.

The first lecture which was delivered in January 1795 was immediately published and called *A Moral and Political Lecture*, an appropriate title for the first of many 'Lay Sermons'.

The first Lecture I was *obliged* to publish, it having been confidently asserted that there was Treason in it. Written at one sitting between the hours of twelve at night and the Breakfast Time of the day, on which it was delivered, believe me that no literary Vanity prompted me to the printing of it—The reasons which compelled me to publish it forbad me to correct it.[1]

The second and third, he assured the same correspondent, George Dyer, were far superior to the first, but there was 'no *necessity* for publishing them'.[2] The allusion to a second and a third refers to the two lectures delivered on the war with France, which were later printed as a single lecture in *Conciones ad Populum* in November 1795, under the title *On the Present War*.[3] The only other lecture to be published was *The Plot Discovered*, an attack on the Two Bills introduced by Pitt and Grenville to suppress seditious publications and to limit the right of public assembly. It came out on 28 November.[4] In the following month the last of the Bristol pamphlets was published; it was not a lecture but a letter written to answer an anonymous attack made on Dr. Fox, a local physician who held radical political views. Entitled *An Answer To 'A Letter to Edward Long Fox, M.D.'*, it was printed a few days after 11 December, the date of the original 'Letter' by A. W.[5]

In *A Moral and Political Lecture* Coleridge excused his youthful incursion into political controversy on the grounds that everyone should be eager to tender advice in a state of emergency. Mere enthusiasm, however, was not enough. He began by stressing the importance of acquiring a 'prompt facility of adverting in all our doubts to some grand and comprehensive truth'.[6] Two lessons were to be learned from the French Revolution: that the restriction of learning to the few 'pointed out the possessors as the victims, rather than the illuminators, of the multitude';[7] and that

---

[1] *C.L.* i. 152.
[2] Ibid. i. 155. For the dating of this letter see *N. & Q.* 15 Oct. 1949.
[3] *E.O.T.* i. 29–55.
[4] Ibid., pp. 56–98. The original paper wrapper bearing the title 'A Protest against Certain Bills', is dated 28 Nov. 1795. The Bills became law on 18 Dec.
[5] Two copies of the pamphlets by A. W. and Coleridge exist. One is in the Bristol Public Library, the other, B.M. Ashley, 2840 (1).
[6] *E.O.T.* i. 7.   [7] Ibid. i. 8.

undisciplined benevolence could easily become a dangerous and destructive force. In order to benefit from France's example it was necessary to consider the difficult question of who were the real friends of freedom in England and to attempt to define what their attitude should be towards the various methods of bringing about reform. He believed that if those who wished to reform society would clarify their position by reference to general principles, England might be saved from the bloodshed that had accompanied the Revolution in France.

He divided the friends of freedom into four classes. Into the first fell all those who were 'prepared to give an indolent vote in favour of reform', and whose opinions depended with 'weather-cock uncertainty on the winds of rumour, that blow from France'; into the second fell the uneducated poor, whose sufferings aroused the desire for revenge and who thus easily became the means by which demagogues or government agents stirred up trouble; into the third fell those who were more interested in stripping off aristocratic titles than in relieving the sufferings of the poor; while into the last class fell 'the small but glorious band, whom we may truly distinguish by the name of thinking and disinterested patriots'.[1] The rest of the lecture, which is taken up with a description of their virtues, marks them out as disciples of Godwin. They are men who have discovered that vice does not originate in man but 'in the surrounding circumstances; not in the heart, but in the understanding'. They place their whole faith in the power of illumination and investigation and regard all things as part of a necessary process. Therefore they are able to look forward 'with gladdened heart to that glorious period when justice shall have established the universal fraternity of love'.[2] Although Godwin is not mentioned by name, Coleridge's message to the audience that attended his first lecture was that the true patriot must believe in the principles that were promulgated in *Political Justice*.

Broadly speaking there were two main lines of approach to the question how to bring about reform in England at this time. At one extreme were those who believed that the most effective method was through the formation of political associations on the model of the London Corresponding Society; at the other extreme were those who, in agreement with Godwin, viewed with the utmost suspicion all forms of political association. What need, they

[1] For the quoted phrases see ibid. i. 12–16. [2] Ibid. i. 17.

asked, for association when man possessed the guiding light of an
independent intellect. When, nine months after its delivery, Coleridge came to revise the text of the first lecture for inclusion in
Conciones ad Populum, where it was given the new title, *Introductory
Address*, he had ceased to advocate a Godwinian solution to the
problem. He now took up a position midway between the extremes. A number of passages attacking the main fallacies of
Godwin's system were added,[1] new sections were introduced
stressing the power of religion on the minds of the poor,[2] and for
the abrupt and unexpected conclusion of the original lecture, of
which the anonymous writer in the *Critical Review* had complained,[3] was substituted a peroration, which ended on the following note: 'Finally, in the words of an Apostle, "Watch ye! Stand
fast in the principles of which ye have been convinced! Quit your-
selves like men! Be strong! Yet let all things be done in the spirit
of love".'[4]

The solution that Coleridge substituted for that of Godwin was
essentially a religious one. The patriot must combine 'the zeal of
the methodist with the views of the philosopher, should be *personally* among the poor, and teach them their *duties* in order that he
may render them susceptible of their *rights*'.[5] He described as
plausible rather than just Godwin's contention that truth by a
gradual descent would at last reach the lower orders. It ignored
the fact that the latter were separated by an impassable gulf from
'the Nobility, Gentry and People of Dress', a phrase that had caught
Coleridge's eye in a perfumer's advertisement.[6] He denied too
the validity of Godwin's treatment of private affections. 'Let us
beware of that proud philosophy, which affects to inculcate philanthropy while it denounces every home-born feeling, by which it
is produced and nurtured.'[7] For Godwin's unreal, academic, and
passive solution was substituted a policy of action, but of action
utterly unlike that advocated by the radical and reform clubs.
'Go, preach the GOSPEL to the poor', he commanded. The vision
of a future state of being for each individual soul which religion

---

[1] *E.O.T.* i. 21.   [2] Ibid. i. 22–23.
[3] 'We . . . think our young political lecturer leaves his auditors abruptly, and that
he has not stated, in a form sufficiently scientific and determinate, those principles to
which, as he expresses it, he now proceeds as the most *important part*. We confess we
were looking for something more, and little thought that we had actually come to the
finis.' *Critical Review*, vol. xiii, Apr. 1795, p. 455.   [4] *E.O.T.* i. 29.
[5] Ibid. i. 22.   [6] Ibid. i. 21.   [7] Ibid. i. 24–25.

offered was more likely, in his opinion, to impress the 'over-worked labourer, skulking into the alehouse' than would God-win's vision of a problematical state of perfection to be enjoyed, not by the individual himself, but by his remote descendants. He saw that the central message of Christianity, that of the individual's importance in the sight of God, could be grasped by the most ignorant, and that its acceptance in the heart of man could bring about a silent revolution in his attitude towards God, the members of his immediate family circle, and his fellow citizens. 'The pater-nal and filial duties discipline the heart and prepare it for the love of all mankind'; and these duties are prescribed by religion.

Coleridge did not take even the most elementary precautions to prevent his remarks from being misunderstood; this applies equally to the original and the revised text. Those who attended the lecture would expect to be given a clear lead how best to effect the reform of society. What in fact they were given were veiled references to Godwin and Godwinism, and as if Coleridge were unaware of the inconsistency involved, allusions to the defend-ants at the Scottish state trial of 1793 who had been sentenced to terms of transportation ranging from seven to fourteen years.[1] Direct reference was made to one of them, Joseph Gerrald.

Withering in the sickly and tainted gales of a prison, his healthful soul looks down from the citadel of his integrity on his impotent persecutors. I saw him in the foul and naked room of a jail—his cheek was sallow with confinement—his body was emaciated; yet his eye spoke the in-vincible purpose of his soul, and he still sounded with rapture the successes of freemen, forgetful of his own lingering martyrdom![2]

While it is true that here and in the reference to Horne Tooke in the revised text, emphasis is laid on the nobility in suffering, and the consciously accepted martyrdom, the mere mention of the names and allusions to their fate was sufficient to suggest to the public that Coleridge sympathized with the activities of the reform

[1] Muir, Palmer, Margarot, and Gerrald were tried before the notorious Scottish judge, Braxfield, for the part they were thought to have played in organizing a national convention of reform associations. They were all found guilty. Gerrald was sentenced to fourteen years transportation.

[2] *E.O.T.* i. 18. In a copy of *Conciones ad Populum*, now in Harvard Library, Cole-ridge wrote in manuscript hand 'Written by Southey. I never saw these men.' In a letter to Thelwall, 22 June 1796, he implies that he was the author of the passage but that he was dependent on someone else for the information about Gerrald's condition in prison. *C.L.* i. 221.

societies, a sympathy which was incompatible with his advocacy of Godwinism. Nor is the revised text of the lecture in *Conciones ad Populum* free from inconsistencies. Although the introduction of passages critical of two of Godwin's main tenets suggests a rejection of the system, the passage relating to the 'glorious band . . . of thinking and disinterested patriots', which is a panegyric in favour of Godwinism, was retained. With justice did H. D. Traill complain that the remarks were 'calculated to bewilder any of the youthful lecturer's well wishers who might be anxious for some means of discriminating his attitude from that of the Hardy's and the Thelwall's of the day'.[1]

As Coleridge had explained at the time, *A Moral and Political Lecture* had been printed in order to prove that it contained no sedition. The lectures that soon followed were not published until several months later, in November 1795. The main objects of these two lectures, which were published as one under the title *On the Present War*, were to prove that the war with France was unnecessary, since it could have been prevented by negotiation; and to draw a comprehensive picture of the war's evil effects on England and France. Throughout the whole of 1794 the Whig Opposition had carried on a strenuous campaign against Pitt's refusal to consider the possibility of negotiation. At the opening of the Session, Fox moved an amendment to the Address in which he recommended that the Ministry should treat as speedily as possible for a peace with France. In December a similar amendment was moved by Wilberforce, who had been an intimate friend of Pitt. In his reply Pitt denied that the Address implied that the Ministry would never make peace with France as long as she retained a republican system of government; but it is clear from his references to the advantages of a monarchical system, that the form of government in France formed the main stumbling block.[2] Here, as in the articles contributed to the *Morning Post* in 1800, one of Coleridge's tasks was to pour ridicule on the contention that dislike of a particular form of government constituted a valid reason for refusing to negotiate.[3]

In the main section of the lecture the evil effects upon England of the war were described and analysed. The details which Coleridge selected resembled those that had figured prominently in the

[1] H. D. Traill, *Coleridge*, 1884, p. 19.
[2] *Annual Register*, 1794, passim.   [3] *E.O.T.* i. 253–68.

speeches of the Opposition during the previous twelve months. There were indignant references to the use of crimping[1] to swell the ranks of the Army, to the suspension of *Habeas Corpus*, and to the State trials of the members of the reform societies. What chiefly distinguished Coleridge's recital of grievances from those of the Opposition was his recognition that the worst feature of the war had been its effect on moral standards, national and individual. And as an example of its effect at the national level he seized on the sudden change that had taken place in British foreign policy during the first six months of the war. At the beginning of the war, Pitt had declared that it was not the policy of the British Government to interfere in the internal affairs of other countries. The policy of non-intervention had since been completely reversed. This inconsistency, for an explanation of which it was only necessary to point to the changes that had taken place in French policy, was a favourite object of attack for Opposition speakers. The point was taken up all the more gladly by Coleridge since at this time he could not admit that any radical change had taken place in France sufficient to warrant such a reversal. The first grave doubts concerning French ambition were not expressed until a year later in *The Watchman*.[2] But in addition to bringing about a serious loss of national character, the war had brought about an even more serious effect in the sphere of private morality. The extensive use of government spies to report on the activities of the reform societies had destroyed mutual trust between individuals; and, in succumbing to the general atmosphere of panic, men had abandoned their high ideals and had sacrificed friends, principles, and everything else to a safe attachment to the Government and the existing constitution. In this context he quoted with approval Paine's dictum from *Commonsense*, which he had probably first met in Godwin: 'Society in every state is a blessing. Government even in its best state but a necessary evil.'[3]

After reflecting bitterly on the loss of personal liberty with

---

[1] 'Crimping.' During this period the Government made much use of agents to entrap men for the Army and the Navy.

[2] See particularly 'Remonstrance to the French Legislators', *The Watchman*, No. 8, 27 Apr. 1796, *W.*, p. 232. The essay is not reprinted in the selection from *The Watchman* in E.O.T. For fuller discussion of this essay see Chap. II.

[3] Godwin quotes the phrase in *Political Justice*. *P.J.* i. 124. In view of the absence of references to Paine elsewhere in the lectures, it is reasonable to presume that Coleridge took it from Godwin.

which the war had been attended, it was natural for Coleridge to
turn his attention to those whom he held responsible for this loss.
In this section his hatred of the union of Church and State was
much in evidence. Pitt, whose eloquence he compared unfavour-
ably with that of Burke, 'mystery concealing meanness, as steam-
clouds invelope [*sic*] a dung hill',[1] came in for a wealth of
invective. But he held the Established Church equally responsible.
The form the attack took was one that Coleridge came to scorn in
later life and one that he held up to reprobation when he revised
the text of his first Bristol lecture. There it was described as
attributing to the system rejected 'all the evils existing under it'.[2]
His judgement upon the Established Church was based upon observations of its outward forms of corruption. It thus became, 'the
religion of mitres and mysteries, the religion of puralities and persecution, the eighteen thousand-pound-a-year religion of epis-
copacy'.[3] His real objection to the Church was twofold: he could
not accept its theology, and he considered it failed completely in
serving society as a result of its exclusive attachment to the
governing class. A footnote in the printed pamphlet asserted that
priests were unnecessary, and to this was added a lively if somewhat laboured parody of Burke's passage on the death of chivalry
in France.

The age of priesthood will soon be no more—that of philosophers
and of Christians will succeed, and the torch of superstition be extin-
guished for ever. Never, never more shall we behold that generous
loyalty to rank, which is prodigal of its own virtue and its own happiness to invest a few with unholy splendours;—that subordination of the
heart, which keeps alive the spirit of servitude amid the empty forms of
boasted liberty! This dear-bought grace of cathedrals, this costly defence
of despotism, this nurse of grovelling sentiment and cold-hearted lip-
worship, will be gone—it will be gone, that sensibility to interest, that
jealous tenacity of honours, which suspects in every argument a mortal
wound; which inspires oppression, while it prompts servility;—which
stains indelibly whatever it touches; and under which supple dulness
loses half its shame by wearing a mitre where reason would have placed
a fool's cap![4]

[1] E.O.T. i. 43.
[2] Ibid. i. 12. For later statement of this principle see *Table Talk*, 'No man can
rightly apprehend an abuse until he has mastered the idea of the use of an institution.' T.T., p. 73. See *Church and State*, passim.
[3] E.O.T. i. 46.
[4] Ibid. i. 47. For the original, see *Reflections*, Everyman ed., p. 73.

The parody probably produced a greater effect on his readers than the intemperate invective he had used earlier to criticize the Church.

The last part of the section relating to the consequences of the war was devoted to its effects on the poor and the Government's futile efforts to solve the problem. Withering sarcasm was employed in describing the punishments meted out to the poor. 'And here we cannot but admire the deep and comprehensive views of ministers, who having starved the wretch into vice send him to the barren shores of New Holland to be starved back again into virtue.'[1] He agreed with Godwin that men were made criminals by their environment and that punishment of this kind was not only useless but dangerous. A government had no right to impose punishment when it had neglected 'the duty of instruction'.[2] It was true, however, that men need neither starve nor steal. The war that had caused all their misery provided a refuge from despair in service in the Army. In one of the Notebooks Coleridge had recorded how he had seen 'a quarter of Lamb and a piece of beef' hung up outside a recruiting office, and in the lecture he referred to this incident as an example of the brutal and cynical attitude that the war had engendered.[3] The whole of this section is filled with genuine compassion for the sufferings of the poor and a strong vein of pacifism reminiscent of passages in Wordsworth's *Female Vagrant*.

The treatment of the effects of the war on France is of less interest. In the main Coleridge merely repeated in their most exaggerated form and with a lamentable lack of restraint the favourite arguments of the Opposition. He asserted that the effect of the Brunswick Manifesto, which among other things had threatened instant death to anyone captured from the French Army, and the effect of the Government's declared policy of pursuing a war of extermination, had been to arouse feelings of terror and indignation in the hearts of the French people, and had thus united them against a common foe.[4] Coleridge followed this with the wildest assertions, the most absurd being that William Pitt was

---

[1] *E.O.T.* i. 48.

[2] Ibid. i. 49. Cf. '. . . instruction is one of the ends of government'. *F.*, p. 161, also *Lay Sermons*, p. 249.

[3] *Gutch Memorandum Book*, B.M. Add. MSS. 27901, f. 5, and *E.O.T.* i. 49.

[4] For an account of the Manifesto and its effect on moderate French opinion see Sir Charles Petrie, *Lord Liverpool and his Times*, 1954, pp. 20–22.

directly responsible for the Terror in France. 'When shall we cease to see this nonsense repeated?' demanded the reviewer in the *British Critic*. There is a marked contrast between the section devoted to England and that devoted to France in this pamphlet; in the latter naked assertion and empty rhetoric take the place of cogent argument. The explanation for this is fairly obvious. Coleridge possessed first-hand knowledge of the effects of the war at home; unlike Wordsworth he had no direct personal experience of what had occurred in France. In his youth he needed perhaps more than most men to subject his imagination and political passions to the discipline imposed by observed facts. The lecture ended with a stirring call to action. 'Are we men? free men? rational men? And shall we carry on this wild and priestly war against reason, against freedom, against human nature? If there be one among you, who departs from me without feeling it his immediate duty to petition or remonstrate against the continuance of it, I envy that man neither his head nor his heart!'[1] But the action, be it noted, is to be through constitutional channels.

The two lectures on the war were delivered during the early part of 1795, before the government had sought to introduce definite legislation to restrict freedom of expression. Coleridge's last lecture, *The Plot Discovered*, was delivered against a very different background. At the beginning of November, the month in which the lecture was given, two Bills had been brought forward, one to prevent the dissemination of sedition through the Press, the other to limit the right of public assembly and thus to stamp out the political associations that were spreading throughout the country. An attack had been made on the King when he was returning from opening Parliament on 29 October. A stone had been thrown at the royal carriage, a shot was said to have been fired, and there had been cries of 'No War' and 'Bread'. Three days earlier a mass meeting had been held by the London Corresponding Society in Copenhagen Fields, on which occasion intemperate language had been used and the abstract right of forcibly resisting oppression had been asserted. As a result the society was held responsible for the attack on the King.[2] The Government had thus an excuse for introducing legislation. It was not, however, the

---

[1] *E.O.T.* i. 55.
[2] J. H. Rose, *William Pitt and the Great War*, 1911, pp. 282–6; and P. A. Brown, *The French Revolution in English History*, 1923, pp. 151–3.

spirit of sedition that led to the attack upon the royal carriage; it
was mainly shortage of food.[1] But what had happened in France
had made it impossible for the Pitt administration to view the
genuine discontents of the people objectively; it lived in a perpetual fear of a popular uprising and was therefore subject to
sudden waves of panic, which resulted in ill-considered prosecu-
tions of individuals and a series of repressive legislative measures.[2]
But the effect of the introduction of these Bills could hardly have
been what the Government expected. In their original form, before they were modified as the result of popular agitation throughout the country and sharp criticism in the House, they gave almost
unlimited powers to the Government. Their wide and undefined
powers and their unreasonable severity, however, had the effect of
bringing together the Radicals and the Whigs in common opposition against this attack on individual freedom. Another mass
meeting was held at Copenhagen Fields. On this occasion the
Dukes of Norfolk and Bedford appeared on the same platform as
John Thelwall and other radical leaders.[3] Meetings were also held
in the large provincial towns. At Bristol Coleridge and Dr. Beddoes attended a loyalist meeting and attempted to pass a motion
condemning the repressive measures. Dr. Beddoes followed this
up with a pamphlet attacking the Bills. At a public meeting called
to protest against them Coleridge proposed that Sheridan and Fox
should be asked to present their petition but it was subsequently
agreed that it should be presented by the member for Bristol.[4]

It is against this background, then, that the last lecture, *The Plot
Discovered*, or as it was entitled on the original wrapper and advertised in *Felix Farley's Journal*, *A Protest against Certain Bills*,
must be seen. When due allowance has been made for the platform rhetoric of the opening section, it is clear that Coleridge did
in fact regard the Bills as forming part of a Government plot to
deprive the people of their freedom. Nor did he change his mind
in later life. An entry in one of the Notebooks for 1830 runs, 'In

---

[1] J. H. Rose, op. cit., chap. xiii, 'Dearth and Discontent'.

[2] '. . . the panic of property had been struck in the first instance for party purposes;
and when it became general, its propagators caught it themselves and ended in believing their own lie; even as our bulls in Borrowdale sometimes run mad with the
echo of their own bellowing'. F., p. 138.

[3] Brown, op. cit., p. 152.

[4] Unpublished letter from Azariah Pinney to Wordsworth, 26 Nov. 1795.
Pinney Papers, Racedown.

1793 & the following years the Jacobinism was indeed for this favored country, then foully slandered by Mr Pitt's Suspension & Gagging Bills, but *an Echo* from afar—an *echo* of the so called Mountain Faction in France.'[1] The growth of discontent in England had been attributed by the Ministry to the 'multitude of seditious pamphlets and speeches daily printed, published and dispersed with unremitting industry and with a transcendant boldness'.[2] This Coleridge denied. The root cause of the increased agitation throughout 1795 was, he asserted, the shortage of food which had reduced the poor to a state of utter starvation. The basic principle on which Coleridge founded his case for the rejection of the Two Bills was the sacred right possessed by every man to communicate what he believed to be the truth. 'To promulge what we believe to be truth is indeed a law beyond law',[3] he declared. He had not yet come to draw the all important distinction between religious and civic rights, a distinction upon which much of the political thought in the later works was based.[4] Believing at this time that such a sacred right existed, he regarded the Bills as a threat to the liberty of the individual. Parodying Burke's style he wrote: 'All political controversy is at an end. Those sudden breezes and noisy gusts, which purified the atmosphere they disturbed, are hushed to death-like silence. The cadaverous tranquillity of despotism will succeed the generous order and graceful indiscretions of freedom.'[5] In addition he considered that they threatened the whole balance of the constitution, since he believed that it was only the right to free speech, the right of association, and the right to petition that prevented the Government from becoming a despotism.

In the first part of the lecture Coleridge was mainly concerned with the effect on the individual. It might be thought at first that he was being merely perverse in suggesting some of the possible interpretations that could be made of clauses in the Bills. When it is realized that it was one of his main objectives to expose their dangerous ambiguities, this form of argument can be seen in its proper perspective. He had already seen how the existing law had

---

[1] *Notebook No. 49*, B.M. Add. MSS. 47544, ff. 15*v*–16.
[2] Coleridge quotes from the first clause of the Grenville Bill. *E.O.T.* i. 57.
[3] Ibid. i. 60.
[4] For the fullest treatment of this distinction in relation to the freedom of the Press see the introductory section of *The Friend*.   [5] *E.O.T.* i. 61.

been interpreted in the State trials, particularly the trial that had taken place in Scotland in 1793, and he now feared that the new Bills would give skilful lawyers unlimited opportunities to obtain convictions on the flimsiest evidence. Coleridge wanted the law to be precise. Then if attempts were made to distort statutory law the independent juries would be able to relate each case to clearly defined and unambiguous statutes. But many years later, in 1814, he wrote that 'the practical law exists in Precedents, far more than in Statutes', and he branded the opposite view as a species of Jacobinism.[1]

Coleridge's treatment of the second Bill, which he neatly summarized in the following words, 'that the people of England should possess no unrestrained right of consulting in common on common grievances: and secondly, that Mr Thelwall should no longer give political lectures',[2] provides a striking illustration of the different attitudes adopted by Coleridge and Godwin towards the same issue. Godwin's method of approach in his *Considerations on Lord Grenville's and Mr. Pitt's Bills*[3] was to examine the actions of the London Corresponding Society and of the popular radical orator, Thelwall, to see how far the Government was justified in legislating against both. His strictures on the Society and Thelwall were nearly as severe as those on the Government, which was what might have been expected after his attack on all forms of association and collective political action in *Political Justice*. Coleridge, on the other hand, made no attempt to examine critically the actions of either the Society or Thelwall;[4] his case rested on the assumption that the legislation proposed was simply part of a Government plot to deprive the people of their freedom. This contrast in approach can be ascribed to a difference of temperament and purpose. Godwin's pamphlet was the work of a cool-headed academic considering dispassionately the justification for introducing the Two Bills at this time; Coleridge's pamphlet was the work of an excitable young man, whose sensibilities had been outraged by the idea of further incursions into the liberties of the individual, and who wished to persuade the public to petition against the Bills.

[1] See Marginalia to *Encyclopaedia Londoniensis*, article on Liberty, published in S. Coleridge, *Memories*, 1913, pp. 212–13.　　　　　　　　　　[2] *E.O.T.* i. 69–70.

[3] The pamphlet is dated 1795, the author is given as 'A Lover of Liberty'.

[4] Coleridge's oblique reference to Thelwall as 'an unsupported malcontent' gave offence and led to the opening of a correspondence in the following year. *E.O.T.* i. 70, *C.L.* i. 204–5.

In this pamphlet he took up the position that only two things prevented the Government of the country from becoming despotic:
the freedom of the Press, which could give the people an '*influential* sovereignty',[1] but which was now threatened, and the right
to petition, which was now impossible except 'with the justice of
the peace at their elbow'.[2] He believed that if the Bills were passed
the delicate balance of power upon which the constitution rested
would be upset.[3]

The Plot Discovered is the only published Bristol lecture that contains any reference to the question of parliamentary reform. This
is indeed surprising, especially when it is remembered that the
various reform and radical societies had come into being in order
to promote this measure. Audiences would expect this subject to
loom large in any political lecture; from all but the last of Coleridge's they would have gone away disappointed. From the
evidence of this lecture it is obvious that he read carefully the
pamphlet prepared by the 'Friends of the People' called *The State
of Representation of England and Wales*, for all the facts and figures
were taken from this source.[4] The whole treatment of the subject
suggests, however, that though he was well informed he was not
personally interested in this method of bringing about improvement in society. While it certainly formed no part of his purpose
to defend the anomalies of the existing system, it is clear that he
neither attributed the miseries of the country primarily to this
source nor anticipated that parliamentary reform would bring
about any marked improvement in society. At this early date he
was already aware of what he described three years later as 'the
error of attributing to governments a talismanic influence over
our virtues & our happiness'.[5] But the report issued by the
'Friends of the People' was not the only work on this subject to
which reference was made. Coleridge also introduced a long quotation from Paley's *Moral and Political Philosophy*, defending the
principle of indirect representation, in order to expose the fallacy
of Paley's view that the welfare of the country was best left in the

---

[1] *E.O.T.* i. 91.   [2] Ibid. i. 93.
[3] Fox declared that the Bills were 'a daring attempt to overthrow the fundamental
principle on which the constitution stood; the universal freedom of discussion'.
Speech, 16 Nov. 1795. *Annual Register*, 1796, p. 38.
[4] Readers of Coleridge's lecture were referred to the report in a footnote. *E.O.T.*
i. 86.
[5] The phrase occurs in a letter to his brother George, *c.* 10 Mar. 1798. *C.L.* i. 395.

hands of the wealthy and that representation should be based on 'interests'. It should be noted that in 1830, in *Church and State*, his idea of the constitution embraces the system of representation of interest and the principle of indirect representation. In 1795, however, as the evidence of *The Watchman Prospectus* suggests,[1] he was drawn into political circles whose main efforts were directed towards obtaining a radical reform of Parliament and though he never at any time advocated a system of universal franchise, he spoke on the reform side and occasionally lapsed into slightly Jacobinical language.

In analysing the social and political problems that faced the people of England in 1795, Coleridge showed himself to be as deeply concerned with the general problem of bringing about the complete reformation of society as with discussing specific topics or with attacking the domestic and foreign policy of the Pitt Ministry. His insistence that the improvement of society was essentially a moral and not a political problem and that the necessary moral reformation must be effected by religion, is in complete harmony with the view expressed in his later political works. In itself the use of the word 'moral' in the title of the first lecture *A Moral and Political Lecture*, was significant; it indicated the nature of the author's approach and perhaps justified the form of address, that of a 'Lay Sermon'.[2] But whereas the writer of the two *Lay Sermons* that appeared at the end of the Napoleonic War inhabited a moral world in which the freedom of the will with all its frightening and tremendous consequences was a reality, the young Bristol orator and pamphleteer was firmly enclosed in the deceptively simple autonomous moral world of philosophical necessity; for the rejection of Godwinism did not involve any diminution of his faith in necessity which he had taken at first hand from Hartley.[3] From Coleridge's necessitarian faith sprang the ebullient optimism and the calm confidence in the ultimate victory of truth which characterize these early works. Again, while stress is laid on the

---

[1] Its chief objects were said to be to co-operate with the Whig Club to procure the repeal of the Pitt–Grenville Acts and with the 'Patriotic Societies for obtaining a Right of Suffrage general and frequent'. The *Prospectus* is printed in *C. Life*, pp. 286–8.

[2] In later life Coleridge referred to the early political works as 'Lay Sermons', thus showing that he himself was aware of fundamental similarities between them and his later work.

[3] It was not until as late as Mar. 1801 that he was able to claim that he had 'overthrown the doctrine of Association, as taught by Hartley'. *C.L.* ii. 706.

power of education in the Bristol lectures and the *Lay Sermons*, in the former it is the education of the masses, while in the latter it is the re-education of the governing classes that Coleridge has in mind.

In attacking the Pitt Ministry Coleridge was led to reflect on one problem that was to engage his attention throughout his life, the principles that should regulate the use of the spoken or written word to influence public opinion on controversial issues. His preoccupation with the rights and duties involved in any attempt to communicate moral and political truth was the natural outcome of his recognition of the power of the written and spoken word. At this early stage, influenced by the dissenting tradition and by his radical associates, he placed greater emphasis on rights than on duties, although in the first lecture and in the lecture *On the Present War*, he recognized the duty of considering 'the character of those, to whom we address ourselves, their situations, and probable degree of knowledge', before uttering truths that might inflame the passions of the unenlightened. Of all the organs for communicating the truth the mightiest was clearly the Press. It was therefore vital that it should not be muzzled.

The liberty of the press, (a power resident in the people) gives us an *influential* sovereignty. By books necessary information may be dispersed; and by information the public will may be formed; and by the right of petitioning that will may be expressed; first, perhaps, in low and distant tones such as beseem the children of peace; but if corruption deafen power, gradually increasing till they swell into a deep and awful thunder, the VOICE OF GOD, which his vicegerents must hear, and hearing dare not disobey. This unrestricted right of over-awing the oligarchy of parliament by constitutional expression of the general will forms our liberty: it is the sole boundary that divides us from despotism.[1]

It can be seen that in eulogizing the power of the Press Coleridge dropped into the language of the Jacobins; and, on the strength of this passage, it has been asserted that he was firmly committed at this time to the doctrine of *vox populi vox Dei*.[2] In later life Coleridge denied that he had ever said that the *vox populi* was the *vox*

---

[1] *E.O.T.* i. 91.

[2] 'Thus once—if only once—Coleridge did say the *vox populi* was of course the *vox Dei* and unquestionably he was stating his conviction.' B. H. Lehmann, *Carlyle's Theory of a Hero*, Duke University Press, 1928.

Dei. 'It may be; but it may be, and with equal probability, *a priori*, *vox Diaboli*. That the voice of ten millions of men calling for the same thing, is a spirit, I believe; but whether that be a spirit of Heaven or Hell, I can only know by trying the thing called for by the prescript of reason and God's will.'[1] In 1827 Coleridge recorded in one of the Notebooks that his 'political creed had always been constitutional'.[2] The evidence of the Bristol lectures does much to substantiate this claim. There he defends the existing constitutional rights and privileges; nowhere in these lectures does he argue for their extension or reform. Apart from the use of the phrases in the passage quoted above, there is no evidence to suggest that he was committed to a belief in the general will and the sovereignty of the people, while there is abundant evidence to prove that he believed that the constitution already provided satisfactory means for airing the people's grievances. In speaking in public and in publishing his lectures, he made use of two of the means; and in *The Plot Discovered* he sought to defend these rights from government attack. The Bristol lectures and pamphlets were not the works of a young Jacobin and Coleridge was thoroughly justified when he wrote in 1818: 'The Conciones are violently anti-polemic, violently anti-Pittite . . . but least of all they are Jacobinical. The only political point, which I have not retained or rather which even then *came out* from Sympathy with those I lived among rather than my steady convictions, is the last sentence about a reform in the House of Commons.'[3]

One of the most surprising aspects of Coleridge's political activities in Bristol in 1795 is the closeness of his attachment to the contemporary political scene. No mention of forming ideal societies is to be found in the published lectures. He had evidently come to realize that the best way of solving problems was to face them and to believe, that in spite of the severe repressive policy pursued by Pitt, the active dissemination of political truth might yet help to prepare the way for the creation of a juster society. But although the subject-matter of the lectures may be said to be of

---

[1] *Table Talk*, entry for 29 Apr. 1832. *T.T.*, p. 160.

[2] *Notebook No. 36*, B.M. Add. MSS. 47531, f. 47. Cf. Crane Brinton's view in *The Political Ideas of the Romanticists*, Oxford, 1926, pp. 69–70, where he convicts Coleridge of having 'a definite revolutionary belief', faith in universal suffrage, and in 'sharing in the deadly rationalism of the age'. It is difficult to see on what evidence this is based.

[3] Letter to J. Morgan, Jan. 1818. MS. Forster 112, ff. 12–13.

national significance, Coleridge's method of treating them frequently reminds the reader how closely he was connected with the
local political scene. When discussing the effects of crimping, he
referred to a pamphlet written by a Bristol doctor, William Bryant,
which described the wretched condition of a regiment that had
recently returned to Bristol from the West Indies. Coleridge's defence of Dr. Fox provides eloquent proof of his active participa-
tion and interest in local politics. To compare the somewhat
abstract classification of the different types of reformers in the first
lecture with the lively gossipy defence of Dr. Fox in this two-
penny broadsheet, is to see how pliant were Coleridge's critical and
political powers. Though this attachment to contemporary issues,
national and local, has meant that these early pamphlets are rarely
read today, it nevertheless remains true that in these works he did
succeed in establishing a fairly satisfactory balance between general
principles and practical politics; and thus showed early promise of
becoming a social critic of no mean order.

It cannot be said, however, that his criticism reached a very wide
audience. Presumably because of their somewhat explosive contents the lectures were not advertised in the Bristol papers as were
those of Southey. For publicity Coleridge was obliged to rely on
the circulation of prospectuses. The price of admission was a
shilling.[1] 'Few attended Mr. C's lectures', writes Cottle, 'but those
whose political views were similar to his own.'[2] But no political
orator can hope to be completely free from hecklers. Evidently the
same weapons of wit and sarcasm that he used to assail the Pitt
administration were employed against any of the Minister's supporters who interrupted the lecture.

On one occasion, some gentlemen of the opposite party came into
the lecture room, and, at one statement they heard, testified their disapprobation by the only easy and safe way in their power; namely, by a
hiss. The auditors were startled by so unusual a sound, not knowing to
what it might conduct; but their noble leader soon quieted their fears,
by instantly remarking, with great coolness, 'I am not surprised, when
the red hot prejudices of aristocrats are suddenly plunged into the cool

---

[1] A *Prospectus* reprinted by Cottle mentions a shilling. *Reminiscences*, p. 18. Sneer-
ing at Coleridge's professions of principles one of his auditors asked, 'Why, if you are
so public spirited, do you take money at the door?' 'For a reason,' said Coleridge,
'which I am sorry in the present instance has not been quite successful—to keep out
blackguards.' *Henry Crabb Robinson on Books and their Writers*, ed. E. J. Morley, i. 59.

[2] *Early Recollections*, 1837, i. 177–8.

water of reason, that they should go off with a hiss.' . . . There was no more hissing.[1]

Not all the opposition came from within the lecture room. Coleridge declared that his life had been threatened by 'two or three uncouth and untrained Automata' and that it was only with difficulty that the mob was restrained 'from attacking the house in which the "damn'd Jacobine was jawing away"'.[2] According to the anonymous writer of the pamphlet *The Observer*,[3] Coleridge cut a sorry figure in public. His personal appearance was untidy and dirty and his method of delivery monotonous. But the same writer singled out his courage for special praise. 'He spoke in public what none had the courage in this city to do before—he told men they have Rights.'

There is an odd lack of harmony between Coleridge's cautious approach to most of the problems tackled and the intemperate language that he frequently employs. A typical example of the latter is his reference to an 'atrocity' story of the American War, made famous by one of Burke's great speeches.[4] These are the words in which Coleridge attacked the use of the Indians by English generals in America. 'The fiend, whose crime was ambition, leapt over into this paradise—hell-hounds laid it waste. *English* generals invited the Indians "to banquet on blood:" the savage Indians headed by an Englishman attacked it. Universal massacre ensued.'[5] The explanation for this general lack of harmony between thought and language is probably that given to Sir George Beaumont in 1803.[6] When his relations and 'the Churchmen and Aristocrats' all treated his opinions as the 'drivel of a babe', he was driven into the camp of the democrats. He strenuously denied that he had ever joined one of the secret

[1] Ibid. i. 177–8. J. Gillman relates substantially the same story in his *Life of Coleridge*, p. 67, and Crabb Robinson alludes to the same anecdote, *Henry Crabb Robinson on Books and their Writers*, ed. E. J. Morley, 1938, i. 59.

[2] *C.L.* i. 152.

[3] *The Observer*, Part I, being a transient glance at about forty youths of Bristol. Bristol Public Library.

[4] It is said that Burke's speech on the employment of Red Indians in the American War moved his auditors to tears. A reference to this well-known atrocity story was likely to arouse the indignation of Coleridge's audience. For Burke's speech see G. M. Trevelyan, *George the Third and Charles Fox*, 1929, i. 202–13.

[5] *E.O.T.* i. 35.

[6] Letter, 1 Oct. 1803, *C.L.* ii. 998–1005. The execution of the young Irish patriot, Emmet, awoke memories of the dangers Coleridge himself had run in youth.

associations, though he had often been 'urged to become a member, now of this and now of that'. The democrats alone appreciated him and performed the offices of love that were so necessary for one who was later to lament:

> To be beloved is all I need,
> And whom I love, I love indeed.[1]

He returned this love by serving their cause in ways and in words that were inconsistent with his most deeply rooted opinions. The following passage, from the letter to Sir George Beaumont already referred to, provides a valuable insight into Coleridge's state in 1795.

> And tho' even to extravagance I always supported the Doctrine of absolute unequivocal non-resistance—yet with an ebullient Fancy, a flowing Utterance, a light & dancing Heart, & a disposition to catch fire by the very rapidity of my own motion, & to speak vehemently from mere verbal associations, choosing sentences & sentiments for the very reason, that would have made me recoil with a dying away of the Heart & an unutterable Horror from the actions expressed in such sentences & sentiments—namely, because they were wild, & original, & vehement & fantastic!—I aided the Jacobins, by witty sarcasms & subtle reasonings & declamations full of genuine feeling against all Rulers & against all established Forms![2]

An excessive love of rhetoric for its own sake is the main fault from which the early political poems and pamphlets suffer. In the poems its cause, as Humphry House suggested, lay in his failure to escape the influence of the eighteenth-century Ode and that of Milton's blank verse.[3] In the pamphlets he seems simply to have enjoyed his power and mastery over words. But it is characteristic of Coleridge's prose writings in general that this undisciplined eloquence should be found side by side with passages whose chief fault lies in their excessive subtlety of reasoning.

No manuscript of the lectures exists and therefore it is impossible to tell exactly what alterations were made to the lectures when they were published. A comparison of the two versions of the first Bristol lecture suggests that considerable changes and additions were probably made.[4] The pamphlets are overburdened

---

[1] 'The Pains of Sleep', ll. 51–52. P.W. i. 391.
[2] C.L. ii. 1000–1.   [3] Coleridge, 1953, chap. iii.
[4] In addition to the changes already noted a long passage comparing Brissot, the Girondist leader, and Robespierre was added. E.O.T. i. 8–10.

with footnotes and quotations from a wide variety of sources, and these for the most part must have been later additions. They indicate an exceptionally well-stocked mind for so young a man. But the wealth of illustrative material and facts concerning British Constitutional history with which *The Plot Discovered* is adorned, came from a single source. Reference to Burgh's *Political Disquisitions*, which Coleridge had borrowed from the Bristol Library in November, enabled him to amass a great deal of information at small intellectual cost.[1] But it was characteristic of Coleridge throughout his life to have at his finger-tips an appropriate phrase or passage from a speech in Parliament or a political pamphlet. Even as a young man he had a good eye for an anecdote or memorable phrase. At the beginning of *The Plot Discovered* he puts to good use Bishop Horsley's foolish and tactless remark in the House of Lords that 'the mass of the people have nothing to do with the laws but obey them'. And in the lecture *On the Present War*, he quoted from Sheridan's speech ridiculing the Government's accusation that the Sheffield Association had been preparing for an armed insurrection. 'And the formidable preparation which was to overturn the constitution was supported by an exchequer containing nine pounds and one bad shilling—*all* to be directed against the armed force and established government of Great Britain.'[2] Finally, a literary flavour is given to the pamphlets by the introduction of quotations from the Greek dramatists and from a great variety of English poets, from Milton, from Akenside, and from Southey's then unpublished poem 'To the Exiled Patriots'.[3] Nor was Coleridge too modest to introduce one of his own passages from the *Fall of Robespierre*.[4]

One essential quality that every successful political pamphleteer must possess is nowhere found in the Bristol pamphlets and that is the command of a consistently powerful style adapted to the needs of a particular public. There is a world of difference between the style of Burke's *Reflections on the French Revolution* and Paine's

---

[1] *Political Disquisitions: or an Enquiry into public errors, defects and abuses*, 3 vols., 1774–5. It contained valuable statistics relating to the electoral system and taxation. When Dr. Parr was asked if he had read it, he replied, 'Have I read my Bible, sir?' Coleridge called it 'an invaluable treasure'. Op. cit. i. 77.

[2] *E.O.T.* i. 41. [3] Ibid. i. 19–20.

[4] Quoted in the lecture *On the Present War*. A footnote refers to *The Fall of Robespierre* as 'A Tragedy, of which the first act was written by S. T. Coleridge'. No mention was made of Southey's joint-authorship. *E.O.T.* i. 54.

Rights of Man, but each writer clearly understood the kind of audience he addressed and knew what were the most effective means of reaching it. Each, as a result, adopted a style wholly appropriate to his purpose. The unevenness and inequalities to be found in the Bristol lectures are partly to be ascribed to sheer inexperience and a boyish desire to show off, but they were also symptomatic of a more radical weakness, Coleridge's inability to come to terms with his public. The consciously superior tone that he adopted for much of the time was little calculated to win the sympathies of his audience, and the passages that he threw in either to amuse, or to satisfy the demand for sensationalism, struck a discordant note. This was the first of many occasions on which Coleridge sought to accomplish what lay outside his range, to please and instruct a mixed public simultaneously.

CHAPTER II

PRIVATE JOURNALISM:
THE WATCHMAN, 1796

IN view of the importance Coleridge attributed, in the Bristol lectures, to the existence of a free and independent Press, it is not surprising to find that he should next have turned his attention to setting up his own journal. As early as December 1794, when his enthusiasm for Pantisocracy was waning and the need to find suitable employment became urgent, his thoughts turned to journalism. He and Southey tried to secure positions as reporters on the *Telegraph*, but nothing came of this project.[1] Shortly afterwards they planned to edit a monthly magazine which was to be called *The Provincial Magazine*,[2] but after they quarrelled the idea was abandoned. 'I must be connected with R. Southey in it, which I could not be with comfort to my feelings', he wrote to Tom Poole on 7 October 1795.[3] A further disadvantage was that it would become 'a thing of monthly *Anxiety* and quotidian Bustle'.[4] Thrown back on his own resources, he called a meeting at the Rummer Tavern to discuss plans for the launching of his own journal, which he proposed to call *The Watchman*. He lost no time in having a *Prospectus* printed, in which he announced that the first issue would appear on Friday, 5 February 1796. In fact, there was a delay and the first number did not appear until 1 March. It is doubtful if Coleridge realized at first the magnitude of the task he had undertaken. To begin with he had to enlist subscribers; that done, he had to produce, almost unaided, an issue of *The Watchman*, consisting of thirty-two pages, every eight days. It was certainly a task involving more than 'monthly *Anxiety* and quotidian Bustle'.

There were many reasons why Coleridge decided to produce his own journal instead of seeking employment with an established

---

[1] *C.L.* i. 152.
[2] Southey said that it was intended to be 'the vehicle of all our poetry'. *Life and Correspondence of Robert Southey*, ed. C. C. Southey, i. 231–2. *The Watchman* later served something of this function for Coleridge.
[3] *C.L.* i. 161.
[4] Ibid.

paper. If he had joined the staff of a national daily he would have had to live in London and this he did not wish. As he said to Estlin a few months after *The Watchman* came to an end, 'I love Bristol & I do not love London'.¹ There were also weighty objections to joining a provincial paper. Most of them were mouthpieces of the Ministry and he could not contemplate helping them 'steal away the people's rights and liberties'.² There seemed, therefore, no alternative but to start his own paper, and this he was encouraged to do by numerous friends and 'sundry Philanthropists and Anti-polemists'.³ By becoming his own master he would in theory be free to print whatever he wished and he would be able to set an example to others how a paper could be conducted without literary or political prejudice. Though he denied that desire for wealth led him to journalism, he had reasonable hopes of making some money out of the project. He canvassed for subscribers in a number of large towns, made arrangements that never matured for the journal to be published in Birmingham as well as in Bristol,⁴ and did what else he could to arrange for a wide circulation; and by being editor, chief contributor, and private distributor he cut down on outgoing expenses. In spite of all his efforts *The Watchman* was not a financial success. The losses amounted to £100.⁵

It is clear that the financial motive was not the only one. From the contents of the *Prospectus* and from the motto subjoined to the title of the paper and the *Prospectus*

> That All may know the TRUTH;
> And that the TRUTH may make us FREE! !

it can be seen that one of Coleridge's main purposes was to find a more effective method of disseminating political wisdom than by lecturing and publishing pamphlets. The general thesis of the *Prospectus* was simple and was boldly stated in large capital letters. First came the assertion,

IN AN ENSLAVED STATE THE RULERS FORM AND SUPPLY THE
OPINIONS OF THE PEOPLE.

---

¹ *C.L.* i. 222. The remark was made after Perry of the *Morning Chronicle* had asked him to come to London and write for him.
² *Prospectus.* See *C. Life*, p. 286.   ³ *B.L.* i. 114.
⁴ An advertisement appeared on 25 Jan. 1796 in *Aris's Birmingham Gazette* announcing that *The Watchman* would be published in Birmingham as well as Bristol. James Belcher was to be the Birmingham publisher.   ⁵ *U.L.* ii. 135.

This was followed by,

A PEOPLE ARE FREE IN PROPORTION AS THEY FORM THEIR OWN OPINIONS. In the strictest sense of the word KNOWLEDGE IS POWER.

At the time he wrote the *Prospectus*, Coleridge envisaged helping the Whig Society to obtain the repeal of the Gagging Acts and intended to co-operate with the Patriotic Societies to obtain 'a Right of Suffrage general and frequent'. By the time the first number appeared, however, his connexions with these bodies had come to an end and his independence of mind reasserted itself. Far from arguing for the repeal of the Gagging Acts in *The Watchman*, he declared that they might serve the useful purpose of rendering the language of political publications 'more cool and guarded', and might encourage writers to confine themselves to first principles. He also refrained from giving any support to the cause of parliamentary reform, since he still adhered to the principle first stated in *A Moral and Political Lecture* and repeated in the following form in the *Prospectus*: 'Without previous illumination a change in the *forms* of Government will be of no avail.' But such illumination could not take place as long as the lower classes were dependent on the provincial papers for information, since with one or two notable exceptions like the *Cambridge Intelligencer*, these were the mouthpieces of the Ministry. Innkeepers feared that they would lose their licences if papers critical of the Ministry were read on their premises.[1] It was, then, to provide a paper that would help to forward political illumination, to disseminate knowledge, and to teach the people to relate everyday political questions to fundamental principles that Coleridge founded *The Watchman*.

He promised that the miscellany would contain recent history, both foreign and domestic; parliamentary reports, and during the recesses, selected speeches from the reign of Charles I onwards; and also, 'Original Essays and Poetry, chiefly or altogether political'.[2] A selection from the latter and from the book reviews was made by his daughter Sara in the first volume of *Essays on His Own Times*, from which it is possible to form a very fair picture of Coleridge's strength and weakness as a journalist.[3] The closely reasoned and impassioned essay *On the Slave Trade* and the *Review*

---

[1] 'Do you take the *Morning Chronicle* or the *Morning Post*?', the publican would be asked, according to Sheridan. 'Take care there is no sedition in it, for if there is, you are liable to punishment!' A. Aspinall, *Politics and the Press*, 1949, pp. 43–44.

[2] *Prospectus*. C. *Life*, p. 287.   [3] *E.O.T.* i. 99–178.

of Burke's Letter to a Noble Lord reveal his strength, while his limitations, particularly of taste and regard for his readers' interests, can be seen in the *Essay on Fasts* and in the *Historical Sketch of the Manners and Religion of the Ancient Germans*. The essays and reviews printed by Sara Coleridge do not, however, give any impression at all of the contents of an average issue of *The Watchman*. In fact about three-quarters of the space was taken up by material reprinted from other sources: out-of-date parliamentary reports, diplomatic news and foreign intelligence, and reports of domestic affairs taken from other newspapers. Her selections do not sufficiently illustrate Coleridge's personal interest in the ideological significance of the events that were taking place in France, nor do they give any indication of the space devoted to the effects of Pitt's repressive policy in the provinces.

It is surprising that Sara Coleridge should not have printed her father's *Remonstrance to the French Legislators*.[1] It marks an important stage in Coleridge's espousal of the revolutionary cause, and it possesses considerable literary merit. 'It contain'd *my* politics', he wrote to the editor of the *Cambridge Intelligencer*;[2] and in form it was something more than a protest against France's aggressive policy and her refusal at this time to negotiate a peace. It was an eloquent plea to the French legislators to recall the original principles on which the Revolution had been based, and Coleridge uttered a prophetic warning of what would befall the whole of Europe if they did not do so.

If however you persevere in your intention, will your soldiers fight with the same enthusiasm for the Ambition as they have done for the Liberty of their Country? Will they not by degrees amid the stern discipline of arms and the Horrors of War, forget the proud duties of *Citizens*, and become callous to the softer charms of domestic life? May not some future Dumourier find a more pliant Army? May not the distresses of the poor drive them to Anarchy? May not the rising generations who have only *heard* of the evils of despotism but have *felt* the horrors of a Revolutionary Republic, imbibe sentiments favourable to Royalty? Will not the multitude of discontented men make *such* regulations necessary for the preservation of your Freedom, as in themselves destroy freedom? Have not some of your supposed Patriots already deemed it expedient to limit the Liberty of the Press? Legislators of France! in the name of Posterity we adjure you to

[1] 27 Apr. 1796, *W.*, pp. 229–30.
[2] 11 Dec. 1796, *C.L.* i. 268. In *U.L.* i. 66, the phrase is printed 'it *contain'd my* politics'.

consider that misused success is soon followed by adversity, and that the adversity of France may lead, in its train of consequences, to the slavery of Europe.[1]

This series of questions was well calculated to stir doubts in the mind of any Frenchman who read it. But who read it? The few who continued to take *The Watchman* were for the most part respectable English middle-class dissenters. But three years later when he again turned to French affairs it was in the *Morning Post* that he wrote his essays and then his denunciations of the new French constitution and his reflections on the despotism of Bonaparte reached across the channel and even Bonaparte himself took an active interest in what Coleridge wrote.[2]

Sara also omitted a large number of passages dealing with the effects of Pitt's repressive policy. Though the writing in these lacks literary distinction, the scattered passages occupy a considerable amount of space in *The Watchman* and indicate the depth of Coleridge's hatred for the system of repression and the employment of government spies and informers. For some of his material he was dependent on contributors. The account of the arrest and trial of John Binns[3] and Gale Jones,[4] two members of the London Corresponding Society who were travelling round the Midlands to revive interest in the reform movement, was supplied by a Birmingham correspondent who called himself 'Phocion'.[5] But

[1] *W.*, p. 232.

[2] Coleridge claimed that Bonaparte ordered Louis Otto to find out from Stuart, the editor of the *Morning Post*, when the promised portrait of himself would appear, *C.L.* ii. 1007. He also claimed that Bonaparte ordered his arrest when he was returning from Malta through Italy on account of the essays he had written in the *Morning Post*. *C. Life*, pp. 150–1. See Chap. III.

[3] John Binns (1772–1860) was born in Dublin, came to London in 1794, and became a member of the London Corresponding Society. Between 1795 and 1801 he was often arrested. In 1801 he emigrated to America and achieved some degree of fame as a journalist. He wrote *Recollections of John Binns* in 1854.

[4] John Gale Jones (1769–1838) was a surgeon and apothecary. An active member of the London Corresponding Society, he was convicted at Warwick in 1797 for uttering sedition. In 1810 he was sentenced to twelve months imprisonment for protesting against the exclusion of strangers from the House during the debate on the Walcheren expedition. Coleridge insisted on making a personal investigation of the reports that he was being ill-treated in prison in 1810. Stuart, *Gentleman's Magazine*, 1838, ii. 127.

[5] Reports of the case appeared in *Aris's Birmingham Gazette*. James Belcher, who was to have printed *The Watchman* in Birmingham, printed *The Trial of John Binns* in 1797. The account was based on the short-hand notes of Henry Binner, who may also have been the author of the reports that appeared in *The Watchman* under the name 'Phocion'.

other examples were to be found on his own doorstep. Two whole pages of one issue were taken up with the account of how a Bristol man, Thomas Gage, had been sentenced to death for throwing stones at the Public Prosecutor's house. Coleridge pointed out that he had been convicted on the evidence of one man, Matthews, a tiler, in spite of the fact that his employer had testified that he had been at work at the time of the offence; and he added that the witness would receive £40 if a conviction were obtained. From this case he drew the general deduction that at no period since the Revolution had 'the lives of so many innocent men been attempted by perjury' and concluded that 'at no period therefore ought the public eye to be more steadily fixed on the courts of Justice'.[1] John Thelwall, the radical orator and demagogue, had drawn the same conclusion in his first lecture entitled *The Moral Tendency of a System of Spies and Informers*. There he related the amazing story of a government agent who had attempted to incriminate a perfectly innocent publican. The agent listened at the keyhole of a room in which the publican had fallen asleep after having read an account of the barbarous treatment of the aristocrats in France; and, hearing him utter violent sentiments in his sleep, he laid information against him. The prosecution alleged that there was '*malice prepense* in the dream'. In his lecture Thelwall poured bitter scorn on 'the crime of dreaming sedition'.[2] Two years later Wordsworth's and Coleridge's habit of taking notes as they walked aroused suspicion and a government agent was sent down to Nether Stowey to watch their activities. Coleridge's motive in reporting the Birmingham and Bristol cases at length in *The Watchman* was the same as Thelwall's in his lecture; it was to rouse public opinion against the system of repression, by showing that the lives of innocent men were at the mercy of government spies and by showing that the magistrates had ceased to be dispensers of justice and had become active agents of the Ministry's policy of repression.

While it is true that Coleridge relied on other papers and correspondents for most of the news concerning the proceedings of the French Legislature, the successes and reverses of the French

---

[1] *W.*, p. 192.
[2] *Lecture the First, The Moral Tendency of a system of Spies and Informers*, 1796, pp. 15–16. There is a copy of this lecture in the British Museum, Press Mark 12270, cc. 24 (5).

Army, and the various examples of misgovernment at home, the actual space devoted to these topics was indicative of the editor's own interests.[1] George Burnett, one of the original Pantisocrats, was to have done the work of sub-editing, but the heavy burden fell on Coleridge's shoulders and he carried it out remarkably well, though it must have been this form of 'Watch drudgery' that precipitated the end of the journal. His policy with regard to reporting news was to state the facts 'simply and nakedly, without epithets or comments'.[2] On occasions the self-imposed restraint produced odd results, as when he placed an asterisk against a report of Mr. Jenkinson's statement in Parliament 'that there never had been a more successful war' and for footnote supplied five exclamation marks.[3] In spite of such oddities it is clear that he made a serious attempt to keep news and views apart, and recognized the principle that underlies all sound editorial policy: 'Comment is free, but facts are sacred.'

The views as distinct from the news, were expressed in the form of separate essays. Coleridge realized that it would be absurd to promise the same degree of impartiality in these as in the presentation of news. 'My bias, however, is in favour of principles, not men', he declared, 'and though I may be classed with a party, I scorn to be of a faction.'[4] It was from the essays, in the main, that Sara Coleridge made her selection. It would be a misnomer to call them leaders, as the subject-matter was not always taken from the events of the day, nor were the essays given special prominence in the layout of *The Watchman*. The choice of theme was highly personal, wayward even, in the last numbers. The paper, however, gave Coleridge the opportunity of continuing the discussion of the two issues that chiefly concerned him at this time: what were the best ways of bringing about social reform; and what were the chief deficiencies of Godwin and his disciples. The essays fulfilled the personal needs of the author rather than those of the subscribers of *The Watchman*; they served in many ways the same function as the Notebooks, in that they enabled Coleridge to clarify, not communicate, his thoughts; though it must be admitted that they contain none of the brilliant intuitive flashes of truth with which the Notebooks are filled. In many respects they

---

[1] Coleridge's connexions with the editors of the *Cambridge Intelligencer* and the *Monthly Magazine* enabled him to reproduce material from these sources.

[2] *E.O.T.* i. 105.   [3] *W.*, p. 96.   [4] *E.O.T.* i. 105–6.

are in marked contrast to the leading articles contributed to the
Morning Post from 1799 to 1802, in which the subjects Coleridge
had to write on were of national importance and the public a large
and established one and therefore easier to address.

In the first of his essays in *The Watchman*, Coleridge connected
his own attempts to use the Press as a medium for the communication of truth with a large-scale historical movement. He considered that he was carrying on the great task of destroying
ignorance and disseminating knowledge that had begun during
the Renaissance and the Reformation. The task had always been
fraught with danger. 'From the reign of Elizabeth to the present
hour, the propagation of civil and religious wisdom has never
been altogether free from danger.' Taxes and stamp duties had
been repeatedly imposed on newspapers to place them beyond the
pocket of the poor man. Pitt had declared that they were fit objects
for taxation on the ground that they were mere luxuries. 'A mere
luxury for the proprietors to be informed concerning the measures
of the directors!' Coleridge indignantly exclaimed. Having already
recognized the constitutional importance of a free Press in *The Plot
Discovered*, he now came to give practical expression to his contention. Indeed, he showed an almost prophetic understanding of the
future importance of the Press. He did not of course see that a
time would come when the popular national Press would debase
rather than elevate the understanding of the people, although his
comments in later life on the methods used by Cobbett and others
indicate that his attitude towards the popular paper of the present
century would have been one of utter contempt.[1] He considered
that the function of the Press was to express the critical spirit of
the nation, and his acute insight into the realities as opposed to the
forms of political life told him that the newspapers could provide
a more accurate index of the state of public opinion than the mere
counting of votes in Parliament. He saw, too, that the Press could
act as a great organ of national education, and that until this
process of political education had reached all classes and taught
'first principles, or the diffusion of that general knowledge which
should be the basis or substratum of politics',[2] it would be premature and dangerous to extend the franchise.

---

[1] *Lay Sermons*, pp. 164–6. In a Notebook entry he accused the Cobbetts and Hunts
of his day of addressing the lower ranks 'as beasts who have no future selves'.
Notebook No. 22, B.M. Add. MSS. 47520, f. 61.   [2] *E.O.T.* i. 105.

In the year 1796 a variety of impediments existed to prevent the carrying out of any such process of political illumination. Apart from the heavy taxes which Coleridge himself avoided by publishing every eight days, there were the two Gagging Acts that severely restricted the freedom of expression. To Coleridge, as to many others, there were far too many people interested in perpetuating the inequalities and injustices of society; and to support his contention he quoted a passage from Arthur Young's *Travels*, a passage that had already been quoted in the *Prospectus*. 'What a mass of the people in all parts of England are some way or other interested in the present representation of the people, in tythes, charters, monopolies, and taxation! and not merely in the things themselves, but in all the abuses attending them.'[1] Even though the impediments to political illumination were immense there seemed to be four ways in which Providence was counteracting them. There was the growth of Methodism, the existence of factories in which it had become the habit for the industrial poor to read a newspaper, the growth of book societies, and the 'increasing experience of the dreadful effects of war and corruption'.[2]

Of these, Methodism and dissent in general received most of Coleridge's consideration. 'The very act of dissenting from established opinions must generate habits precursive to the love of freedom', he declared. 'Man begins to be free when he begins to examine.' In view of the frequency with which it has been suggested that Methodism acted as an anodyne for the people's sufferings,[3] one should note that Coleridge firmly denied that a religion that inculcated faith in mysteries prepared the way for a passive acceptance of tyranny. On the contrary, he asserted, religion by directing the mind to the thought of an after life teaches a self-discipline and self-government that make the individual critical of all forms of public misgovernment, particularly of measures that interfere with the liberty of the individual. The special value of the

---

[1] Ibid. i. 102. Arthur Young (1741–1820) wrote extensively on economics and agriculture. His most famous work was *Travels in France*, 1792, in which he attacked the *ancien régime*. He subsequently changed his political opinions and served under Pitt. See Coleridge's attack in a *Morning Post* article, *E.O.T.* ii. 395–403.

[2] Ibid. i. 102–5.

[3] A suggestion strongly denied by R. F. Wearmouth in *Methodism and the Common People in the 18th Century*, 1945, p. 221. The Hammonds were obliged to revise sections of *The Town Labourer* in the light of Dr. Wearmouth's research into Methodist history. See the preface to the Guild Books ed. of the Hammonds' work.

contribution Methodism was making towards the conquest of ignorance and the training for citizenship depended on certain features of the movement. Its high degree of organization gave it an advantage over the efforts of a 'myriad of detached metaphysical systematizers', a phrase directed at the disciples of Godwin; its close connexion with the poor established strong bonds of affection 'that must necessarily lead to a blameless indignation against the authors of their complicated miseries'; while its tendency to induce sobriety and domestic habits would, Coleridge believed, make the people susceptible of liberty.[1]

But Coleridge himself moved in Unitarian and not Methodist circles and in the pages of *The Watchman* can be detected his growing dissatisfaction with the former. Their characteristic defects were described as a smug self-satisfaction, a somewhat cold and calculating benevolence,[2] and a frequent failure to carry philanthropy beyond the sphere of good intentions and high principles. The ill-judged tone of irritation that he allowed to enter the essays *On Fasts*, on *Modern Patriotism*, and *We See Things with Different Eyes* arose partly from this source. Although he had spoken in the Bristol lectures and in the first number of *The Watchman* of his intention to bring political illumination to the poor peasant, he must have soon realized that the method of presentation adopted in his miscellany made this impossible. He saw that the only way of reaching the minds of the poor without inflaming their passions and stirring up a violent spirit of revolt, as the democrats tended to do, was to join the Methodists, but this he was prevented from doing because he objected to the 'absurdity' of their enthusiasm and the nature of their theological beliefs. In the Bristol lectures, however, he had already laid down the principle that the true patriot should 'plead *for* the oppressed, not *to* them'. To succeed in doing this it was first necessary to win the confidence and support of the members of the middle classes whom he addressed on behalf of the poor, but this he proved incapable of doing. Instead of attempting to gain their confidence and make them forget their differences in the common task of improving the lot of the poor,

---

[1] *E.O.T.* i. 102–4.
[2] Cf. the lines from *Reflections on Having Left a Place of Retirement*:

> And he that works me good with unmov'd face,
> Does it but half: he chills me while he aids,
> My benefactor, not my brother man!
>
> (*P.W.* i. 107.)

he constantly reminded them of these very differences and increased their disunity.

Thus, in the essay *On Modern Patriotism* which appeared in the third issue, he denied the right of many people to call themselves patriots and drew caricatures of various types of reformers: the tavern demagogue, the uncritical disciple of Godwin, the middle-class radical whose chief activity seemed to be attending public dinners, the rich Whig aristocrat with a taste for gaming, and the opponent of slavery who complacently enjoyed the benefits of the vile trade; all these were made the subject of vivid satirical thumbnail sketches.[1] At the time the reference to the Whig fond of gaming would certainly have been interpreted as a veiled attack on Fox; nor would it have required much ingenuity to associate Horne Tooke with the democrat who appeared at all public dinners.

The short section on the disciples of Godwin adds nothing to our knowledge of Coleridge's attitude towards Godwin's political philosophy. It consists largely of sarcastic references to his treatment of the domestic affections, a section of *Political Justice* that he had already attacked in the revised version of the first Bristol lecture. The letter *To Caius Gracchus*, which appeared in the fifth issue and was an answer to a correspondent's complaint of his treatment of Godwin in the earlier essay, is equally disappointing.[2] Sarcasm was heaped on the already much-ridiculed passage in which Godwin had chosen an unfortunate example to illustrate the future conquest of mind over matter. Godwin had envisaged the time when a plough might be turned into a field and 'perform its offices without the need of superintendence'. It was in this sense, he declared, that Franklin had conjectured that 'mind would one day become omnipotent over matter!'[3] Alluding to this passage in *Political Justice* and another in which Godwin had written of the ultimate conquest of death itself, Coleridge replied to Caius Gracchus's charge that the editor of *The Watchman* was a mere 'Enthusiast' by saying: 'You deem me an *enthusiast* . . . because I am not quite convinced with yourself and Mr. Godwin that mind will be omnipotent over matter, that a plough will go into the field and perform its labour without the presence of the agriculturist, that man may be immortal in this life, and that death is an act of the will ! ! !'[4] In this essay, as in his letters to his friends

---

[1] *E.O.T.* i. 135–6.   [2] Ibid. i. 160–5.   [3] *P.J.* ii. 503.
[4] *E.O.T.* i. 164.

and in his Notebooks, he promised to write a full critique of
Political Justice, but nothing came of his promises.[1] He claimed that
since writing his sonnet *To William Godwin* in 1795 he had 'studied
his work', a claim that is not substantiated by the evidence of *The
Watchman* essays, where the gibes are those which could have been
made by anyone with only a second-hand knowledge of the work.
Some light is thrown on Coleridge's assertion that he had devoted
further study to the work and that he was in fact preparing an
answer or critique of Godwin by the correspondence with Thelwall during 1796. Two facts emerge clearly from this exchange of
letters: that Coleridge's increased hostility to Godwin owed more
to the anecdotes about his character and personal life that he had
heard, than to a continued study of *Political Justice*; secondly, that
the projected critique of the work existed only in Coleridge's
brain.

It was strangely inconsistent for one who claimed that his bias
was 'in favour of principles, not men'[2] to allow stories of a man's
personal life to affect his judgement of a work. The cause of this
inconsistency is not far to seek. Coleridge was a profoundly religious man and a devoted father at this time, and thus the stories
of Godwin's egotistical atheism and vague rumours concerning
his domestic life were sufficient to awaken personal prejudice.
Though he asserted that it was Godwin's character that had increased his hatred of atheism, the facts point to the opposite
conclusion. Thelwall accused him in one letter of 'industriously
collecting anecdotes unfavourable to the character of great men';[3]
and an example of this practice is the humorous anecdote related for
the amusement of Benjamin Flower. 'A young man of fortune,
(his name, Gurney) wrote & published a book of horrible Blas-
phemies . . . —& after a fulsome panegyric adds that the name
of *Godwin* will soon supersede that of Christ.—Godwin wrote a
letter to this Man, thanking him for his *admirable* work, & solicit-

---

[1] On 2 Nov. 1796 he announced to Benjamin Flower that he would shortly 'be
delivered of an Examination of Godwin's political Justice'. *C.L.* i. 247. Among a
long list of projected works in the Gutch Memorandum Book appear 'Strictures on
Godwin, Paley etc.' and number 17 on a longer list, 'Letters to Godwin'. *N.* i. 161
and 174.

[2] *E.O.T.* i. 105.

[3] Coleridge defends himself from the charge in a letter to Thelwall, 22 June 1796,
C.L. i. 221, but his susceptibility to malicious gossip about Godwin is amply illus-
trated in an earlier letter in which he refers to a series of anecdotes detrimental to
Godwin's good name. Ibid. i. 214.

ing the honour of his personal friendship!!!'[1] It is clear from the
letter written to Thelwall that Coleridge had allowed his mind to
be poisoned through listening to malicious talk.

The correspondence has a further interest, for it provides first-
hand evidence of the reaction of a Jacobin and atheist to *The
Watchman*. Thelwall opened the correspondence by writing to
complain of Coleridge's use of the phrase 'Unsupported Malcontent' in *The Plot Discovered*.[2] Feeling that since they were both
engaged in the same occupation of disseminating political knowledge they 'should not be strangers to one another', Coleridge
wrote an apologetic reply in which he disingenuously explained
that the passage had originally read ' "unsupported Malcontents"
meaning myself and you', but that he had been seized afterwards
with a fit of modesty and omitted himself.[3] This conciliatory
gesture led to an exchange of letters throughout the remaining
months of 1796. Thelwall made two main charges against the
editor of *The Watchman*. He accused Coleridge of having allowed
sectarian prejudice to enter into his critique of Godwin, and of
having failed to prove his thesis that in order to be a good democrat it was first necessary to be a good Christian. Since the latter
charge struck at the root of Coleridge's approach to social and
political problems, he was led to amplify what he had already said
in the *Introductory Address* and in the pages of *The Watchman*. The
Christian religion was specially fit for democrats, he asserted.

It certainly teaches in the most explicit terms the rights of Man, his
right to Wisdom, his right to an equal share in all the blessings of
Nature; it commands it's disciples to go every where, & every where to
preach these rights; it commands them never to use the arm of flesh, to
be perfectly non-resistant; yet to hold the promulgation of *Truth* to be
a Law above Law, and in the performance of this office to defy 'Wickedness in high places,' and cheerfully to endure ignominy, & wretchedness, & torments, & death, rather than *intermit* the performance of it;
yet while enduring ignominy, & wretchedness, & torments & death to
feel nothing but sorrow, and pity, and love for those who inflicted
them; wishing their Oppressors to be altogether such as they, 'except-
ing these bonds.'—Here is *truth* in theory; and in practice a union of
energetic *action*, and more energetic *Suffering*.[4]

When a few lines later Thelwall came upon the phrase 'Christianity regards morality as a process', he might well have wondered

[1] Ibid. i. 269.   [2] C. Cestre, *John Thelwall*, New York, 1906, p. 140; *E.O.T.* i. 70.
[3] *C.L.* i. 205.   [4] Ibid. i. 282.

whether there was any essential difference between Coleridge's necessitarian brand of Christianity and Godwin's political philosophy. But a vital difference between Coleridge and both Thelwall and Godwin is in fact laid bare by this correspondence; Coleridge believed that it was more important to seek the moral reformation of the vicious than to preach to the virtuous, while the other two were content to address the politically elect. But it is one thing to believe in the unique power of religion to bring about a radical moral reformation of the individuals that constitute society, and quite another to convince others of this power, and to persuade them to abandon all methods that are exclusively political. Even if it is accepted that the Christian religion possesses this unique power, it is nevertheless true that the critic of society who adopts a specifically Christian viewpoint will probably find himself addressing only the faithful.

The main interest, then, of the essay on *Modern Patriotism* and the letter *To Caius Gracchus* does not lie in their intrinsic literary merit, or in their effectiveness as propaganda, in both of which they are sadly deficient, but in the light that is thrown on Coleridge's final rejection of Godwinism. For intrinsic literary and polemical merit one has to turn elsewhere; to the essay *On the Slave Trade*, for example, a model of its kind. Though the arguments on both sides are clearly stated, the author's opinion is never in doubt. This method of presenting an argument bears out Coleridge's contention in *The Friend*, that 'the first duty of a wise advocate is to convince his opponents, that he understands their arguments and sympathizes with their just feelings'.[1] In attacking the apologists of the slave trade, however, he did not side with the Abolitionists. Referring to Wilberforce's Bill, he asserted that 'the application to the Legislature was altogether wrong'.[2] It was wrong because it was superfluous. According to Coleridge the best method of killing the Slave Trade was for every Christian to refrain from using the unnecessary luxuries, sugar and rum; and by means of a violently rhetorical passage he attempted to make his readers see that the West Indian commodities came stained with human blood. 'Then with our fleshly eye should we behold what even now Imagination ought to paint to us; instead of conserves, tears and blood, and for music, groanings and the loud peals of the lash.'[3] It will probably be objected that Coleridge

[1] *F.*, p. 135.   [2] *E.O.T.* i. 149.   [3] Ibid. i. 150.

should have accepted the necessity of State legislation and that he ought therefore to have persuaded his readers to support Wilberforce's Bill. In fact his solution struck at the heart of the problem, for it was an attempt to change the attitude of the individual and through him ultimately the attitude of society as a whole. His purpose in painting the sufferings of the slaves in such vivid colours was to awaken the consciences of his readers by laying the responsibility for this inhumanity on the shoulders of each of those who continued to use any goods from the West Indies. Although it can now be seen that Coleridge was too optimistic in believing that individual abstention would kill the trade and thus make legislation unnecessary, he was certainly right in thinking that the evil needed to be brought home forcefully to the individual and that in this question as in all others some degree of illumination must precede reform.[1] But here, as on other occasions, he did not sufficiently recognize the reciprocal relationship that exists between legislative act and the force of public opinion.

Only in his *Two Addresses on Sir Robert Peel's Bill*, 1818, did Coleridge attribute sufficient importance to legislation as an instrument of reform; then he used his literary talents to rally support of Peel's Bill to control the use of child labour in the cotton mills.[2] Apart from this radical difference in approach, the essay *On the Slave Trade* and the two later *Addresses* have much in common. In both, the arguments of the opposition are fairly set out and decisively destroyed, in both, Coleridge's generous humanity and sympathy for human suffering is much in evidence, and in both, he substitutes for the abstract arguments of his opponents concrete references to the actual sufferings of those whose misery he hoped to alleviate. In the pamphlets on factory legislation he took his facts from the 'Report of the Committee on the State of Children and Manufacturers, 1816',[3] and the same serious and painstaking study of the evidence is seen in the essay *On the Slave Trade*. In both cases, the effect of a wealth of concrete

[1] Ibid. i. 21.

[2] *Remarks on the Objections which have been urged Against the Principle of Sir Robert Peel's Bill* (18 Apr. 1818) and *The Grounds of Sir Robert Peel's Bill Vindicated* (24 Apr. 1818). The two *Addresses* were edited and privately printed by Sir Edmund Gosse in 1913. Reprinted in L. E. Watson, *Coleridge at Highgate*, 1925, pp. 171–8.

[3] The Committee was set up by Peel. 'It took the evidence of forty-three witnesses, not one of them a worker.' J. L. and B. Hammond, *The Town Labourer*, Guild ed., i. 162.

detail was to show that not only were the arguments of the opposition baseless but that they sprang from a cold calculating self-interest and a thorough disregard for the sufferings of others. Coleridge's experience of politics and politicians—and here is the clue to his intense hatred of Pitt—led him more and more as time went on to distrust abstract arguments and generalizations unrelated to already established principles and observed fact. The attitude is best summed up in the following passage from one of the pamphlets on the Factory Bill. 'Generalities are apt to deceive us. Individualise the sufferings which it is the object of this Bill to remedy, follow up the detail in some one case with human sympathy, and the deception vanishes.'[1] Once you imagined the sufferings of an individual, it was impossible to accept the argument that the Factory Bill should be opposed because it might arouse false hopes in the workers and therefore increase industrial discontent. Similarly once you imagined the sufferings of the slaves you could never accept the specious arguments of the slavers.

The book reviews in *The Watchman* formed a no less important part of the miscellany than the essays. Coleridge's views on the subject of reviewing appeared in the introductory essay in the first number. There he declared that it was his intention never to review more than one work in each issue and only works 'of apparent merit, whether such as teach true principles with energy, or recommend false principles by the decorations of genius'. The *Critical Review*, for example, mechanically dispatched anything up to fifty volumes an issue, and this was by no means exceptional. Hence the low standard of the reviews. Coleridge was equally critical of the extent to which the reviews were affected by political bias and by the connexion of periodicals with the booksellers. Literary excellence was to form the sole criterion of merit in *The Watchman*; and declaring that he was free from all external attachments, the editor promised his readers that his book reviews would contain neither flattery nor resentment.

On the whole Coleridge remained faithful to the avowed policy of including one review in each issue. There was in practice, however, a considerable deviation from the general policy laid down in the first essay. It is impossible to believe that the decision to review an *Essay on the Public Merits of Mr Pitt*[2] by Thomas Beddoes,

---

[1] L. E. Watson, *Coleridge at Highgate*, p. 177.
[2] *W.*, pp. 16–23.

or Count Rumford's *Essays*,[1] was based purely on their literary excellence. In reviewing Beddoes's pamphlet he was doing a friend a favour,[2] and his motives in drawing attention to Count Rumford's *Essays* were no less personal. He had made a discovery and he wished to share it with his readers. He had experienced a proud delight, he declared, when he had found 'that Count Rumford was an Englishman', and he now bracketed him with Howard, the prison reformer, and the thought of them restored his faith in England.[3] It can be seen that the editor's freedom from attachment to booksellers and political parties led not to a policy of responsible independence but to one the irresponsibility of which arose from an arbitrary exercise of his personal tastes and interests.

The best of these reviews appeared in the first issue of *The Watchman*. This was a *Review of Burke's Letter to a Noble Lord*,[4] a work which had aroused much interest at the time of publication. The review illustrates two characteristic qualities of Coleridge's best controversial writings: the attempt to do full justice to the strength and power of an opponent, and his sure skill in selecting the main points in the opponent's argument in order to reduce them to absurdity by cumulative ridicule and inspired rhetoric. The academic discipline learned in the study of classical literature served him well when he ventured into the world of political controversy. He frequently approached the point of view or work to be criticized as if it were an academic exercise; this is particularly true of his remarks on style, in his perception of any dangerous ambiguities of phrase, and in his detection of false logic and omission of relevant fact. Quotation from the work under

[1] Ibid., pp. 140–4.

[2] It is not known when Coleridge first met Beddoes. In Nov. 1795 they attended a public meeting to protest against the Pitt–Grenville 'Gagging Bills'. It was through Beddoes, who was in charge of the Pneumatic Institute at Bristol, that Coleridge met Humphry Davy, who was his pupil at this time.

[3] Sir Benjamin Thompson, Count Rumford (1753–1814) was actually an American by birth. He was a scientist, soldier, and statesman. In 1779 he was elected a Fellow of the Royal Society and was later knighted by George III. The Elector of Bavaria honoured him for his service to the State from 1783 to 1795. The collected edition of his works that appeared in 1796, *Essays Political, Economical, and Philosophical*, helped to disseminate his ideas on the improvement of hospitals, workhouses, cooking of food, warming houses economically, and on how to cure smoky chimneys. Coleridge particularly welcomed the last of these since boy chimney sweeps would no longer be required.

[4] Lamb selected this review as containing 'the best prose'. Letter to S. T. C. 31 May 1796. *Letters of Charles and Mary Lamb*, 1905, i. 8.

discussion also played an important part in his political writings. In *The Plot Discovered*, for example, long sections from the two Bills were quoted to illustrate the potential danger that lay behind some of the more ambiguous clauses, while in the essay *On the Slave Trade* the false logic of the trade's apologists was successfully exposed. This trained critical sense, which was ultimately literary in origin and character, later enabled him to detect and demonstrate to the readers of the *Morning Post* that the French Constitution of 1799 was nothing but an elaborate façade to hide the reality of despotic rule, and, in the following year, to hold up to ridicule the muddled thinking and general illiteracy of the British reply to the French overtures for peace.[1]

At the beginning of the *Review of Burke's Letter to a Noble Lord*, Coleridge paid generous and heart-felt tribute to Burke's style of oratory, to his great vigour of intellect, and 'almost prophetic keenness of penetration'. The characteristic of true eloquence, he noted in connexion with his oratory, is to 'reason *in* metaphors; of declamation, to argue *by* metaphors'.[2] He singled out for special praise the tender passages referring to Burke's son and the eulogy of Lord Keppel. However, once justice had been done to the virtues that the work undoubtedly possessed and once Burke's genius had been fairly recognized, Coleridge subjected the four main sections to a merciless destructive analysis; these were Burke's attack on Frenchmen and French principles, his contempt for geometry, chemistry, and metaphysics, the personal attack upon the Duke of Bedford, and lastly the defence of his pension. The review ended on a characteristic note.

It is consoling to the lovers of human nature, to reflect that Edmund Burke, the only writer of that Faction 'whose name would not sully the page of an opponent,' learnt the discipline of genius in a different corps. At the flames which rise from the altar of freedom, he kindled that torch with which he since endeavoured to set fire to her temple. Peace be to his spirit, when it departs from us: this is the severest punishment I wish him—that he may be appointed under porter to St. Peter, and be obliged to open the gate of heaven to Brissot, Roland, Condorcet, Fayette, and Priestley![3]

---

[1] See Chap. III for a full discussion of these articles.

[2] *E.O.T.* i. 108.

[3] Ibid. i. 118–19. The passage had first appeared in Dec. 1795, in *An Answer to 'A Letter to Edward Long Fox'*, p. 8. It was a life-long habit to use passages he valued several times.

This last passage, which had first appeared in *An Answer to 'A Letter to Edward Long Fox'*, was perhaps worth more than the whole of the rest of the review. It was the kind of *jeu d'esprit* in which Coleridge excelled and might be compared with the poems *Fire, Famine and Slaughter* and *The Devil's Thoughts*, and with the *Letter From Liberty to Famine*, printed as the first item in *Conciones ad Populum* and subsequently echoed by Shelley in *Swellfoot the Tyrant*.[1]

The *Watchman* came to an end when the tenth number appeared on Friday, 13 May 1796. In a farewell address to his readers Coleridge explained that he was obliged to give it up for the simple reason that the work did not pay its expenses. This was not the only reason. G. L. Tuckett, a friend of Robert Allen and Coleridge had prophesied in the beginning what would happen. 'I'll lay any wager, Allen, that after three or four numbers the sheets will contain nothing but parliamentary debates and Coleridge will add a note at the bottom of the page; "I should think myself deficient in my duty to the public if I did not give these interesting debates at *full* length".'[2] Throughout the first ten issues there was a steady decrease in the amount of original material; and in the last three there was hardly anything that was original at all.[3] Even some of the material presented as being original had in fact appeared elsewhere. Such unacknowledged borrowing was common editorial practice, however, and should not be used as evidence to impugn Coleridge's honesty.[4] Taken with all the other evidence, however, it shows unmistakably that fairly soon after beginning his own journal Coleridge discovered that he had embarked on a far more onerous course than he had expected and that he lost interest once the 'Watch drudgery' overwhelmed him. A further reason for its failure was that he never seems to have decided for which classes of reader he was writing, nor to have understood that the success of any journal depends on its capacity to please a known section of the public. Coleridge's difficulty in establishing a satisfactory relationship with the public has already been pointed out in connexion with the lectures and pamphlets composed in the previous year. His excuse for his failure there and in *The Watchman* would

---

[1] K. N. Cameron, 'Shelley and the *Conciones ad Populum*', *M.L.N.*, Dec. 1942.

[2] Quoted in L. Hanson, *The Life of S. T. Coleridge: the Early Years*, 1938, p. 99.

[3] S. F. Johnson, 'Coleridge's *The Watchman*: Decline and Fall', *R.E.S.*, N.S. iv, 1953, pp. 147-8.

[4] L. Patton, 'Coleridge and the "Enquirer Series"', *R.E.S.* xvi, 1940, pp. 188-9.

probably have been that his sole object was to communicate the truth to whoever would listen, and that this was incompatible with seeking to please certain classes; yet it seems as if he deliberately went out of his way to alienate the sympathies of the democrats, dissenters, and Godwinites alike, and it was from these three groups that he had to look for subscribers.

His final words of farewell are not without pathos. 'I have endeavoured to do well. It must be attributed to defect of ability, not of inclination or effort, if the words of the Prophet be altogether applicable to me, "*O Watchman! thou hast watched in vain!*"'[1] Convinced of his unfitness for public life he retired to Nether Stowey and left the work of political illumination to such firebrands as John Thelwall. 'I am not *fit* for *public* life;' he wrote to Thelwall, 'yet the Light shall stream to a far distance from the taper in my cottage window. Meantime, do *you* uplift the *torch* dreadlessly, and show to mankind the face of that Idol which they have worshipped in Darkness!'[2] Frequent correspondence had evidently made Coleridge think more favourably of Thelwall, in spite of the latter's continued protestations of atheism, and opposition to all forms of religion. The phrase 'do *you* uplift the torch dreadlessly', appears to echo lines in the sonnet *To the Honourable Mr Erskine*, printed in the *Morning Chronicle* in December 1794.

> When British Freedom for an happier land
> 　　Spread her broad wings, that flutter'd with affright,
> 　　Erskine! thy voice she heard, and paus'd her flight
> Sublime of hope, *for dreadless thou didst stand*
> 　　(Thy censer glowing with the hallow'd flame)
> 　　A hireless priest before the insulted shrine,
> 　　And at her altar pour the stream divine
> Of unmatch'd eloquence.[3]

The mantle of Erskine, the counsel for the defence and hero of the treason trial of 1794, had evidently come to rest, however incongruously, on the shoulders of Thelwall, and Coleridge was content to retire for a time from active politics.[4]

---

[1] *E.O.T.* i. 178.　　　　　　　　　　　　　　　　　　　　[2] *C.L.* i. 277.
[3] *P.W.* i. 79–80. The italics are mine.
[4] 'For a time, Thelwall stood in his eyes as the hero of the struggle for social justice.' C. Cestre, *John Thelwall*, New York, 1906, p. 142.

CHAPTER III

PUBLIC JOURNALISM:
THE *MORNING POST*, 1799–1802

THE light that streamed from Coleridge's cottage window at Nether Stowey was lurid and fitful. After the death of *The Watchman* and until he became a leader-writer on the *Morning Post* in November 1799, he relied wholly on verse for the communication of his political views. The use of this medium was not in itself a new departure, for he had been writing or revising verse of political significance during the time that he gave the Bristol lectures and also when he ran his own journal. In addition to the *Morning Chronicle* 'Sonnets on Eminent Characters', he had written 'Reflections on having left a place of Retirement', in which he had publicly committed himself to

> . . . go, and join head, heart and hand,
> Active and firm, to fight the bloodless fight
> Of Science, Freedom, and the Truth in Christ;[1]

while the long amorphous blank verse poem *Religious Musings*, begun as early as December 1794 but not completed until 1796, was a not wholly successful attempt to use the Miltonic style to express his radical politics and philosophical speculations.[2] His frequent practice of quoting his own poetry in his early prose works indicates that he thought of his work in prose and verse as forming a single whole. But during the period of retirement at Nether Stowey, it was natural for a variety of reasons to rely on poetry as the medium for political propaganda.

Two of these poems, the *Ode on the Departing Year* and *France: An Ode*, form landmarks in the development of Coleridge's political thought. The dominant note of the first is a deep disgust

---

[1] *P.W.* i. 107–8. The original sub-title, 'A Poem that affects not to be Poetry', and the motto 'Sermoni propriora', indicate that Coleridge was searching for a verse form in which he could deal with the affairs of common life, personal and political.

[2] For excellent analyses see H. House, *Coleridge*, 1953, p. 64, and C. Cestre, *La Révolution française et les poètes anglais*, Dijon, 1906, p. 328.

with his native land for associating herself with the armed ambition of the continental powers, particularly with Russia. In form it exhibits many of the characteristic weaknesses and excesses of the eighteenth-century political ode, nor does Coleridge avoid the danger inherent in all political poetry, that of substituting empty declamatory phrases for the language of genuine passion. The second ode, Coleridge called it 'a kind of Palinodia',[1] is an altogether finer thing. Passion, thought, and form are beautifully fused; and within the narrow compass of the five richly orchestrated but regular stanzas he presents a moving account of the hopes and disillusionment aroused in him by the course of events in France. He frankly admits, as did Wordsworth in *The Prelude*,[2] that when Britain first joined the continental alliance against France he

> sang defeat
> To all that braved the tyrant-quelling lance.[3]

Though blasphemy, bloodshed, and foreign conquest stained the purity of the revolutionary ideal, he continued to hope that France might come as a deliverer and 'compel the nations to be free'; but France's attack on Switzerland in 1798 brought about the complete and final disillusionment. He then came to realize, as Shelley did later, that freedom resides in the spirit and not in the outward form.

> The Sensual and the Dark rebel in vain,
> Slaves by their own compulsion! In mad game
> They burst their manacles and wear the name
>   Of Freedom, graven on a heavier chain!
> O Liberty! with profitless endeavour
>   Have I pursued thee, many a weary hour;
> But thou nor swell'st the victor's strain, nor ever
>   Didst breathe thy soul in forms of human power.[4]

Thus did Coleridge make his public 'Recantation' of his earlier views.[5] The period of residence in Germany awoke moods of

---

[1] *P.W.* (J. D. C.), p. 588.

[2]
> 'I rejoiced,
> Yea, afterwards, truth most painful to record!
> Exulted in the triumph of my soul
> When Englishmen by thousands were o'erthrown.'
>   (*The Prelude*, 1805, x. 259–63.)

[3] *France*, ll. 36–37.   [4] Ibid., ll. 85–92.

[5] Its original title in the *Morning Post* was 'Recantation: An Ode'. G. Bonnard, 'The Invasion of Switzerland and English Public Opinion', *English Studies*, xxii, 1940, pp. 1–26.

poignant nostalgia. A year later, in *Lines: Written in the Album at Elbingerode in the Hartz Forest*, he invoked the spirit of his native land in tones of untroubled patriotism.

> O thou Queen,
> Thou delegated Deity of Earth,
> O dear, dear, England! how my longing eye
> Turned westward, shaping in the steady clouds
> Thy sands and high white cliffs!
>   My native Land!
> Filled with the thought of thee this heart was proud,
> Yea, mine eye swam with tears.[1]

Though he was still bitterly critical of Pitt's policy on his return, there was no question of any further sympathy for the French cause or disloyalty to the land of his birth.

In the autumn of 1799 he began to write political leaders for the *Morning Post*. His connexion with this paper had been established two years earlier through James Mackintosh, who introduced him to his brother-in-law, Daniel Stuart, the editor, who agreed to pay him a guinea a week in expectation of receiving items of verse regularly. Before leaving England he contributed eight pieces, only two of which have political significance, *Fire, Famine and Slaughter* and *France: An Ode*. On his return and after patching up his quarrel with Southey he collaborated with him in producing the highly successful piece of political drollery, *The Devil's Thoughts*. The resumption of poetical contributions was followed up by a single prose article, 'On Peace', published on 6 November 1799.[2] Stuart was evidently pleased with it and offered him regular employment on the staff of his paper. At the time Coleridge seems to have expected that this would in fact last about four or five months. Although Coleridge writes in the *Biographia Literaria* of his being engaged 'to undertake the literary and political department', a phrase to which Stuart later took exception, his position was evidently what we would call today a 'Leader Writer'. Even this phrase is something of an anachronism since it was the work

---

[1] Ll. 24–30.

[2] Although Coleridge mentioned an essay on 'Peace' in a letter to Southey, 24 Dec. 1799, *C.L.* i. 552, Sara did not include it in her collection in *E.O.T.* It was first attributed to Coleridge by Mrs. Glickfield in *P.M.L.A.* lxix, No. 3, June 1954 pp. 681–5. See Appendix A.

of Mackintosh and Coleridge that made the leader a familiar feature of the newspapers of the nineteenth century.[1]

The first subject on which Coleridge was called to write when he arrived in London on 27 November 1799 was the new French constitution devised by Sieyès and Bonaparte. Reliable information about its exact form was not available until the end of December when the *Morning Chronicle* and its rival the *Morning Post* printed a copy of the complete text.[2] Before that, rumour and speculation supplied the deficiency. Nevertheless, as early as 4 December the *Morning Post* promised its readers an account of the new constitution. Two days later it printed a brief description of its main features, while making it perfectly clear that the details had come through unofficial channels. It was from these meagre details that Coleridge built up a masterly description of the new constitution in an essay that appeared on 7 December. Great credit must go to him for his imaginative interpretation of the bare details with which he had been supplied. He admitted that the sketch printed in the previous day's issue might turn out to be grossly inaccurate, but working on the basis of this rough sketch he produced an article that revealed an almost prophetic anticipation of the chief features of the constitution, together with its chief weaknesses. Coleridge had won a notable triumph by his article; and the *Morning Post* had stolen a march on its chief rival the *Morning Chronicle*.

The new French constitution was an expression of the thesis 'confidence comes from below, power from above'.[3] An ingenious electoral system which was superficially based on universal manhood suffrage had been produced. This form of suffrage was rendered nugatory, however, since it applied only to the preliminary stages of election, while above that a series of decimations reduced those eligible to vote until six thousand, called Notabilities of the Nation, remained. From these the executive selected representatives to sit in the legislative chambers. This system of 'filtra-

---

[1] The phrase 'leading paragraph' was in current use. See *C.L.* i. 552, and ii. 728. For its growing importance, see Coleridge's story of the family who complained in 1809 that there was nothing in one issue of the *Courier* because it contained no leading paragraph. *U.L.* i. 450.

[2] Copies of the *Morning Chronicle* and the *Morning Post* for 1799 may be consulted in the B.M. Burney Collection, Nos. 943 and 949 respectively.

[3] J. H. Rose, *The Life of Napoleon*, 1902, i. 229. The account that follows is based on Rose.

tion', as Coleridge called it, had been created in order to appease
the people with some semblance of power while retaining control
all the more firmly at the centre. It also provided an elaborate
system of checks and balances at the legislative and executive
levels, the theoretical purpose of which was to prevent either from
becoming supreme.

In all, Coleridge wrote four articles on the new constitution and
it was in these that he first related the foundation of government
to the protection of property. Little documentary evidence exists,
however, to indicate the stages through which his thought on this
subject passed or the reasons that led him to reverse his early ideas
on the communal ownership of property. In the *Morning Post* essays
he laid down two principles: that in the present state of man and
society, government must be founded on property; and that in a
country in which 'the physical strength of the nation is in the poor,
the government must be in the hands of the rich'.[1] The latter
phrase, based as it is on the application of the balance of power to
the social structure of the country, suggests a naïve and illiberal
attitude; but when it is related to the world in which Coleridge
lived, it can be seen for what it is: a clear-sighted recognition of
fact. The fullest and clearest statement in the *Morning Post* of Coleridge's views on property shows that he had not become an
apologist for the Tories, nor the rich aristocratic Whigs. 'For the
present race of men Governments must be founded on property,
*that government is good in which property is secure and circulates; that
government the best, which, in the exactest ratio, makes each man's power
proportionate to his property.*'[2] Here the reference to the circulation
of property indicates that Coleridge's view of society was dynamic
not static, although it must be admitted that nowhere in his
writings is to be found any satisfactory account of how this process
was to operate. A great deal of what he wrote in these four essays
criticizing the founding of a system of government upon universal
franchise, anticipated the political theory he advanced ten years
later in *The Friend* and which was worked out in fuller detail in the
Lay Sermons and *On the Constitution of the Church and State*. The four
essays on the new French constitution clearly illustrate the way in
which Coleridge's political theory was developed in response to
the challenge of great events. It was not the product of solitary
speculation divorced from the political realities of his day.

[1] *M.P.* 7 Dec. 1799, *E.O.T.* ii. 331.   [2] Ibid.

In spite of the lack of positive evidence to account for the change in attitude towards property, it is nevertheless probably safe to attribute it to two causes. A study of the various stages through which the French Revolution had passed must have considerably modified his original views. In a later article 'Once a Jacobin Always a Jacobin'[1] and also in his attack on the Rights of Man school of political philosophy in *The Friend*,[2] he demonstrated that the main lesson that he had learned from the experiment carried out in France was that something more secure than a doctrine of abstract rights or the ever-shifting shoals of public opinion was needed to form the basis of a stable government. The second cause lay in the nature of his employment. Although he was not the man to compromise his principles for the sake of adhering to the general policy of the paper, which in fact 'held a watching brief on behalf of monied liberalism',[3] it is probable that a knowledge of the audience he addressed led him to take this opportunity of formulating for the first time in print his slowly maturing opinions on government, and the circles of rich Whigs into which he had been introduced affected the direction and accelerated the rate of this development.

In letters to friends he expressed more daring and speculative opinions on the subject of property. On 25 January 1800 he wrote to Southey:

You say, I illuminize—I think, that Property will some time or other be modified by the predominance of Intellect, even as Rank & Superstition are now modified by & subordinated to Property, that much is to be hoped of the Future; but first those particular modes of Property which more particularly stop the diffusion must be done away, as injurious to Property itself—these are, Priesthood & the too great Patronage of Government.[4]

Two months earlier in an essay in the *Morning Post* he had dismissed the notion of such evolutionary modification as 'a useless and impertinent speculation'. So it was for a leader writer on a national paper. It had no rightful place in an article whose function

---

[1] *M.P.* 21 Oct. 1802, *E.O.T.* ii. 542–52. Sara was unable to assign a date; this has been done by reference to a file in the B.M.

[2] *F.*, pp. 115–27.

[3] E. H. Coleridge, 'Fragmentary and Unpublished Life', printed in *Coleridge: Studies by Several Hands*, ed. E. Blunden and E. L. Griggs, 1934, p. 39.

[4] *C.L.* i. 563–4.

was to inform the public of the chief features of the French constitution. In April 1801 in a letter to Poole he suddenly gave vent to his pent-up feelings: 'O there are ways enough, Poole! to *palliate* our miseries—but there is not honesty nor public spirit enough to adopt them.—Property is the bug bear—it stupifies the heads & hardens the hearts of our Counsellors & Chief Men!— They know nothing better than Soup-shops.'[1] No such sentiments had found their way into essays in the *Morning Post*. A comparison of the essays with passages in letters to friends exhibits the unexpected manner in which Coleridge, applying a rigorous form of self-control, disciplined his mind to the task of commenting publicly on public affairs. The two passages quoted from the letters would undoubtedly have found their way into a *Watchman* essay; but when he wrote for the *Morning Post* the magnitude of events, the sense of occasion, and the knowledge that his words would be widely read, compelled him to develop a sober and responsible attitude towards his role as critic of foreign and domestic affairs.

Coleridge's insight into the realities as opposed to the forms of a constitution is well illustrated in his treatment of the system of checks and balances which was supposed to maintain the independence of the French legislative and executive. He recognized this for what it was, a mere trick to deceive the people into believing that the revolutionary principles had been retained while the power was actually being taken from them and lodged in a military dictatorship. 'The whole process of popular election is therefore a mere trick', he wrote, 'a miserable masquerade domino, to throw around the nakedness of despotism.'[2] He recognized, too, that the mere division of function among a number of chambers would be useless unless it represented a real division of interest. 'Checks and counterpoises can only be produced by real diversity of interests, of interests existing independent of legislative function', he declared.[3] This part of the constitution appeared to him as 'a skein of threads tangled rather than divided'. His final judgement upon the whole framework was forceful and uncompromising; it was, he declared, 'the mere ornamental outworks of a military despotism'.

The next issue of national importance upon which Coleridge

---

[1] Ibid. ii. 721.   [2] *M.P.* 27 Dec. 1799, *E.O.T.* ii. 345.
[3] *M.P.* 31 Dec. 1799, *E.O.T.* i. 188.

was called to write was Bonaparte's move towards ending hostilities. On 25 December 1799 the latter dispatched notes to Francis II
and George III proposing peace. Pitt, who interpreted this move
as an attempt to break up the Anglo-Austrian alliance, treated the
proposal with some suspicion. His first reaction to the new French
constitution had been to hope that it might prove 'a very moderate
American kind'. Canning, to whom he confided this view, soon
opened his eyes. He advised Pitt to reply that he would treat with a
monarchy, and to say that to a monarchy restored to its rightful
owners he 'would give not only peace, but peace on most liberal
terms'.[1] On 31 December Pitt wrote to Dundas to tell him that he
had decided to repel the overtures for peace on the grounds that
the conditions in France 'did not provide a solid security for
peace'. This decision was conveyed to Bonaparte in Grenville's
note, which according to J. H. Rose 'ranks amongst the greatest
mistakes of the time. It made the name of the Bourbons odious
and that of Bonaparte popular throughout France.' It is a judgement with which Coleridge would have completely agreed.

His attitude towards Pitt's policy was forcefully expressed in a
series of articles contributed to the *Morning Post* during the early
months of 1800. In these he asserted that it was absurd and insult-
ing to offer to confirm France in her ancient territory; that the
harsh, unconciliatory tone of the British note would increase
Bonaparte's popularity until his flight from Egypt became 'a call
from heaven';[2] that the note was in effect an attempt to convey
'into a country a proclamation against its government, under the
pretence of an official answer to a pacific overture made by that
government';[3] that the effects of continued war must, if successful,
revive the spirit of Jacobinism and if unsuccessful, arouse the
spirit of French ambition; lastly, and most important, that there
now existed a hope that with the conclusion of a peace the spirit of
permanent property might reassert itself, and a government come
into existence founded on this basis and not on the dangerous doctrine of natural right. These were to be the arguments advanced by
the opposition speakers when the peace proposals were later
debated in Parliament. After reporting part of the debate he remarked to Wedgwood how pleasant it was to listen to your 'own
particular phrases in the House of Commons—& quietly in the

[1] J. H. Rose, *William Pitt and the Great War*, 1911, pp. 383–4.
[2] *M.P.* 8 Jan. 1800, *E.O.T.* i. 221.   [3] *M.P.* 7 Jan. 1800, *E.O.T.* i. 214.

silent self-complacence of your own Heart chuckle over the pla-
giarism, as if you were grand Monopolist of all good Reasons'.[1]
Many years later, when complaining to Stuart that he had never received any acknowledgement of his services from those in power,
he claimed that 'by a mere reference to dates, it might be proved
that no small number of fine speeches in the House of Commons,
and elsewhere, originated, directly or indirectly'[2] in his essays or
conversations. This claim is substantiated in the specific case of
the debate on Bonaparte's overtures for peace.

In his examination of the British notes to Bonaparte he succeeded in making both the policy and the personalities of the
Ministry ridiculous. One essay in particular, entitled *Lord Grenville's Note*, deserves special attention, for according to Stuart it
was one of Coleridge's most successful contributions.[3] Charles
Lamb expressed his joyous approval of this *jeu d'esprit* and con-
gratulated its author on the very novel and exquisite manner in
which he had 'combined political with grammatical science'. In
light-hearted mood he remarked, 'It must have been the death
blow to that Ministry. I expect Pitt and Grenville to resign.'[4] In
this essay much of the essential Coleridge is to be found: his theory
that language is the organ of thought and not its decoration; his
instinctive distaste for all forms of slovenly writing and his ability
to make such work appear utterly ridiculous by means of skilfully
selected quotations; passionate indignation that the welfare of the
country should depend on men of such inferior talents as Windham, to whom he rightly attributed the authorship of the British
Note. Although Coleridge's article is a polished and finished piece,
it possesses some of the spontaneity and vigour of his marginalia
and may well have taken its origin from jottings on the text of the
published note. For example, having quoted a sentence from the
original, which alleged that professions of peace had been repeatedly held out by all those who had successively directed the
resources of France, Coleridge remarked in a homely off the cuff
manner, 'young children, who have been lately *held out* by their
nurses, often talk as vulgarly'; and he noted that the latter part of
the offending sentence should have been 'who successively have

---

[1] 4 Feb. 1800, *C.L.* i. 569.
[2] 12 Sept. 1814, *L.* ii. 628.
[3] 22 Jan. 1800, *E.O.T.* i. 261–6. Sara Coleridge was unable to ascribe a definite
date to this essay.
[4] *The Letters of Charles and Mary Lamb*, ed. E. V. Lucas, 1905, i. 154.

directed' and not 'who have successively directed', demanding
contemptuously, 'is not Mr W. metaphysician enough to perceive
the difference?' But the essay was more than an attack on a political
mediocrity; behind the banter and wit lay the grim recognition
that false reasoning might lead to needless slaughter. 'False
reasoning is perhaps never wholly harmless; but it becomes an
enormous evil, when the reasoning, and the passions which accom-
pany it, are to be followed by the sacrifice of tens of thousands.'[1]
A highly critical attitude towards language was one of Coleridge's
most valuable assets as a political journalist.

Whereas Coleridge expressed his view on British policy clearly
and unequivocally, his treatment of Bonaparte's character and
policy was not wholly consistent. The question that was on everyone's lips at the beginning of 1800 was: 'Can Bonaparte be sincere
in his desire for peace?' In attempting to answer this question
Coleridge exhibited the fault which is often in evidence in his
philosophical and religious writings but which is less often found
in his essays in the *Morning Post*. He made his argument rest on
distinctions the force of which would not have been grasped by
the average reader. In the first of these articles he appeared to
throw doubt on Bonaparte's sincerity.

Propositions of peace, or proposals for negotiation, at this time, can
only have for their object the popularity of the new government. They
enable Buonaparte at once to throw the odium of continuing the war
on the allies, while he secures to his own government the character of
moderation and justice, and fulfils the promises he has made, of being as
forward in pacification, as he has been brilliant in warfare.[2]

In the two following issues of the paper Coleridge asserted firmly
and unequivocally that Bonaparte was sincere. Inevitably he was
charged with inconsistency. This he set out to answer on 6 January.[3] He drew his reader's attention to a distinction applicable to
Bonaparte's conduct. 'To make offers without *expectation* that they
will be accepted, does not constitute insincerity, provided a real
wish exists that these offers *may* be accepted.' Although he had
drawn a similar distinction between wishing and expecting in the
first article he did not apply it closely to the question of Bonaparte's sincerity at all. In addition, whatever force the distinction

---

[1] *E.O.T.* i. 261.   [2] *M.P.* 2 Jan. 1800, *E.O.T.* i. 196.
[3] First attributed to Coleridge by Mrs. David Glickfield in *P.M.L.A.* lxix, No. 3,
June 1954, pp. 681–5.

might have possessed had been vitiated in the original by the per-
suasive force of the passage which so firmly called his sincerity in
doubt. The inconsistencies in phrasing suggest either that Coleridge was genuinely unable to make up his mind on this difficult
issue, or that in order to forward a policy of peace he was led to
use his reason 'as a hired advocate' and to turn a blind eye to the
threatening aspects of Bonaparte's character and policy. To use
one's reason in this way is a temptation that besets every journalist
and it is surprising how seldom there is any suspicion of Coleridge's having done so, especially when it is borne in mind that the
leader writers of his day were expected to write to a brief.

Coleridge's subsequent account of the conditions that made the
rise of Bonaparte possible reveals acute political insight. In what
he later came to call 'the age of personality',[1] he nevertheless
recognized the importance of the large impersonal forces that
mould society; he recognized also the important part played by
public opinion in the evolution of various kinds of government.
Of the rise of Bonaparte he wrote:

> The real causes of the usurpation must be sought for in the general
> state of the public feeling and opinion; in the necessity of giving con-
> centration and permanence to the executive government; and in the in-
> creasing conviction that it has become good policy to exchange the
> forms of political freedom for the realities of civil security, in order to
> make a real political freedom possible at some future period.[2]

He believed that there were three main reasons why the French
people preferred Bonaparte to a restored monarchy. The large
class of *nouveaux riches* need fear no sudden revolution of property;
the position of the Chief Consul allowed a choice of person; and
the French genuinely thought that the new form of government
would draw together the various parties. It is to Coleridge's credit
that national prejudice did not blind him to Bonaparte's undoubted
genius. 'They have seated on the throne of the republic', he wrote,

> a man of various talent, of commanding genius, of splendid exploit,
> from whose policy the peaceful adherents of the old religion anticipate
> toleration; from whose real opinions and habits the men of letters and
> philosophy are assured of patronage; in whose professional attachment
> and individual associations the military, and the men of military talent,
> look confidently for the exertions of a comrade and a brother; and,

[1] *F.*, p. 237.   [2] *M.P.* 11 Mar. 1800, *E.O.T.* ii. 314.

finally, in whose uninterrupted felicity the multitude find an object of superstition and enthusiasm.[1]

But from the beginning his praise was not without important qualifications. He condemned absolutely the means Bonaparte had used to gain power. The great unanswered question that faced Europe was to what use he would put his power, and this was a question that time alone could decide. All depended on one thing, whether his virtue was as great as his genius. Coleridge prophesied that if it were, he might do for the old world what Washington had done for the new. In an earlier article, assigned to Coleridge by Dr. D. V. Erdman, he had already spoken of Washington as a man who possessed 'the character of a commanding genius', and he clearly believed that the great American's virtues were equal to his genius.[2] Bonaparte's proved not to be. As soon as events began to show to what evil ends he was directing his great gifts, Coleridge immediately set out to awaken the nation to the danger in a series of articles published in the autumn of 1802.[3]

A character study of Pitt was his greatest single triumph in journalism. Seen in relation to the essays on Bonaparte it indicates that Coleridge was already feeling his way towards the distinction that plays so important a part in his literary criticism, that between the man of genius and the man of mere talent. Upon this distinction the whole portrait of Pitt turns. While it leads to a somewhat one-sided picture it bestows an added dimension, a philosophical depth, which, whatever we may think of the ultimate validity of the distinction, makes the portrait convincing and consistent. Hazlitt called it 'masterly and unanswerable'.

In the portrait of Pitt, as in the discussion of Windham's reply to France, Coleridge shows special interest in language as a measure of intellectual power. He contended that the education in words that Chatham had given his son had inevitably destroyed the seeds of genius and fostered mere talent. Thus Pitt acquired 'a premature and unnatural dexterity in the combination of words, which must of necessity have diverted his attention from present objects, obscured his impressions, and deadened his genuine feel-

---

[1] *E.O.T.* ii. 315–16.

[2] 'Coleridge on George Washington: Newly Discovered Essays of 1800', *Bulletin of the New York Public Library*, vol. lxi, no. 2, pp. 81–97.

[3] A series of three articles in which France under Bonaparte was compared with Rome under the Caesars. *E.O.T.* ii. 478–514.

ings'.[1] To this form of early training Coleridge ascribed the two main weaknesses in his character: his love of abstractions, and the coldness of his affections, seen alike in private and public life. In discussing his worship of abstractions he drew an important and valuable distinction between generalizations based upon a coherent system of thought and those 'generalities—Atheism and Jacobinism—phrases, which he learnt from Mr Burke, but without learning the philosophical definitions and involved consequences, with which that great man accompanied those words'.[2] His method of thinking was neatly summed up as 'Abstractions defined by abstractions! Generalities defined by generalities!' In dealing with his other great weakness, the coldness of his affections, Coleridge asserted that it was impossible to believe that Pitt who loved neither man nor nature was a fit person to guide the destinies of a great nation. He was, he said,

A plant sown and reared in a hot-house, for whom the very air that surrounded him, had been regulated by the thermometer of previous purpose; to whom the light of nature had penetrated only through glasses and covers; who had had the sun without the breeze; whom no storm had shaken; on whom no rain had pattered; on whom the dews of heaven had not fallen!—A being, who had had no feelings connected with man or nature, no spontaneous impulses, no unbiassed and desultory studies, no genuine science, nothing that constitutes individuality in intellect, nothing that teaches brotherhood in affection! Such was the man—such, and so denaturalised the spirit, on whose wisdom and philanthropy the lives and living enjoyments of so many millions of human beings were made unavoidably dependent.[3]

This passage illustrates fairly clearly some of the qualities Coleridge hoped to find in a statesman. Mere statecraft and powers of oratory were of no avail without a generous love and a noble imagination. The latter were to be cultivated by ordering one's life in harmony with the natural forces of the universe. Even when writing political leaders for the *Morning Post* Coleridge did not cease to be the poet and philosopher of nature; and the belief that a harmonious relationship with man and nature indicated the existence of genius is remarkably similar to the idea expressed in the philosophical lectures of 1818, where he declared that 'to have a genius is to live in the universal, to have no self but that which is reflected not only from the faces of all around us, our fellow

---

[1] Ibid. ii. 320.   [2] Ibid. ii. 326.   [3] Ibid. ii. 323.

creatures, but reflected from the flowers, the trees, the beasts, yea from the very surface of the [waters and the] sands of the desert'.[1]

Nothing in the actual character of Pitt or in his actions can fully explain Coleridge's bitter hostility towards him; it is only explicable if one recognizes that he became a symbol for all that Coleridge most despised in the world of contemporary politics: the whole machinery of secret influence and intrigue disguised behind the façade of a 'decorous profession of religion'; the overbalance of the commercial interest;[2] and the rigorous system of repression that stemmed from the 'panic of property' aroused by the French Revolution. He came, too, in some sense to symbolize in his person not only a whole political system but an alien philosophy of life. He was the embodiment of Lockian empiricism; or to use a phrase from a later letter, he was a perfect 'Little-ist' a man of mere talent.[3] Circumstances moulded him; he lacked the imagination to mould circumstances. 'He was cast, rather than grew',[4] and behind that epigram lay a distinction that possessed the utmost importance for Coleridge. For the application of this distinction to politics in general he was indebted to Burke, from whom he learned to revere the processes of slow growth and the accumulated wisdom of antiquity, but for its application to men he drew on the wealth of his own psychological observations and philosophical deductions. The standards that he applied to statesmen and to works of art were similar; men who were the products of outward circumstances and not of a vital principle working from within fell into the same category as works of art in which a mechanical as opposed to an organic form operated.

A note was appended to the essay on the character of Pitt promising 'Tomorrow of Bonaparte'. Although Coleridge continued to promise to write the companion piece for many years it never in fact appeared. There are, I think, three possible reasons why it was not written at the time. To begin with 'constitutional indolence' probably played its part. On two other occasions a promised article did not appear immediately but was in fact published several weeks later. On 27 November 1801 Coleridge promised to write an article on the report that Grey was to succeed Lord

---

[1] *Philosophical Lectures*, ed. K. Coburn, 1949, p. 179.

[2] Cf. Coleridge's analysis of post-war discontents in the *Lay Sermons*, 1816–17, when he ascribed the root cause to the overbalance of the commercial interest.

[3] Letter to T. Poole, 23 Mar. 1801, *C.L.* ii. 708.

[4] *E.O.T.* ii. 320.

Hobart; it did not appear until 11 December. At the end of an article of 23 February 1802 he promised an essay on Addington's Administration; it did not appear until 22 March.[1] In this case, a month after the character study of Bonaparte had been promised, Louis Otto, who was in England negotiating with the British Government for the exchange of prisoners, approached Stuart privately on his master's behalf to ask when the essay would appear. Bonaparte had been so impressed with the portrait of Pitt that he was eager to read his own, and wished, if possible, to ensure that it would be a complimentary one.[2] Such interference by the interested party was sufficient to silence Coleridge. But it may well be that he was unable to fulfil his promise for the simple reason that he had already said all he had to say on the subject in two earlier articles called *Bonaparte in his Relations to France* and *Bonaparte in his Relations to England*, which had been published before the character of Pitt on 11 and 19 March respectively. These earlier articles probably suggested a comparison between the Chief Consul and the Prime Minister of Great Britain, between the 'man of commanding genius' and the man of mere talent, a comparison modelled on Plutarch's method of taking a pair of famous men, but with this important qualification, that these portraits were to illustrate how similar positions had been reached by the most dissimilar means. It has always been assumed that it was the essay on Pitt which first came into Coleridge's mind and suggested the idea of composing a pair of lives on the modified Plutarchan model, but it may not have been so. Having rashly allowed the promise 'To-morrow of Bonaparte' to appear, he could either repeat much of what he had already said in the two previous articles on Bonaparte and produce an article that would form a disastrous anti-climax to the portrait of Pitt, or he could keep his readers in a state of eager expectation and persuade himself that he really would produce the promised article in the future. I think he did the latter.

If Coleridge's attitude towards a man of genius and a man of talent is evident in his essays on Bonaparte and Pitt, his contempt for a man of 'small talent' comes out strongly in the essay on *Mr Addington's Administration*. Addington became Prime Minister in February 1801 when Pitt resigned office to salve his conscience on

---

[1] For the article of 27 Nov. 1801, see Glickfield, op. cit., pp. 681–5; for the second see my note 'Coleridge on Addington's Administration', *M.L.R.* liv, 1959, pp. 69–72.
[2] *C.L.* ii. 1007.

the issue of Catholic Emancipation and in order to make it possible
for a new Ministry to treat with France 'on terms which he himself
would have found it mortifying to accept'. In the autumn of 1801
Addington's negotiation of the Preliminaries for the Peace of
Amiens was well received by the nation, but by winter and the
spring of the next year he was obliged to try to win over some of
the Whigs, including Grey. Coleridge warned the Whigs of the
danger of joining a Ministry that had continued the rigid system
of domestic repression inaugurated by Pitt; and some time later
Grey wrote to Fox expressing his relief at escaping from this unhappy coalition.[1] By the spring of 1802 Addington's position had
worsened. The imminent downfall of the Ministry seemed an
appropriate moment for a general summing up of its achievements
and the character of its leader. In setting out to do this it was
inevitable that Coleridge should have drawn some sort of comparison between the two Ministries and their respective Ministers,
Pitt and Addington. The essay begins with a reference to the
category, 'men of small talent' into which Addington so clearly
fell. 'We easily forget, or forgive, or perhaps overlook', declared
Coleridge, 'the faults and errors of men of small talent.' This fact,
according to him, explained why Addington's Administration had
not been considered objectionable by those who had been bitterly
opposed to that of his predecessor, Pitt. He noted how Addington
imitated Pitt in debate, but there was an important difference to be
noted.

Mr. PITT puzzles his audience by his ingenuity, Mr. ADDINGTON by
his confusion. The one renders himself unintelligible by his sophistry;
the other is not understood, because that which is not clearly conceived,
can never be clearly and definitely expressed. He never displays dexterity in debate, expansion or vigour of mind, a strong discriminating
power, originality of thought, or richness of fancy. His intellect is too
shortsighted to see beyond the point immediately before him, and
hence, in a case of complexity, it is mere chance if one part of his
argument does not contradict the other.

He felt that it was a national disgrace that the destiny of the
country had been placed in such unsuitable hands.

This, is, perhaps, the most critical aera in our history, and it will

---

[1] 'My escape, from the scheme of last year I think one of the happiest of my life.'
G. M. Trevelyan, *Lord Grey of the Reform Bill*, 1920, p. 127.

require the most skilful talents to carry us through it. That Mr. ADD-
INGTON is equal to the task, standing as he does, without system or
principles to guide his conduct, embracing to-day what he rejected
yesterday, confounded by the least difficulty, a Tory one hour, a Whig
the next, changing with every new breeze; that he is fit to guide the
helm no man of sense will believe.

He had made the dangerous experiment of being 'all things unto
all men' hoping that 'all men would be of one mind and temper to
him' and had only succeeded in proving his own unfitness for
high office. With somewhat perverse ingenuity Coleridge suggested that his very faults had saved the country. Had he possessed
greater powers of mind 'we should be now upon a dangerous
sea with the double disadvantage of a bad pilot, and that pilot
possessed of our utmost confidence'. As it was, he had lost the
people's confidence; they had recognized that he was a poor
pilot. Two months later Canning reminded the nation that they
would be obliged to look to Pitt if 'again the rude whirlwind
should arise'. Then prophesied Canning,

> The regrets of the good, and the fears of the wise,
> Shall turn to the Pilot that weathered the Storm.[1]

But his words, and those of Coleridge went unheeded; the incom-
petent Addington remained at the helm.

Coleridge's main purpose in the last series of articles, which he
contributed to the paper in the autumn of 1802, was to awaken
the nation to the danger of the 'perilous designs and unsleeping
ambition' of Bonaparte. The Preliminaries of London were signed
on 1 October 1801 and the news of the peace was greeted with
riotous acclamation by the London crowd. At first Coleridge
accepted the necessity for making peace. To Poole he wrote, 'We,
i.e. Wordsworth & myself, regard the Peace as necessary, but the
Terms as most alarming';[2] a judgement not unlike Sheridan's
more epigrammatic 'a peace every man should be glad of, but no
man can be proud of'. But Coleridge soon came to reverse his
opinion of its necessity. Among the marginal comments in his
copy of Godwin's *Thoughts Occasioned by the Perusal of Dr Parr's
Spital Sermon* is the following: 'It is with Jacobinism as with the
French Empire, we made peace just at the very time that war *first*

---

[1] C. Petrie, *George Canning*, 2nd ed., 1946, p. 62.
[2] 21 Oct. 1801, *C.L.* ii. 771.

became just and necessary.'[1] Having recognized this he felt that it was his duty to expose the unreal basis on which the Peace of Amiens was founded. In later life he was justly proud of the part he had played in uniting public opinion against France. Fox attributed the renewal of the war against France to the influence of the *Morning Post*. Although Coleridge recognized this for what it was, 'a violent hyperbole of party debate', he said that he would be proud to have the words inscribed on his tombstone.[2] The Peace of Amiens provided a breathing space in which men of all parties could take stock of their positions. The time had come when, 'Both parties had found themselves in the wrong. The one had confessedly mistaken the moral character of the revolution, and the other had miscalculated both its moral and physical resources.'[3] Afterwards it therefore became possible for all those who, like Coleridge, had been 'conscientiously an opponent of the first revolutionary war', to give their full and unqualified support to the war against Napoleon.

Coleridge's 'alarum trumpets' in the *Morning Post* took three forms: an attack on Napoleon and his régime; an attack on Fox's behaviour in Paris; and a discussion on the circumstances that appeared to favour the restoration of the Bourbons. The first and the third well illustrate Coleridge's habit of looking for historical analogies when writing about contemporary problems. He firmly believed that 'we anticipate the future only by the analogies of the past',[4] and that historical knowledge was essential for any kind of political prophecy.

Armed with the two-fold knowledge of history and the human mind, a man will scarcely err in his judgement concerning the sum total of any future national event, if he have been able to procure the original documents of the past, together with authentic accounts of the present, and if he have a philosophic tact for what is truly important in facts, and in most instances therefore for such facts as the DIGNITY OF HISTORY has excluded from the volumes of our modern compilers, by the courtesy of the age entitled historians.[5]

Even if history teaches no simple lessons it provides experience from which we may derive knowledge and wisdom. In the first

---

[1] *Thoughts*, p. 7, B.M. C. 45, f. 18 (3). Coleridge first acquired the pamphlet in Aug. 1801, see *C.L.* ii. 751. It is impossible to be certain when he added the comment quoted, but presumably during the course of the year.

[2] *B.L.* i. 145.   [3] Ibid. i. 123.   [4] *E.O.T.* ii. 573.   [5] *B.L.* i. 148.

series of articles he resorted to a figure of speech which is to be found in a number of other places in his writings. He there took comfort in the fact 'that experience will not be always like the lights in the stern of the vessel, illuminating the tract only which we have already passed over'.[1] On the other hand, he was well aware of the danger of a too facile use of historical analogy to prove a point or prophesy the future course of events; and in a passage in the manuscript *Observations on Egypt*, which he prepared when Public Secretary in Malta, he declared that 'a blind faith in false analogies of the Past' was one of the characteristic faults of the unthinking.[2] The series likening France under Bonaparte to Rome under the Caesars illustrates how valuable a tool historical analogy might become, while the series in which he compared the conditions in France in the autumn of 1802 to those existing immediately before the restoration of Charles II fails to carry any conviction at all. It is a piece of special pleading which gains little from the appeal to history.[3]

The similarity in the names of titles and offices in the French and Roman Empire made the form of the first analogy an obvious one. The analysis, however, penetrates beyond the superficial resemblances. Coleridge shows that similar large-scale social and economic forces were at work. These he enumerated as being the great influx of wealth, which led to a disproportionate influence being exerted by the commercial interest; the popularity of the philosophy of Epicurus which produced a predominantly utilitarian view of life; the rise of unprincipled demagogues; and finally the effect of the military machine in teaching the soldiers to owe allegiance to the generals and not to the law. He also noted a number of ways in which the French Empire differed from that of Rome. France could not claim to be spreading the light of civilization by her conquests, nor had she any excuse for basing her system of government on despotic rule for a great advance in political science had been made since Roman times, namely the discovery of a representative system of government based upon the ownership of property. He also insisted that the mere existence of close similarities did not mean that the rise and fall of the

---

[1] *E.O.T.* ii. 492. Repeated in *Table Talk*, 18 Dec. 1831, *T.T.*, p. 146, and in the Notebooks.   [2] Egerton 2800, f. 124.

[3] R. F. Brinkley, however, describes it as 'one of the most brilliant examples' of historical analogy. *Coleridge on the Seventeenth Century*, Duke University Press, 1955, p. 4.

French empire would follow the exact course of the Roman; it did not even mean that it was doomed to fall. But he took great pains to stress that the period of Roman history to which Bonaparte's France bore closest resemblance was the time when 'Rome ceased to be a Republic, and the government was organized into a masked and military despotism'.[1] In this lay Europe's danger.

In these three articles Coleridge's insight into the potential power of the Press, particularly the newspaper, is well illustrated. In Roman times no equally powerful organ for ventilating the opinions of the people existed, but by Bonaparte's day the newspapers had already begun to assume something of their modern importance. Coleridge saw that the existence of a free Press was incompatible with despotic rule. In a letter to his brother George he described his feelings after Bonaparte had asked when his portrait would appear in the *Morning Post*. 'Stuart immediately came to me, & was in very high spirits on the occasion—I turned sad, & answered him ["] Stuart, that man will prove a Tyrant, & the deadliest enemy of the Liberty of the Press".'[2] He went on to add, 'Stuart has often talked of publishing this conversation of mine as an instance of political prophecy'; and indeed it was. In addition to realizing that a dictatorship must always seek to destroy the freedom of the newspapers, he also saw that the probable duration of despotic rule had been considerably lessened on account of the growth in importance and increase in independence of the Press in most European countries. In the second of the essays in which he worked out the historical analogy between France and Rome, he summed up the function of a free Press in memorable words:

When God sent Christianity into the world, he made men capable of freedom; when he permitted the discovery of printing, he gave men the means of acquiring and perpetuating it. The press is the only '*infernal machine*,' which is truly formidable to a modern despot. And only the enemies to the freedom of their country, either fear or have cause to fear. At this moment, the illumination of all Europe, and the European world, is acting upon each part of it. The rapid intercommunication of thoughts and discoveries, the amiable social vanity, that is the result of this free intellectual commerce; and the awe, in which each government stands, of the opinions of its nation, and in which each nation stands, of the opinions of its neighbours; these are the most effectual guards and

---

[1] *E.O.T.* ii. 480.   [2] 2 Oct. 1803, *C.L.* ii. 1007.

warrants of mutual freedom: these will make all actual despotism short-lived; and will convert (and, in some measure, have already converted) formal despotisms into virtual free states. Prussia and Denmark are existing instances.[1]

It was not, therefore, surprising that he should have protested indignantly against the attempt made by some English politicians to persuade the London newspapers to modify the tone of their attack on Bonaparte. Clearly he believed that his writings and those of other enlightened journalists contained a vital message, to silence which would be a tacit acquiescence in the triumph of France, a triumph which would have been achieved at the expense of all principle and the rights of other nations. 'Her present power, her present form of government so closely resemble those of Rome', declared Coleridge, 'that all the Powers of Europe, that remain unsubjugated, are called upon to suspicion, watchfulness, and prompt and firm courage.'[2] It was his ambition to awake those qualities in his readers and his subsequent pride that he had done so in spite of all external threats.

The dominant note struck in the articles on Bonaparte was one of lofty contempt. A tone of noble indignation, however, prevails throughout the two letters addressed to Charles James Fox. On the pretext of gathering material for his history, Fox visited France during the Peace of Amiens and outraged English public opinion by paying obsequious court to Bonaparte. Accounts of his behaviour reached Coleridge through newspaper reports and these were supplemented by letters from his friend Tom Poole who was in France at the time.[3] In the two letters in the *Morning Post* he set out to rebuke Fox publicly for his present conduct, and to review in some detail the policy Fox had pursued during the period from the beginning of the French Revolution to the Peace of Amiens. He considered that his worst fault lay in his continued defence of France long after she had deserted her original principles. He did not blame him for hoping that France would inaugurate a new world order. His main charge against him was not that he had expected too much from the French Revolution and the reform movement at home, but that he had deliberately closed his eyes to the excesses that had accompanied each. At no time was Coleridge

---

[1] *E.O.T.* ii. 500–1. [2] Ibid. ii. 514.
[3] Sandford, *Thomas Poole and His Friends*, ii. 87–88.

an uncritical admirer of Fox. In the first Bristol lecture, in *The Watchman*, and in some of the early articles in the *Morning Post*,[1] he had attacked the so-called friends of freedom who, like Fox, worshipped everything French and were always ready to defend France as long as they might thereby attack Pitt's Ministry. His final verdict on this statesman was not given until later in life, when according to Thomas Allsop he declared:

The grand mistake of Mr Fox was, that he did not separate the causes of the war from the consequences, but acted as though, having espoused the cause of the French Revolution, he must in every instance advocate its measures. This lost him his party, and swelled the ranks of Mr Pitt, a man utterly unfitted for the conduct of a war, all his plans being based upon so called expediency, and pernicious short-sightedness, which would never allow him to take into his calculation the future.[2]

This passage expresses succinctly the substance of the two *Morning Post* letters to Fox. It was easier to see the events and personalities with complete objectivity twenty years after than when he was close to them; and in recording Fox's political career in 1802 he was in part retracing the steps of his own, for he, too, had hoped too generously of the outcome of the French Revolution and the English reform movement. Unlike Fox, however, he saw the later developments of each with a steady and clear eye. Nevertheless, the texture of the prose bears the stamp of the degree to which he was making a personal confession. And the same may be said of the article *Once a Jacobin Always a Jacobin*, in which much of the same ground is covered and which also forms a personal testament.[3]

Coleridge's work on the *Morning Post* was not restricted to writing leaders; he also tried his hand at parliamentary reporting. Stuart, at whose instigation he undertook the work, later ridiculed his efforts; and Gillman told the picturesque story of how Coleridge fell asleep after listening for half an hour to Pitt's great speech on the British war aims, delivered on 17 February 1800. According to Gillman he 'volunteered' a speech for the Prime Minister; and it was of this report that Canning was alleged to have remarked 'it does more credit to the author's head than to

---

[1] For example, 'Advice to the Friends of Freedom', 12 Dec. 1799.
[2] Allsop, i. 134–5.
[3] Not dated by Sara Coleridge, but appeared on 21 Oct. 1802. *E.O.T.* ii. 542.

his memory'.[1] In fact the accounts given by Coleridge's friends and biographers are colourful rather than informative. Fortunately it is possible to reconstruct the pattern of his activities from his letters and notebooks. On the first two occasions when he visited the House the debate on British policy was postponed. On the third occasion he arrived at 7.45 a.m. on 3 February and remained until 3 a.m. on the following morning, when he returned to the newspaper's office, wrote his report, and corrected other men's work until 8 a.m. As he informed Wedgwood, to whom he sent a copy of the paper, he reported only a part of Pitt's speech, actually the second half.[2] The anecdote that he told Gillman about falling asleep probably referred to this occasion. It could not refer to the report of the speech of 17 February, since Notebook No. 10 proves unmistakably that Coleridge was awake and jotting down notes throughout the speech. His next visit occurred on 10 February. He then took down fairly full notes of Sheridan's speech opening the debate on the expedition to Holland.[3] His last visit, on 17 February, was the most successful one. On this occasion Pitt was challenged to define the object of the war with France in one sentence and he promptly did so in one word, 'Security'. On the following day he wrote to Southey telling him to read Pitt's speech in the *Morning Post*. 'I reported the whole', he said, 'with notes so scanty, that—Mr Pitt is much obliged to me. For by heaven he never talked half as eloquently in his Life time.'[4] These notes, which are almost illegible and bear the unmistakable signs of having been hastily and furtively scribbled in the poorly lit reporter's gallery, are scanty indeed, but they cover the whole speech and were at least full enough to remind Coleridge of the substance of Pitt's speech when he came to compose his report. A comparison of the first section in the Notebook with the opening sentences of the report in the *Morning Post* illustrates how much he had to work on and what was supplied by memory and imaginative reconstruction. The passage from the Notebook runs,

Security—against a danger the greatest that ever threaten'd that never threaten'd that it is a danger that it is a danger—which no nation so

[1] *Life of Coleridge*, 1838, pp. 207–8.

[2] *C.L.* i. 568–9. A comparison of the jottings in Notebook No. 4, *N.* i. 651, with the speech as published in the *M.P.* on 4 Feb. shows that he was responsible for the second half. This report is not the 'abstract' of the debate printed by Sara, *E.O.T.* i. 285, as has often been assumed. The latter was also by Coleridge and appeared on 6 Feb.   [3] *N.* i. 652.   [4] *C.L.* i. 573.

successfully—because no nation so energetic—because none other perceived abroad—but here—that we are attractive [. . .] That which we
did not dream of under tyr. of Robes[pier]re 5 directors shifting of that
scene—mocking name of Liberty to that Usurpation because all Hope
united under one person, the nursling & champion—& pars ipse sine
of Jacobins.[1]

This subsequently became,

The honourable gentleman calls upon ministers to state the object of
the war in one sentence. I can state it in one word: it is Security. I can
state it in one word, though it is not to be explained but in many. The
object of the war is security: security against a danger, the greatest that
ever threatened this country; the greatest that ever threatened mankind;
a danger the more terrible, because it is unexampled and novel. It is a
danger which has more than menaced the safety and independence of
all nations; it is a danger which has attacked the property and peace
of all individuals; a danger which Europe has strained all its sinews to
repel; and which no nation has repelled so successfully as the British;
because no nation has acted so energetically, so sincerely, so uniformly
on the broad basis of principle; because no other nation has perceived
with equal clearness and decision the necessity, not only of combating
the evil abroad, but of stifling it at home; because no nation has
breasted with so firm a constancy the tide of jacobinical power; because
no nation has pierced with so stedfast an eye, through the disguises of
Jacobinical hypocrisy; but now, it seems, we are at once to remit our
zeal and our suspicion; that Jacobinism, which alarmed us under the
stumbling and drunken tyranny of Robespierre; that Jacobinism, which
insulted and roused us under the short-sighted ambition of the five
Directors; that Jacobinism, to which we have sworn enmity through
every shifting of every bloody scene, through all those abhorred
mockeries which have profaned the name of liberty to all the varieties
of usurpation; to this Jacobinism we are now to reconcile ourselves,
because all its arts and all its energies are united under one person, the
child and the champion of Jacobinism, who has been reared in its principles, who has fought its battles, who has systematised its ambition, at
once the fiercest instrument, of its fanaticism, and the gaudiest puppet
of its folly![2]

A comparison of other parallel passages suggests that in the introduction Coleridge allowed himself more freedom to expand
and adorn than elsewhere, but as far as can be judged from the
accounts that appeared in *The Times* and the *True Briton* his report

---

[1] *N.* i. 653.   [2] *E.O.T.* ii. 293–4.

was substantially accurate, while as regards literary finish it far
surpassed the other reports.[1] Coleridge did not add the rhetorical
and literary flourishes in order to enhance Pitt's reputation as a
public speaker; he added them because the Johnsonian tradition of
parliamentary reporting still exerted an influence on current practice. Believing that one of the most important functions of the
newspaper was to provide readable parliamentary reports, he
seized the opportunity to demonstrate what a fine piece of writing
such a report could be.

The value of Coleridge's political journalism on the *Morning
Post* has been variously assessed. Coleridge thought sufficiently
highly of his contributions to wish to see them collected and republished in book form. Jottings in the Notebooks suggest that the
title would probably have been 'Men and the Times'[2] and Sara
may have had this projected title in mind when sixteen years after
her father's death she published her collection of the miscellaneous
political writings under the title, *Essays on His Own Times*. Coleridge's nearest approach to making such a collection was to retain
a number of cuttings from the paper and to print a typical promis-
sory note at the end of the second issue of *The Friend*, on 8 July
1809. Subscribers were then informed that he intended to publish
'Essays from the *Morning Post*', and other essays relating to
America, the Mediterranean, and Egypt. As if to persuade himself
of the reality of this plan he added the following circumstantial details. 'The work will be presented in two volumes on crown octavo,
woven paper, the price not exceeding 16 shillings.'[3] It need hardly
be added that nothing came of this project.

His motives in wishing to see their republication were complex.
As long as they lay hidden away in out-of-date newspapers and
therefore almost completely forgotten by the public, the sense of
having lived and written in vain, and of having 'wasted the prime
and manhood'[4] of his intellect in Stuart's service, must have been
overwhelming. Stuart was justified in denying the accuracy of the
quoted phrase,[5] but it was a pardonable hyperbole in the circum-

---

[1] Stuart, however, claimed that the reports in the *True Briton* and *The Times* were
better than Coleridge's report. See parallel excerpts in Michael Macdonagh, *The
Reporters' Gallery*, 1913, pp. 299–307; see also W. Hindle, *The Morning Post, 1772–
1837*, 1937.

[2] See *N.* i. 1577 and 1673 for the occurrence of the phrase in connexion with
Coleridge's journalism.   [3] *F.* (1809), p. 32.

[4] *B.L.* i. 145.   [5] *Gentleman's Magazine*, May 1838, p. 485.

stances, for Coleridge had certainly devoted the full strength of
his intellect and critical powers to the actual essays he had written.
Quite apart from showing the extent of his contributions and
demonstrating the vast amount of labour and creative energy he
had spent in Stuart's service, he believed that their republication
would be of great contemporary interest, since it would reveal that
in all essentials he had correctly anticipated the future course of
events. Their appearance would provide a concrete illustration of
the truth that a journalist who related the events of the day to
general principles became something of a seer and prophet. And
in 1814 he proudly boasted to Stuart that very many of his essays
'would read to you now, AS HISTORY'.[1]

Coleridge considered that his chief contribution to journalism
lay in substituting principles for the rule of expedience, of 'placing
the questions and events of the day in a moral point of view; in
giving a dignity to particular measures by tracing their policy or
impolicy to permanent principles, and an interest to principles by
the application of them to individual measures'.[2] Only one qualification needs to be made. When he wrote for the *Morning Post* he
had not yet formulated any fully consistent set of political principles; the gradual formulation arose from the challenge of events.
In fact what gives such vitality to these articles is the impression
they convey of a great and original mind grappling with complex
problems and reaching out to relate each in turn to something permanent in the nature of man or the organization of government.
He believed that 'armed with the two-fold knowledge of history
and the human mind, a man will scarcely err in his judgement,
concerning the sum total of any future national event';[3] and again
and again in these essays this twofold knowledge is brought to
bear on contemporary events, with the result that like Edmund
Burke he saw 'all things, actions, and events, in relation to the
laws that determine their existence and circumscribe their possibility'.[4] Recognizing the importance of 'Facts of the Mind', which
form the permanent and unchanging data of any problem, he
came to refer all political and social problems to what he called
'the System of our Nature'. The clearest evidence of this is found
in the unpublished sermon from which these phrases have been
quoted. It was written on 6 October 1799, that is a month before

---

[1] 12 Sept. 1814, *L.* ii, 629–30.
[2] *B.L.* i. 146.   [3] Ibid. i. 148.   [4] Ibid. i. 125.

he began contributing political articles to the *Morning Post*, and is in the main an attack upon the New Philosophy as enshrined in the French Revolution. The following passage well illustrates Coleridge's method of relating all things to the basic facts of human psychology.

There is a false and dangerous Philosophy which addresses itself to Men, as to Beings of pure Intellect, and either forgets our Passions and Affections, or argues for their Extinction. Instead of considering that as a moral Truth which is suited to the System of our Nature, the Professors of this Philosophy would fain suit the System of our Nature to that which *they* consider as moral Truth.[1]

Thus Coleridge worked outward from his knowledge of the human mind, supplementing this with a knowledge of men and events derived from a philosophical reading of history.

But knowledge of Man, whether derived from personal observation and introspection or from books needed to be related to knowledge of men. For the latter he was indebted to Stuart. In a letter dated 8 May 1816 he wrote: 'I dare affirm my belief, that my greater knowledge of *man* has been useful to you; though from the nature of things, not so useful, as your knowledge of *men* has been to me.'[2] Stuart was 'a very knowing person' not in the derogatory sense in which the phrase was used in the first edition of *Table Talk*, but in the sense that he was on familiar terms with many of the leading politicians and was certainly more experienced than Coleridge in the difficult business of interpreting personal and party gossip. It was his custom, he told the readers of the *Gentleman's Magazine* in 1838, to call on Coleridge 'in the middle of the day, talk over the news, and project a leading paragraph for the next morning'. Much hangs on the interpretation of the word 'project'. From its context the reader is encouraged to think that all the fundamental brainwork was supplied by Stuart and that Coleridge merely added a little literary eloquence. Often, the editor suggests, he failed to do even that, for 'the thought of compulsion disarmed him'. But whatever rancour may have developed

---

[1] *The original | of | a discourse | Written for whom | I neither know or care | as a College Commemoration | Sermon—Oct 6th 1799*, B.M. Add. MSS. 35343, f. 33. See promise to write the sermon in a letter to George Coleridge, 29 Sept. 1799, *C.L.* i. 532. See my note, *N. & Q.*, n.s. v (Apr. 1958), 150-2.

[2] *L.* ii. 660-1. But cf. 'Without the knowledge of Man, the knowledge of Men is a hazardous acquisition'. *Lay Sermons*, p. 132.

in later life, making it impossible for either to write impartially about this period in retrospect, the evidence of Coleridge's articles and the increased success of the paper during the years 1799–1802 prove that the collaboration was an extraordinarily fruitful one.[1] Nevertheless, it is very unlikely that Stuart made any formal offer of a partnership. In March 1800 Coleridge confided to Poole the news that Stuart had offered him 'half shares in the two Papers, the M.P. & Courier', if he would devote himself to them. He said that he refused on the grounds that he preferred 'the lazy reading of Old Folios'; and requested Poole not to hint a word to anyone about the offer. From the evidence of this letter it is fairly clear that Coleridge thought that some kind of offer had been made, but that it was contingent on his willingness to devote all his time and energies to journalism. After Coleridge's death, Wordsworth wrote to his daughter Sara saying that he had been so convinced of the great services rendered by Coleridge to the *Morning Post* that he had 'urged him to put in his claim to be admitted a proprietor, but this he declined, having a great disinclination to any tie of the kind'.[2] It has been suggested that the fact that so intimate a friend as Wordsworth had heard nothing of an offer proves that none was ever made.[3] But this point of view fails to take into consideration Coleridge's plea for secrecy in the letter to Tom Poole. Certainly Stuart himself recognized that such a partnership might have been a profitable one. 'Could Coleridge and I place ourselves thirty years back, and he be so far a man of business as to write three or four hours a day, there is nothing I would not pay for his assistance. I would take him into partnership and I would enable him to make a large fortune.'[4] But the admission is not without an important qualification; and almost certainly Stuart's original tentative offer was similarly hedged round with various saving clauses.

The task of writing on a great variety of subjects for a large public exerted a beneficial influence on Coleridge's prose style.

[1] In the first edition of *Table Talk* Coleridge is reported as having said: 'I raised the sale of the *Morning Post* from an inconsiderable number to 7000 per day in the course of one year.' It was withdrawn in subsequent editions. Stuart demonstrated that the claim was not borne out by the figures; but undoubtedly Coleridge's work helped to increase the circulation, as Stuart was forced to admit when he considered individual contributions, e.g. the character of Pitt.

[2] *C. Life*, p. 110.

[3] By Campbell for example, op. cit.

[4] Quoted by Sara Coleridge in the Introduction to *E.O.T.*, pp. xci–xcii.

The excessive rhetoric that disfigured so many passages in the Bristol pamphlets and *The Watchman* essays disappeared almost entirely. Its presence in the earlier works had been symptomatic of his uncertain relationship with his public and of a failure to come to terms with political realities, which resulted in the substitution of the creatures of the author's indignant imagination for the men and measures to which he was opposed. As a leader writer on the *Morning Post* he wrote for a known public. He also closed the distance between himself and the subjects on which he was called to write. The extraneous personal element disappeared from his writing, and the personality of the writer and idiosyncracies of style no longer obtruded themselves between the reader and the topic under review. This is particularly true of his essays on the new French Constitution and the character studies of the leading statesmen of the day, although it must be admitted that the gap was not fully closed in the case of the portrait of Pitt, who retained something of the personal symbolic importance for Coleridge that Castlereagh later attained for Shelley. The essays on the French Constitution and Bonaparte's Peace Overtures were based on a close study of the relevant documents. As a result Coleridge no longer beats the air in vain; the punches have a definite object, are accurately aimed, and land home. There is no more political shadow-boxing. But the self-control imposed on his natural exuberance led to no diminution in the variety of his prose style. It ranges in irony from the inspired flippancy of the essay on *Grenville's Note* to the impassioned nobility of the first letter *To Mr. Fox*, reminiscent of, though not closely modelled on, the *Letters of Junius*. It rises occasionally to lofty flights of poetry as in the passages already quoted from the portrait of Pitt. More often the prose style is an effective medium for expressing vividly and memorably a subtle piece of dialectical argument or for drawing general deductions from contemporary events:

It is the fate and nature of revolutions, that the people at first are more than *angels* in their notions of rights and liberties; and less than men in the enjoyment and practice of them. It is equally natural, that the consequent failures should induce disgust; and that arguments should be deduced from the first outrages of a transient hope, to *justify* the despotism which has its best foundation in an equally transient despondency. A sick stomach, and a throbbing head, are as little favourable to just conceptions, as the gay madness of the midnight carousal. This

is the morning after a debauch.—As we would not rely on the promises
of France, in her drunken mood, so neither shall we calculate on her
passiveness and languor, now that she is *getting* sober. We must wait till
she *is* sober. We shall then see, that as the despotism and ambition of
the French Government have no plea of necessity or advantage, derived
from the circumstances of Europe at large, and consequently cannot be
justified; even so, and for even the same reasons, it cannot be permanent.[1]

Coleridge frequently sums up a complex political process with
the kind of simple but memorable antithetic sentence with which
this passage begins. The figures of speech are often of the
simple homely kind but are invariably worked out with great ingenuity and daring. The sentence structure is very much more
varied than in his other prose works. He learned how to use the
short sentence effectively. For example, in the above passage the
sentence 'this is the morning after a debauch'. And he does not
scorn to make the most of italics for emphasis. Nevertheless, few
phrases from these essays have survived. The epithet 'an upstart
Corsican'[2] and the phrase the 'child and champion of Jacobinism',
both applied to Bonaparte, are the only ones that have achieved
anything like common currency; and the latter was not a Coleridgean coinage but Stuart's correction of the phrase from Pitt's
'Security' speech that Coleridge had originally jotted down as 'the
nursling & champion' of Jacobinism.[3] Although only one of Coleridge's biographers, H. D. Traill, has done anything like justice to
the fine prose to be found in the journalism, a contemporary, De
Quincey, recognized the true worth of this work.

Worlds of fine thinking lie buried in that vast abyss, never to be dis-
entombed, or restored to human admiration. Like the sea it has swal-
lowed treasures without end, that no diving bell will bring up again.
But no where, throughout its shoreless magazines of wealth, does there
lie such a bed of pearls, confounded with the rubbish and '*purgamenta*' of
ages, as in the political papers of Coleridge. No more appreciable monument could be raised to the memory of Coleridge than a re-publication
of his essays in *The Morning Post*, but still more of those afterwards
published in *The Courier*.[4]

[1] *E.O.T.* ii. 499–500.

[2] Ibid. ii. 566. The use of the same phrase at the end of the second letter to Mr.
Fox is a conjectural reading supplied by Sara, who had an imperfect copy of the
article. The *M.P.* article actually reads 'low born'.

[3] *N.* i. 653. Stuart's claim that he supplied the alteration was made in the *Gentleman's Magazine*, May 1838, p. 488.

[4] Quoted by Sara in her Introduction to *E.O.T.*, p. xv.

Such a monument was raised through the devotion of his daughter when she published *Essays on His Own Times*. It is hoped, too, that this discussion will have illustrated the 'worlds of fine thinking' and will have the effect of reviving interest in the articles entombed in Sara's little-consulted volumes.

CHAPTER IV

POLITICS FROM 1804 TO 1814

1. *Public service in Malta*

IN April 1804 Coleridge left England for Malta in search of health. Soon after his arrival on the island on 18 May, he found himself caught up in the business of official administration; and far from being a period of rest and recuperation it proved to be one of strenuous activity. Within six weeks of landing he agreed to act as temporary Private Secretary to Sir Alexander Ball, the Civil Commissioner, or as it is more convenient to call him, the Governor of Malta. On 18 January 1805 Mr. Macaulay, the Public Secretary, died, and from that date Coleridge assumed the senior position. He was installed in 'cool and commanding rooms' in the Palace and for the first time in his life felt with pride and pleasure the responsibility of high office.[1] He told Southey of how he had some fifty times a day subscribed himself 'Segretario Publico dell' Isole di Malta, Gozo, e delle lore dipendenze',[2] and he cut off one of these official signatures and stuck it proudly in one of the Notebooks.

Both as Private and as Public Secretary he was called on to prepare a great number of official documents. He wrote State papers on British foreign policy in the Mediterranean, drafted a vast quantity of official letters, and dispatched reports on what he observed in Sicily, which he visited in the autumn of 1804. He also submitted memoranda on the legal system.[3] His work as Secretary was more onerous and exacting than he had expected when he agreed to help the Governor. He complained to Stuart of the excessive amount of work that he had to do, and reported that on some nights after preparing official letters and memoranda he was almost too tired to undress himself.[4] Of this vast amount of official correspondence little or nothing has survived. Papers sent home by the 'Arrow, the Acheron, and a Merchant Vessel' all

---

[1] *C. Life*, chap. viii, also *C.L.* ii. 1142 n.

[2] 2 Feb. 1805, *C.L.* ii. 1162.

[3] Details of his varied activities are contained in the letters he wrote from Malta, for example on 21 Aug. he writes to his wife of 'having examined into the Law-forms of the Island'. *C.L.* ii. 1170.   [4] 1 May 1805, *C.L.* ii. 1166.

failed to reach their destination, while most of the papers remaining in Malta were destroyed when old documents were burned in order to make room for new in 1851.

The subject-matter of the State papers he composed is indicated in a letter to Southey. There he writes: 'I have been working in memorials concerning Egypt, Sicily, & the Coast of Africa.' A paper entitled *Observations on Egypt* exists in manuscript in the British Museum but has never been published.[1] In addition the paper printed in the twenty-second issue of *The Friend*, on the subject of Malta and the renewal of war with France, was in origin a State paper. 'The considerations I am about to submit to the Reader, were written by me during my residence at Malta—were written at the instance of Sir Alexander Ball, and after many conversations with him on the subject, and when written, were read and approved by him.'[2] How much of the essay as published in *The Friend* was written in Malta, how much was added subsequently, what modifications were made, it is impossible to say. Certainly the version of the *Observations on Egypt* in the British Museum does not correspond with the form in which it was first submitted to the Ministry. Telling Stuart in 1806 what he had salvaged from his stay in Malta, he mentioned two notebooks and 'a valuable paper on the present state of Egypt much fuller of facts & more sober reasoning than the one written for Sir A. B. to be sent to the ministry'.[3] No trace of the original paper is to be found in the Public Record Office and so it is not possible to compare the texts to see exactly what changes were made.[4]

His work was highly valued by Sir Alexander Ball; this is proved by passages in Coleridge's letters, his unfinished life of Ball in *The Friend*, and the Governor's references to him in his own letters. Hungry for human affections and genuine appreciation of his talent, Coleridge was almost pathetically grateful that someone in high office recognized his political acumen and was eager to employ him in the service of the State. Even the rather extravagant claim that Ball expressed his willingness, had he been a man of means, to pay Coleridge £500 a year for the mere pleasure that he received from his conversation,[5] is rendered less improbable when it is compared with a passage in a letter from the Governor of

---

[1] 2 Feb. 1805, *C.L.* ii. 1164. B.M. Egerton MSS. 2800, f. 118.
[2] *F.* (1809), p. 354.   [3] 22 Aug. 1806, *C.L.* ii. 1178.
[4] P.R.O. C.O. 158, 8–10.   [5] Letter to Sara, 21 Aug. 1805, *C.L.* ii. 1171.

Malta to G. F. Leckie, the British Consul at Syracuse. Having promised that Coleridge's company would be a feast for the Consul's mind, Ball went on to add: 'we must prevail on him to draw up a Political Paper on the Revenue and resources of Sicily'.[1] His services, then, were highly valued.

The two letters Coleridge wrote from Syracuse, describing the circumstances relating to the capture of a British merchant vessel by a French privateer, prove that he was capable of writing extremely efficient and fully documented reports. On this occasion he took great care to obtain copies of every document that could be of use to Ball in unravelling what had occurred. All purely private views were excluded and his literary powers strictly subordinated to the task in hand. But the same subordination of his personal views is not so strongly in evidence in the State paper called *Observations on Egypt*. Its purpose was to consider the necessity for Britain to maintain her interest in Egypt and to deny this sphere of interest to France. In the twelve months that preceded Coleridge's arrival, Sir Alexander Ball had been actively engaged in extending Britain's influence in Egypt through an agent, Vincenzo Taberna, who had been instructed to discover the extent of French influence and to explore the possibility of a disguised form of British control.[2] Ball had also circularized officials with an extract from the *Gentleman's Magazine* which drew attention to the strategic importance of Egypt.[3] Thus when Coleridge arrived a great deal of thought was being given to the subject. In his *Observations* Coleridge expressed the opinion that France wanted Egypt primarily on its own account, and only 'secondly and distantly as a means of subverting Britain's Eastern Empire'. Nevertheless, he set out to consider what effect a threat to this sphere of influence might have, and expressed his confidence in his native country's power to rise to the occasion. Faced with this threat, 'I should still hope', he said,

that the genius of the country would remain triumphant, that the genius of G. Britain, by which I mean that blended result of Laws, Language,

---

[1] The letter is printed in a footnote in *C.L.* ii. 1157. For the original see Add. MSS. 35344, f. 263.

[2] Shafik Ghorbal, *The Beginnings of the Egyptian Question and the Rise of Mehemet Ali*, 1928, p. 215.

[3] A review of *A Summary Account of Liebnitz's Memoir* on the conquest of the Nile by France, *G.M.* 1803, ii. 943–8. The review expressed arguments similar to those expressed by Coleridge in his paper on Malta. *F.*, p. 177.

Customs, long enjoyment of personal and political Independence, illustrious Forefathers and whatever else constitutes a Grand national character and makes a Nation more than an aggregate of Individuals, I should still cherish a faith, that this would oppose to the new and strange Peril new and equal resources.

However interesting this may be as marking his earliest attempt to define what constituted a nation, it forms something of a digression in a paper the function of which was to discuss the main problems of British foreign policy in relation to Egypt. But it does in fact provide a striking example of the way in which Coleridge developed his political theory in response to specific problems.

The stay in Malta certainly brought him into close contact with the difficulties of political administration. In *The Friend* he declared that 'in many respects', these months were 'the most memorable and instructive' in his life;[1] and in a letter written to Stuart soon after his return from Malta he summed up what he had gained from his residence there in the following words.

In short, tho' no emolument could ever force me again to the business, intrigue, form and pomp of a public situation, yet beyond all doubt I have acquired a great variety of useful knowledge, quickness in discovering men's characters, and adroitness in dealing with them / I have learnt the *inside* character of many eminent living men / & know by heart the awkward & wicked machinery, by which all our affairs *abroad* are carried on.[2]

'Years of waste'[3] they may have been as regards the development of his poetic genius, disastrous in their effect on his health and opium-taking habits as his friends noted with pity and regret, but they were nevertheless an invaluable apprenticeship to statecraft. In Malta he was led to develop his ideas on what constituted the wise statesman or governor. The *Morning Post* essays on Pitt, Addington, and Fox provide abundant evidence of his dissatisfaction with the characters of the leading English statesmen; and a letter to Poole complaining of the general dearth of wisdom in

---

[1] *F.*, p. 351.
[2] 22 Aug. 1806, *C.L.* ii. 1178.
[3] 'The influence of Wordsworth was withdrawn; and these were years of waste, and, to speak plainly, ruin.' H. W. Garrod, *Coleridge, Poetry and Prose*, 1925, p. viii. Morchard Bishop writes of the 'spiritual loneliness and the intolerable society of administrative officials, in a Mediterranean climate' as almost completing his destruction. *The Complete Poems of Samuel Taylor Coleridge*, Macdonald Illustrated Classics, p. xxi.

England, illustrates Coleridge's faith in the incalculable powers that might be wielded by one good and wise man.

O merciful Heaven! if it were thy good Will to raise up amongst us *one* great good man, only *one* man of a commanding mind, enthusiastic in the *depth* of his Soul, calm on the *surface*—and devoted to the accomplishment of the *last End* of human Society by an Oath which no Ear of Flesh ever heard, but only the omnipresent God!—Even this unhappy nation might behold what few have the courage to dream of, and almost as few the goodness to wish.[1]

Now in Sir Alexander Ball he had discovered 'the abstract Idea of a wise & good Governor'.[2] But even after one has read Coleridge's unfinished sketch of Ball's life in *The Friend*, it is a little difficult to understand what it was that led him to praise Ball so highly.[3] Certainly his private life as husband, parent, and master is shown to have been irreproachable; while the same strict regard for the moral law was illustrated in his dealings with subordinates as a naval commander in his youth and as an administrator in later life. He never refused to listen to the opinions of others, even of weak men. 'It was one of his maxims', said Coleridge, 'that a man may suggest what he cannot give.' He was free, too, from the fault 'so frequent in Englishmen, and so injurious to our interests abroad, of despising the inhabitants of other countries'. But what most impressed Coleridge and made Ball fit his 'abstract Idea' of a Governor was that his rule was based on principle and not on mere expedience. It was founded on the assumption that those he ruled were rational creatures, each of whom possessed a conscience to which appeal might always be made. Ball recognized 'that no body of men can for any length of time be safely treated otherwise than as rational beings, and that, therefore, the education of the lower classes was of utmost consequence to the permanent security of the empire, even for the sake of our navy'.[4] Coleridge had expressed similar views in the Bristol lectures, but it came as a surprise and a delight to find that his opinions were shared by a distinguished public administrator, the Governor of Malta. He discovered also that Ball was a convert to the monitorial system of Andrew Bell[5] and that he was in favour of introducing

---

[1] 18 Apr. 1801, *C.L.* ii. 721.   [2] *C.L.* ii. 1141.   [3] *F.*, pp. 350–85.   [4] *F.*, p. 355.

[5] Andrew Bell (1753–1832) devised a monitorial system to solve the special difficulties at the Madras Male Orphanage. Hence it was often called the 'Madras System'. In 1797 Bell published an account of his experiment and introduced his method in a number of schools. In 1808 he published a 'Sketch of a National Educa-

a national system of education. No wonder that when he returned his conversation was, as De Quincey complained, nothing but 'Ball and Bell—Bell and Ball'.[1]

Coleridge's residences abroad correspond with important stages in the development of his political ideas. While it is obvious that the main importance of the period spent in Germany in 1798–9 was that it introduced him to the German philosophers, absence from England appears to have contributed something to the development of a more sober and balanced view of English and European politics; and the result can be studied in the essays in the *Morning Post*, particularly in the passages dealing with property and the historical importance of the landed gentry. The feeling of nostalgia that sent Wordsworth on a voyage of imaginative rediscovery into his own past and which produced some of the greatest passages in *The Prelude*, made Coleridge think more kindly of his native land and recall its glorious history. His second residence abroad in Malta intensified his innate patriotism. In a foreign country dissension fell into proper perspective. 'Many a party man', he remarked in one of the Notebooks, 'talks as if he hated his Country, saddens at her prosperous events, exults in her Disasters, and yet all the while is merely hating the opposite party, & would himself feel & talk as a Patriot were he in a foreign Land.'[2] Distance from England with its accompanying nostalgia, contact with the 'abstract Idea' of a Governor, the complex responsibilities of office, the recognition of the vast superiority of the system of government in England over those that he had seen in Sicily and Italy, a superiority to which his mind returned again and again after his foreign travels; all these facts played their part in reconciling Coleridge to his homeland with all its faults and in providing a substratum of experience upon which to build his political theory in the periodical, *The Friend*, the last of his ill-starred ventures in private journalism.

II. *Private journalism again: 'The Friend', 1809–10*

It was certainly not the encouragement of his advisers that led Coleridge to found *The Friend* nearly three years after his return

tion', and three years later helped to found the National Society for Promoting the Education of the Poor in the Principles of the Established Church. Coleridge eulogizes him in *The Friend*, F., pp. 60–61, and *Lay Sermons*, p. 45.

[1] *The Collected Writings of Thomas De Quincey*, ed. D. Masson, 1889–90, ii. 185–6.
[2] *Notebook No. 11*, B.M. Add. MSS. 47508, f. 38.

from Malta. A *Prospectus* sent to Charles Lamb only aroused the doubt whether he would ever accomplish anything at all.[1] He remembered, as Coleridge himself should have remembered, the total failure of *The Watchman*; and in a letter to Charles Lloyd he reminded him of that earlier unlucky attempt to produce a private periodical. When the first issue did actually appear, Lloyd complained that the style was 'abstruse and laboured' and contrasted the 'lamentable want of voluntary power' with the spontaneous and sprightly vivacity of Coleridge's conversation.[2] Wordsworth was one of the gloomiest of the prophets, though indeed he did not refuse his active help. After remarking to Poole that it would have been better if Coleridge had never thought of making the attempt, he wrote: 'I give it to you as my deliberate opinion, formed upon proofs which have been strengthening for years, that he neither will nor can execute anything of important benefit either to himself his family or mankind.'[3]

The ultimate grounds of this uncharitable judgement were moral not literary. Nevertheless, in spite of Wordsworth's gloomy forebodings—'it cannot go on for any length of time. I am *sure* it cannot'—twenty-eight issues in fact appeared. It is true that the publication of *The Friend*, far from making the profit of £12 to £20 a week that Coleridge had at first prophesied,[4] involved him in further debts to his friends amounting in all to about £300;[5] and to this extent Wordsworth's opinion was confirmed by subsequent events. But that Coleridge proved that he was incapable of benefiting mankind is a judgement with which few will concur who have read *The Friend*.

Coleridge regarded this work as 'both the reservoir and the living fountain' of his mind. He believed that he was in possession of vital truths and he wished to communicate these to all who were prepared to grapple with them. He wished to 'uphold those truths and those merits, which are founded in the nobler and permanent parts of our nature against the caprices of fashion', and to 'recom-

---

[1] Letter to Sarah Hazlitt, 10 Dec. 1808, *Letters of Charles and Mary Lamb*, ed. E. V. Lucas, 1905, i. 392.

[2] *Charles Lamb and the Lloyds*, ed. E. V. Lucas, 1898, p. 244.

[3] 31 May or 1 June 1809, *Letters of W. and D. Wordsworth, Middle Years*, i. 321.

[4] Letter to Wordsworth, May or June 1808, printed in full in an appendix in E. K. Chambers, *Coleridge*, 1938, p. 350.

[5] This is the conclusion reached by Miss Barbara Rooke in *An Edition of The Friend*, unpublished London doctoral thesis, p. 55.

mend *principles* instead of mere *expedience*'. He had already begun
to prepare materials for a comprehensive philosophical work before he left for Malta. At that time the title of the work, which was
evidently not to be issued in periodical form, was 'Consolations
and Comforts'. 'Consolations and Comforts from the exercise and
right application of the Reason, the Imagination, the Moral Feelings, Addressed especially to those in sickness, adversity, or distress of mind, from speculative gloom.' The phrase 'speculative
gloom' which appears here in a letter to Tom Poole, dated 15
January 1804, actually appeared five years later in the *Prospectus* to
The Friend, an indication of the connexion between the two works.
The Notebooks for the Malta period and those he kept on his
return to England contain a good deal of material that was
earmarked for 'Comforts and Consolations' or 'The Soother of
Absence' alternative titles for the same projected philosophical
and meditative work. They also contain material that was not recorded with this work in mind, but which was later incorporated
in one or other of the essays in *The Friend*. The work was thus the
product of a period of meditation and reflection extending over at
least five years.

With such an ambitious aim in mind it seems at first curious that
Coleridge should have chosen the periodical form. The idea of
founding another periodical, a successor to *The Watchman*, may be
dated as far back as 1804, when, before his departure for Malta, he
recorded in his Notebook that he would '*like* to dare to look forward to the time, when Wordsworth and I with contributions
from Lamb & Southey, & a few others—should publish a Spec-
tator'.[1] The periodical form possessed no advantages for carrying
out his purpose. As Dorothy Wordsworth commented with her
characteristic good sense, the 'mode of publication is not the
proper one for matters so abstract as are frequently treated of—for
who can expect that people whose daily thoughts are employed on
matters of business, and who *read* only for relaxation should be
prepared for or even capable of serious thought when they take up
a periodical paper, perhaps to read over in haste?'[2] Nevertheless,
Coleridge succeeded in persuading himself that it was an appropriate medium for his ideas. He considered that it suited the nature

[1] *Notebook No. 15*, B.M. Add. MSS. 47512.
[2] Letter to Jane Marshall, 18 Feb. 1810, *Letters of W. and D. Wordsworth, Middle Years*, i. 356.

of his own mind, and in this he showed considerable self-know-
ledge, for although he could never produce copy on time, the
obligation to do so compelled him to exertions that he would not
otherwise have made. With less justice he considered that the delay between issues would enable the reader to familiarize himself
with the strange, unfashionable ideas propounded. Had each essay
formed a self-contained unit instead of being an 'arbitrary section
of a continuous treatise, which required continuous reading to
effect its purpose'¹ and had the contents of each issue born a closer
relation to what had preceded it and what was to follow, the
periodical form might have possessed this advantage. The incon-
gruity between the matter and the form did not go unnoticed in
the reviews. 'Though coming with some of the exterior marks of a
newspaper, [it] was yet to derive nearly as little aid from the
stimulant facts and questions of the day, as if it had been a commentary on Aristotle or Plato.'² Thus remarked the anonymous
writer in the *Eclectic Review*.

The first issue of *The Friend*, which appeared on 1 June 1809
contained a typical Coleridgean promise. 'I shall dedicate my
second number', he wrote, 'entirely to the views, which a British
Subject in the present state of his country ought to entertain of its
actual and existing Constitution of Government.'³ The promise
was not immediately fulfilled. The following issue was largely
taken up with a personal defence against the attacks on his morals
and politics that had been made long ago in 1799 in *The Beauties of
the Anti-Jacobin.*⁴ He then ran out of stamped paper. When this
again became available in August there followed not the essay on
the 'existing Constitution of Government' but a series of essays
On the Communication of Truth and the Rightful Liberty of the Press.
The subject extended through four issues of *The Friend*, being
concluded in the sixth issue on 21 September.⁵ It was very charac-

¹ E. K. Chambers, *Coleridge*, p. 228.
² The *Eclectic Review*, Oct. 1811, p. 914. According to Crabb Robinson, Coleridge
wrote and thanked the editor for the 'flattering review'. *Henry Crabb Robinson on
Books and their Writers*, ed. E. J. Morley, i. 55.
³ *F.* (1809), p. 12.
⁴ Dorothy Wordsworth disapproved of this pointless raking up of the past; she
was probably not the only reader to find it distasteful. *Letters of D. and W. Wordsworth, Middle Years*, i. 306. The chief charge made in 1799 was that he had abandoned
his wife and children. There were also reflections on his supposed Jacobinism.
⁵ These essays formed the introductory section in the rifacimento edition of *The
Friend*, 1818.

teristic of Coleridge that he should think it necessary to address his readers at length in order to prove that he was morally entitled to address them at all. Quite apart from a natural inclination for elaborate schemes of self-justification and the desire to bring his conduct into line with first principles, there can be seen in these essays unmistakable evidence of Coleridge's continuous preoccupation with the problems attending the freedom of the Press. But whereas in *The Plot Discovered* and *The Watchman* he had placed the main emphasis on the abstract right of speaking the truth regardless of its consequences, he now devoted much of his attention to the grave responsibilities that fell on anyone who wished to address a wide heterogeneous public on controversial issues, and to the related problem of what degree of freedom a State could safely give the citizen in the expression of opinion.

It was also expedient for the author of *The Friend* to state his views clearly on this subject in view of the notoriety that his early political writings had won.[1] The period 1808–10 saw a rapid increase in the number of charges brought against journalists. Between 1801 and 1807 the average yearly number did not exceed two, but between 1808 and 1810 there were forty-two *ex-officio* informations and eighteen trials of journalists.[2] Wordsworth's anxiety concerning the passages in his *Convention of Cintra* that reflected on the character and ability of the generals in the Peninsula Campaign proves how real the fear of prosecution was in 1809. He had been reminded of the danger by coming across a reference to the savage sentences that had been passed ten years earlier on Benjamin Flower and Gilbert Wakefield for their attacks on Richard Watson, Bishop of Llandaff;[3] and he drew Coleridge's attention to these trials and to the general danger.[4] Almost certainly Wordsworth's references acted as a timely warning and prompted Coleridge to establish his respectability in the first issues of *The Friend* and to consider at length the function of the Press and its relations with the State.

Coleridge made no very significant changes to this section when

---

[1] It was Coleridge's political poetry not his prose that led to the attack in the *Anti-Jacobin*.

[2] E. Halévy, *A History of the English People in the 19th Century*, 1949, i. 161–2.

[3] Wakefield was sentenced in May 1799 to two years' imprisonment, Flower, editor of the *Cambridge Intelligencer*, to six months and a £100 fine, for alleged libels on Richard Watson.

[4] *Letters of W. and D. Wordsworth, The Middle Years*, i. 296–309.

he came to revise the original papers for publication in the rifacimento edition of *The Friend*. This is all the more strange when it is
borne in mind that the freedom of the Press and State control had
once again become very much a live issue about this time. In
November 1816 Cobbett decided to publish a popular edition of
his *Political Register* at twopence a copy. He was thereby able to
reach a new class of reader, and the change in publishing policy
coincided with his public espousal of Cartwright's programme for
universal suffrage and annual Parliaments.[1] The spirit of Jacobinism was again abroad. But both Southey and Coleridge noted a
significant difference between the Jacobinism of the 1790's and
that which seemed to be overwhelming the country. It had now
'sunk to the rabble', noted Southey in a letter to Lord Liverpool,
and in a letter to G. C. Bedford he recommended that transportation should be used to 'curb the *licentiousness* of the Press'.[2] Coleridge advocated no such illiberal measure though he felt strongly
on the subject. The reasons why he did not seize the opportunity
of attacking Cobbett and the popular demagogues when he issued
The Friend in 1818 were twofold. Apart from adding a whole new
section on Religion and Philosophy Coleridge made no real attempt to revise the old material. Secondly, he had already written a
vigorous attack on the new spirit of Jacobinism in the *Letters to
Judge Fletcher* printed in the *Courier* in 1814, and a further attack
two years later in the second *Lay Sermon*.[3] He did add one short
passage when he prepared the rifacimento;[4] it was not in the main
an attack on the popular demagogues and their methods but directed
against what he called here and in a letter to Daniel Stuart, 'Legislative Jacobinism'.[5] By this phrase he meant the intervention of
the State to compel the fulfilment of duties of imperfect obligation.
This was to confuse the proper spheres of religion and government. The example he gave was Lord Erskine's Bill for the pre-
vention of cruelty to animals. It is odd to think of the author of the
last stanzas of *The Ancient Mariner* being opposed to so humane a
measure. He opposed it on the grounds that it was an example of

[1] *Political Register*, 23 Nov. 1816. See also G. D. H. Cole, *The Life of William
Cobbett*, 3rd rev. ed., 1947, pp. 201–7.

[2] 19 Mar. 1817. See C. D. Yonge, *Life and Administration of Robert Banks, Second
Earl of Liverpool*, 1868, 2 vols. ii. 298–9. 7 Sept. 1816. *Letters of Robert Southey*, ed.
M. H. Fitzgerald, 1912, p. 265.

[3] E.O.T. iii. 677–733; *Lay Sermons*, pp. 157–69.

[4] *F.*, pp. 54–58.   [5] 30 Oct. 1814, L. ii. 635.

the dangerous principle of 'extending PERSONALITY to *things*'.[1] The section certainly ends with a reference to the contemporary situation, to 'one of those viperous journals, which deal out profaneness, hate, fury, and sedition throughout the land', a reference which, from its context, appears to refer to Cobbett's paper.[2] His most pointed comment on the methods employed by the popular demagogues, however, is to be found in one of the Notebooks and belongs to the year 1816 or 1817. There he remarked 'that the Cobbetts & Hunts address you (= the lower Ranks) as beasts who have no future selves—as if by a natural necessity you must *all* remain poor & slaving'.[3] A few more simple straightforward comments of this type would have added force to Coleridge's somewhat oblique treatment of the freedom of the Press in the rifacimento edition of *The Friend*.

The principles regulating the communication of truth and the rightful liberty of the Press were considered in *The Friend* under two heads; in relation to the individual and his own conscience, and in relation to the State. Fundamental to the argument in the first part was the distinction drawn between what constitutes moral truth and what mere verbal accuracy. The behaviour of Blifil in *Tom Jones* provided an apt illustration of the fact that moral truth involves some reference to the intention of the speaker. It was not sufficient for a man to be able to prove a correspondence between his words and certain facts, he must consult his conscience as the sole arbiter of his conduct. 'The conscience, or effective reason, commands the design of conveying an adequate notion of the thing spoken of, when this is practicable; but at all events a right notion, or none at all.'[4] To illustrate the sense in which he was using the words 'right' and 'adequate', Coleridge recalled to the reader's mind how a schoolmaster teaches arithmetic empirically; he does not teach the necessary truth involved in each rule, since this would demand a knowledge of higher mathematics. Nevertheless, 'he conveys a right notion, though he cannot convey the adequate one'.

He then asks two questions. When is a man justified in communicating a right though inadequate notion? And, second,

---

[1] The Bill was introduced in 1809 and was resolutely opposed by Windham, whom Coleridge praises for his action. *F.*, pp. 55–56. See *L.* ii. 635 n. and 636.

[2] *F.*, p. 58.

[3] *Notebook No. 22*, B.M. Add. MSS. 47520, f. 61.   [4] *F.*, p. 23.

under what circumstances should he refrain absolutely from the attempt? The answer supplied to the first is that a man may do this if he can satisfy his conscience on the following grounds: that it is his desire to convey truth only and that if his words should lead to positive error, it is the fault of the receiver and not the communicator; that the error involved should not materially vitiate the imperfect truth; that it does not prevent the acquiring of knowledge that will subsequently destroy that error. The answer to the second is simple and unequivocal. The existence of ignorance and of predominant passions in the public lays a moral obligation on the conscience to abstain from the attempt, for at best it can produce only nominal proselytes.

Coleridge anticipated the objection that would inevitably be made. How, it would be asked, could an author foresee into whose hands his book might fall, either in the present or, even more difficult, in the future. All would be well, Coleridge asserted,

if the author have clearly and rightly established in his own mind the class of readers, to which he means to address his communications; and if both in this choice, and in the particulars of the manner and matter of his work, he conscientiously observe all the conditions which reason and conscience have shown to dictate, in relation to those for whom the work was designed.[1]

In addition he thought that there existed little danger in communicating heterodox views as long as they were treated with due seriousness, since the number of men capable of understanding the implications of original ideas was at any time limited. The writer who forced his readers to think ruled out the possibility of his work falling into the wrong hands.

In turning to consider the attitude of the State to the individual writer, Coleridge began by asserting that the State must always act on the principle of self-preservation. 'Every depository of the supreme power must presume itself rightful.'[2] But he saw that it was important for the welfare of the State that it should not concern itself exclusively with self-preservation; it should also attend to the 'condition of its growth, and of that adaptation to circumstances, without which its very life becomes insecure'. Towards that growth and orderly development the writer had much to contribute. The main problem that confronted the state was the

[1] F., p. 30.   [2] Ibid., p. 39.

problem of how to institute laws which, while making seditious libel an offence, would not unduly restrict the legitimate and constructive work of the critic of society. Quoting with approval Milton's dictum that 'a book should be as freely admitted into the world as any other birth', he dismissed any system of State licensing or censorship as an undesirable and impracticable method of preventing sedition. He was content that the existing law was based on the right principle, namely, that only after publication had taken place could the State intervene. The chief difficulty, however, was to decide when an offence had taken place. Whereas in theft and murder the act constitutes the criminality, in questions involving libel, or any other misuse of words 'the degree makes the kind, the circumstances constitute the criminality'. Since the State owes an incalculable debt to the civilizing influence of the Press, the law should take notice of virtuous intention and allow this due weight in considering whether an offence had been committed. 'It is to the press that we owe the gradual ascendancy of those wise political maxims, which casting philosophic truth in the moulds of national laws, customs, and existing orders of society, subverted the tyranny without suspending the government.'[1] The general matter, style and method of publication provides the State with external proof of the writer's intention. Two examples are given. Coleridge relates how he came upon workers in a large factory reading a sixpenny pamphlet 'containing a selection of inflammatory paragraphs from the prose works of Milton'. From the principle on which the passages had been selected, from the price and method of circulation, it was clear that the intention of its compiler was to subvert the allegiance of the ignorant and uneducated labourers. As an example of a work where the author's good intention mitigated what would have otherwise have constituted an offence, he refers to the articles that had appeared in the *Morning Post* during the Peace of Amiens—many of them by Coleridge himself—'not a paragraph warning the nation, as need was and as most imperious duty commanded, of the perilous designs and unsleeping ambition of our neighbour, the mimic and caricaturist of Charlemagne; but was a punishable libel'.[2]

[1] Ibid., p. 45.
[2] Ibid., p. 46. For a more detailed working out of the comparison of Napoleon and Charlemagne see p. 48.

Coleridge had noted earlier in the discussion that the existence of ignorance on a large scale enormously increased the danger of any publication becoming the innocent cause of evil. He realized that the ultimate solution to this problem lay in 'the rational spirit of freedom diffused and become national' and the 'consequent influence and control of public opinion, and its most precious organ, the jury'.[1] Rather surprisingly he did not refer to the Fox Act of 1792, the theoretical effect of which was to transfer from the judge to the jury the responsibility for deciding whether a libel had been committed. Earlier the jury's function had been limited to deciding whether the defendant had published the work in question, and, secondly, whether the work had the meaning alleged in the indictment or information. But even after 1792, the Solicitor-General's ruling that the judge should be free to exercise his discretion in allowing the jury to decide on the whole issue did much to vitiate the force of Fox's Act.[2] Quite apart from this limitation of the jury's powers and the fact that it was often very carefully handpicked, its usefulness clearly depended on how well its members understood the law. It was of the utmost importance, asserted Coleridge, that the jury should realize that the degree, the circumstance, and the intention, constitute (not merely modify) the offence, but give it its being, and determine its legal name.[3] The 'Pole Star', the leading principle upon which judgement must rest is the more or less remote connexion of the work with 'overt-acts, as the cause or occasion of the same'. It was easier, he thought, to apply this principle to works attacking individuals than to those directed at institutions of government.[4] In deciding on the latter the jury had a difficult calculation to make. Whereas the overt-acts that might follow from a libel on a government—for example, the attempt to put some of Tom Paine's theories into practice—would be far more serious than anything that could be caused by a libel

[1] F., p. 53.

[2] W. H. Wickwar, *The Struggle for the Freedom of the Press*, 1928, pp. 40–48; A. Aspinall, *Politics and the Press*, 1949, pp. 37–38.

[3] F., p. 53.

[4] Throughout this discussion Coleridge fails to distinguish between civil and criminal libel. Personal loss of character is the essence of a civil libel, and the object of bringing an action damages to the injured party. The essence of a criminal libel is a tendency to cause a breach of the peace by libels defamatory, obscene, blasphemous, or seditious. It is with seditious libel that Coleridge is mainly concerned throughout. Had he used a more precise terminology it would have greatly improved this section of *The Friend*.

on an individual, the likelihood that such theories would be carried into practice was relatively small.

Throughout this lengthy discussion that took up the third to the sixth issues of *The Friend* in 1809 and formed the introductory section of the rifacimento of 1818, it can be seen that Coleridge considered that the dangers of subversion that the law attempted to prevent were largely the product of ignorance. He believed that this could be eradicated by two main means: by formal education —and a generous tribute was paid to Andrew Bell's monitorial system—and by the communication of knowledge by the Press, 'the Thames of our intellectual commerce'. A too rigorous application of the law would prevent this dissemination of valuable information; fear of the ignorant and unprincipled would guarantee that they should remain so, thus constituting a perpetual threat to good order and social stability. A vicious government has little real choice in its legislation relating to the Press. It must either 'fall by the people if they are suffered to become enlightened, or with them, if they are kept enslaved and ignorant'.[1] But Coleridge writes on the assumption that in England the Government was not vicious and could safely, and to its own advantage, permit the diffusion of knowledge through the Press. Individuals have two related duties, one to themselves and one towards others. 'To make use of all the means and appliances in our power to the actual attainment of rectitude, is the abstract of the duty which we owe to ourselves: to supply those means as far as we can, comprises our duty to others.'[2] It therefore becomes the duty of a wise State to allow the individual the greatest degree of freedom compatible with its own self-preservation in carrying out the second of these responsibilities; and it was Coleridge's self-dedicated task in all his journalism to carry out this duty he acknowledged he owed to others.

After the series on *The Communication of Truth* came to an end in the sixth number of *The Friend*, 21 September 1809, the long-promised and long-delayed political essays began to appear. Some were essays on the principles of political philosophy, others were retrospective accounts of the political scene in England between the year 1793 and the Peace of Amiens, others dealt with questions relating to international law and to the subject of taxation. Inter-

[1] F., p. 40.
[2] F., p. 61 and repeated in *The Statesman's Manual*, see *Lay Sermons*, p. 52.

H

mingled with these essays was a great deal of miscellaneous matter in prose and verse; and when Coleridge produced the rifacimento in 1818 he relegated the miscellaneous prose items to the sections he quaintly called 'Landing Places' and printed the political essays in a separate section entitled *On the Principles of Political Knowledge*.

This section of *The Friend* represents Coleridge's first attempt to formulate in any systematic fashion his ideas on the main problems of political philosophy. His earlier political writing had been mainly concerned with contemporary events, and though it was his proud boast that he had always related these to principles, no opportunity had yet arisen for a full statement of the principles that he had been slowly evolving. *The Friend* provided him with this opportunity. The essays in this periodical may be said therefore to contribute more to our understanding of Coleridge as a political philosopher than as a critic of contemporary society. Nevertheless, it is true that his attitude towards the events of the day is not fully intelligible without reference to the political theory expressed in *The Friend*. Professor Muirhead regretted that Coleridge sought to bribe the attention of the reader with discussions of contemporary problems and thus was prevented from fully developing his political theory.[1] But this view fails to take into consideration the integral relation which existed between the two. It was natural and inevitable that there should be countless references to recent events and current issues since Coleridge was usually led to consider the fundamental problems of political philosophy in relation to specific issues. Thus his ideas on representation, on constitutional theory and the function of property were developed when faced with the task of examining the new French Constitution in the *Morning Post*. Nor could he discuss the philosophy of the Physiocrats without reference to the course of English and European history since the fall of the Bastille. The same intimate relation between contemporary events and political theory may be observed in the essays on taxation and international law.

In the essays *On the Principles of Political Knowledge* Coleridge set out to consider three major theories of the origin and nature of government. He began by relating each to the theory of knowledge of which it was the natural and inevitable product. He saw Hobbes's political system as the logical outcome of a philosophy

[1] J. H. Muirhead, *Coleridge as Philosopher*, 1930, chap. vi.

of human nature that asserted that the human mind was 'nothing but manifold modifications of passive sensation'.[1] For Hobbes, then, man is a kind of higher animal, and he is led to found his system of government on the law of the jungle. Behind Rousseau's system of government, on the other hand, lies the assumption that men are creatures of pure reason. Midway between these two extremes is the system based on the assumption that man is a creature of understanding, 'or the faculty of suiting measures to circumstances'. It is essentially an attempt to attribute the basis of government to 'expedience founded on experience and particular circumstances'.[2] This is the system that, with certain important modifications, Coleridge accepts.

Coleridge's analysis of these three systems of political theory does not deserve to be considered seriously as a technical exposition of the subject. While the general method of approach is sound the treatment of each is uneven. The section devoted to Hobbes is too brief; and nothing much is said about the system to which Coleridge inclines except as it arises from criticism of the other systems. Only the section devoted to the theory of Rousseau and the Physiocrats is developed sufficiently to illustrate the main outline of the theory being criticized and Coleridge's objections to its basic assumptions and the superstructure built thereon. He concentrated his attention on this theory because he believed it was of vital practical importance to show that it was untenable. Nevertheless, it is presented with some degree of sympathy, partly because he could hardly treat with contempt a system whose worst fault was to over-emphasize the supreme faculty of reason in man, partly because he recognized that it was a bad policy 'to represent a political system as having no charm but for robbers and assassins, and no natural origin but in the brains of fools or madmen, when experience has proved, that the great danger of the system consists in the peculiar fascination it is calculated to exert on noble and imaginative spirits'.[3] This was the mistaken policy that had been pursued by Anti-Jacobins in England. They had failed to recognize the genuine attraction of the revolutionary ideas for noble minds, and instead of trying to win over the English Jacobins by means of rational persuasion they had used the power of the State to stamp out all heterodox political views and had sought to brand anyone for life who had at any time sympathized with the

---

[1] F., p. 102.   [2] Ibid., p. 127.   [3] Ibid., p. 116.

French Revolution. 'Once a Jacobin always a Jacobin', Pitt had declared in Parliament. This Coleridge had indignantly denied in the *Morning Post*;[1] and the whole plan of the political section of *The Friend* is based on the assumption that men are always open to rational argument. The best means of permanently discrediting a false political theory was not by suppression but by 'an intelligible and thorough exposure of the error, and, through that discovery, of the source, from which it derives its speciousness and powers of influence on the human mind'.[2] Coleridge believed that it was vitally important to examine Rousseau's political theory in 1809, because even though the revolutionary principles as a complete system had ceased to exert much influence on English opinion, many of the arguments used by the radicals and reformers were indirectly based on these untenable principles. He hoped that: 'By detecting the true source of the influence of these principles, we shall at the same time discover their natural place and object; and that in themselves they are not only truths, but most important and sublime truths; and that their falsehood and their danger consist altogether in their misapplication.'[3] He himself found in Rousseau at least one divine truth, for in his critique he was first led to formulate a distinction that plays an important part in all his mature political writings, the distinction made between a person and a thing and the attitude appropriate to each.[4] He began by pointing out that Rousseau's political theory was based on an undeniable truth, that all voluntary actions are moral actions and are grounded in the reason. The possession of reason distinguishes a person from a thing and thus a thing 'may rightfully be used, altogether and merely as a means', whereas a person 'must always be included in the end, and form a part of the final cause'.[5] The acceptance of such a distinction is implicit in Coleridge's earlier political criticism, in *The Watchman* essay on the slave trade, for example; but it was not until 1809 that he gave a clear and explicit statement of the principle. It has recently been called 'the leading principle of the Conservative tradition of political obligation'.[6] Whether this be true or not it certainly became in Coleridge's

---

[1] 'Once a Jacobin Always a Jacobin', *M.P.* 21 Oct. 1802; *E.O.T.* ii. 542–52.
[2] *F.*, pp. 114–15.
[3] Ibid., p. 115.
[4] See *Lay Sermons*, p. 237; *Church and State*, pp. 15–16.
[5] *F.*, p. 118.
[6] *The Conservative Tradition*, ed. R. J. White, 1950, p. 43.

hands a powerful critical weapon with which to attack the Utili-
tarian spirit of the early nineteenth century.

Not only does Rousseau's theory begin with this undeniable
truth but it states the central problem involved in any attempt
to create a satisfactory account of political obligation. Coleridge
states this problem as follows: 'Man must be free: or to what
purpose was he made a spirit of reason, and not a machine of instinct? Man must obey; or wherefore has he a conscience?'[1] In
order to illustrate Rousseau's solution, Coleridge gives a brief
outline of the whole system. He is also thereby able to point out
how Rousseau's disciples had made unjustifiable deductions from
his solution. He points out how the doctrine of the General Will
provides an answer to this central problem of political obligation
and then proceeds to concentrate on the section of the *Social Contract* in which Rousseau distinguished between the General Will
and the casual overbalance of wills, since he realized that a failure
to recognize the real force of this important distinction had
brought about disastrous results in France and elsewhere. He
asserts that it is impossible to deduce from the theory as stated by
Rousseau that the right of universal legislation resides in the
people nor could the National Assembly claim with any justification to be the organ of the General Will. He reminds his readers
that the pure will that flows from universal reason cannot be attributed to any one person or society 'and least of all to the mixed
multitude that makes up the people; but entirely and exclusively
to reason itself, which it is true, dwells in every man potentially,
but actually and in perfect purity is found in no man and in no
body of men'.[2] Neither the Jacobins nor Bonaparte were justified
in claiming to be the embodiment of the universal reason. He concludes that the *Social Contract* affords no grounds for preferring
one system of government or representation to another.

The undeniable truth that the work contains is one which,
according to Coleridge, is applicable only to the sphere of private
morality. In that sphere the reason issuing its commands through
the conscience 'is the one universal and sufficient guide to morality'. The chief error of Rousseau and his disciples lay, therefore,
in the unjustified assumption that reason had the power to prescribe the rules that should regulate the external actions of 'particular bodies of men, according to their particular circumstances'.[3]

[1] F., p. 119. [2] Ibid., p. 121. [3] Ibid., p. 122.

But, for these things, declared Coleridge, 'we must rely on our understandings, enlightened by past experience and immediate observation'; and determine our choice 'by comparisons of expediency'.[1] The whole critique of Rousseau can thus be seen to rest on two distinctions, that between the spheres of private and political action and their appropriate schemes of morality, and that between reason and understanding. The first of these he himself had failed to observe in his earliest political works owing to the force of the dissenting tradition.[2] The latter he had come to develop in order to separate what might be called the legislative from the executive functions of the human mind; and in one of the *Courier* essays he refers explicitly to the understanding as the 'calculating faculty, which is properly the executive branch of self-government'.[3] The ultimate grounds for his rejection of Rousseau's system lie in the recognition that it is built on an erroneous theory of human nature. For Rousseau and his French and English disciples man was a creature of pure reason; for Coleridge he was nothing of the sort. Reason was only one of the elements that went to make up 'his mixed and sensitive nature'. In an unpublished sermon written in October 1799, the inadequacies of the revolutionary principles had been exposed by a similar reference to what he there called 'the *System* of our Nature'.[4] If reason were only a part of this system of human nature it was absurd to expect it to be capable of governing the complex relations of men in society. 'It ought not to do this, because it cannot. The laws of reason are unable to satisfy the first conditions of human society.'[5] But this does not mean that reason can contribute nothing. From it alone 'can we derive the principles which our understandings are to apply, the ideal to which by means of our understandings we should endeavour to approximate'.

One of the effects of the distinction made between the operation of the understanding and the reason is to set up a dual system of morality in *The Friend*. This can be seen in the essays *On the Communication of Truth* and in the main political section. One law applies to the individual in the sphere of private morality and another to the citizen in the sphere of public morality. The main weakness in

[1] *F.*, p. 123. [2] For example in the Bristol Lectures. See Chap. I.
[3] 22 Dec. 1809, *E.O.T.* ii. 656.
[4] *The original of a discourse, Written for whom I neither know or care as a College Commemoration Sermon—Oct. 6th 1799*, B.M. Add. MSS. 35343, f. 40.
[5] *F.*, p. 125.

Coleridge's use of this dual system is that in a number of passages he is led to write as if expedience, unrelated to principles evolved from the reason, were a sufficient justification for any particular form of political action. He is sometimes guilty of the fault of which he held Burke to be guilty, 'if his opponents are theorists, then everything is to be founded on prudence . . . calculators? Then calculation itself is represented as a sort of crime.'[1] The same is in some measure true of Coleridge. In arguing against the abstract principles of Rousseau and the Rights of Man school of thought he places the whole emphasis on the rule of expedience, while in attacking the statesmen of his age and their policies he changes his ground and lays the whole emphasis on the need for principles. The reader loses sight of the important qualification, 'from reason alone can we derive the principles which our understandings are to apply',[2] and the rule of expedience appears to be divorced from the rule of universal reason.

The *Social Contract* contained no satisfactory account of the origin and function of property. It is impossible to deduce the right of property from the reason. According to Coleridge the chief object for which men formed a state was the protection of their property not their lives. He considers what would happen if the land were state-owned and if labour and produce were equally divided. Far from bringing into existence an era of universal justice as he had once thought when he planned Pantisocracy, it would involve great injustice, unless—and he implies that this is impossible—'the reason of all and each was absolute master of the selfish passions of sloth, envy, &c.'.[3] If such angelic creatures were to exist, so unlike human beings as we know them, then government would be superfluous. Once you recognize the inequalities of the human mind and the natural inequalities of the earth, you are obliged to acknowledge that individual ownership of land necessarily involves unequal property. 'To property, therefore, and to its inequalities, all human laws directly or indirectly relate, which would not be equally laws in the state of nature'[4] he concludes, and this conclusion prepares the way for his attack on the attempt to establish the right of universal suffrage. It also provides the basis for his tentative outline of the true ends of government in the fifteenth number of *The Friend*.

---

[1] Ibid., p. 117.   [2] Ibid., p. 125.
[3] Ibid., p. 126.   [4] Ibid.

One of the Notebooks in which Coleridge jotted down his meditations on a great variety of subjects during the composition of *The Friend* contains a number of passages of varying length relating to the subject of property. Two of these reveal that Coleridge was by no means unaware of the danger of accepting uncritically the importance often assigned to property. 'The great object in writing on the Constitution is to avoid being imposed on by the names of *things*, as of *Property* & to keep the attention steadily fixed on men, and their actual and actuating principles, motives, and impulses—Custom, Law &c.'[1] In another passage of approximately the same date he wrote: 'By no means convinced of the Truth of the late simplifying schemes of our Constitution, which reduce all to the influence of Property. I deem them false, 1 from the *growth* of the Constitution, 2 from the nature of the human mind *in toto*, and 3 from the actual state of things at present.'[2] In succeeding passages in this Notebook one can trace the stages through which Coleridge's thought passed as he strove to evolve some satisfactory account of the origin of property and its relation to the constitution. He noted that the 'very status belli of all savage tribes with their neighbours', seemed to indicate that the desire to acquire and preserve property was natural to man. 'What was not felt in the Individuals could never have been felt in the Tribe',[3] he noted. Observation of the behaviour of the swans on Hawkshead Lake suggested that a sense of property was natural even to animals.[4] He turned to John Locke; and though he considered that his notion of founding the right of property on the principle that the sweat of man was mixed with the soil was ridiculous, he recognized that 'as a mere metaphor, and translating it into a general proposition' it was both true and important. This general proposition he then states as follows.

That a man who by an act of his mind followed by the *fact* of bodily usufructure has impropriated an object, a spot of land, for instance, has combined with it many parts of his Being—his knowledge, memory, affections, a sense of right as well—and that this field is therefore to him what it is not to any other man. Therefore the other takes from him, what he cannot take himself—the good to himself does not equal the evil to his equal.[5]

---

[1] *Notebook No. 18*, B.M. Add. MSS. 47515, f. 119*v*.
[2] Ibid., f. 19. [3] Ibid., f. 117.
[4] Ibid., f. 118. [5] Ibid.

To this he adds what he considers to be a more important argument,

the *necessity* of individualist action to moral agency, & an individual sphere to Individual scheme of action and of property to them.—That without which a necessary end cannot be realized, is itself necessary—therefore lawful.[1]

If these passages are compared with the treatment of property in the political essays in *The Friend*, it will be seen that much of the freshness, originality, and intellectual excitement disappears in the essays. There the treatment is too dogmatic, the faith in property is insufficiently related to principle and the whole leaves the reader with the impression that Coleridge had in fact allowed himself to 'be imposed on by the names of things', which was the very fault he had hoped to avoid. Such a comparison of Notebook jottings with a published work suggests what a further comparison of parallel sections in later works confirms, that had Coleridge found means to incorporate more of these passages into the published works he would have appeared to his contemporaries a more stimulating and forthright social critic.

In the sections of *The Friend* devoted to the subject of parliamentary reform, Coleridge criticizes three distinct kinds of reformers: those who based their claim on abstract metaphysical reasoning, those who appealed to ancient statutes, and those who rested their case solely on expedience. Major Cartwright is introduced as a typical example of the first class.[2] On the grounds that he 'confounds the sufficiency of the conscience to make every person a moral and amenable being, with the sufficiency of judgement and experience requisite to the exercise of political right',[3] Coleridge asserts that his case for reform was ultimately based on physiocratic principles and that it falls with the discredited system on which it was based. But to treat a demand for reform based on the confusion of religious and civil liberties as if it had its only origin in the theories of the Physiocrats was to ignore altogether the most characteristic feature of the English dissenting tradition, which was the transference of ideas of Christian liberties and moral freedom to the world of political action. It was surprising that

---

[1] Ibid.

[2] All Coleridge's references were to Cartwright's *The People's Barrier against Undue Influence and Corruption, 1780*. He confessed that this was the only one of his works that he had read.   [3] *F.*, pp. 129–30.

Coleridge's earlier connexions with dissenting circles did not reveal the strength of this tradition, for his own Bristol lectures illustrate its influence.

In one of the Notebooks he declared with an air of triumph: 'I flatter myself, that I have knocked on the head the reasonings of Cartwright & the Antiquarians for Reform as *founded solely* on the Law of the Land.' Nevertheless, all the evidence suggests that the second class proved a hard nut to crack. The chief stumbling block was the fact that, 'the whole force of their cause depends on undoubted principle of the common Law of England which I must cheerfully admit to be of higher authority than any particular statute can be, and so constitutional—greatly deprecating, as I do, the assertions concerning the Omnipotence of Parliament'.[1] In *The Friend* Coleridge was content to lay down the principle that 'the wisdom of legislation consists in the adaptation of laws to circumstances', and that consequently it was only necessary to establish that the circumstances under which the ancient law was passed had ceased to exist in order to prove the law inapplicable.[2]

Our ancestors established the right of voting in a particular class of men, forming at that time the middle rank of society, and known to be all of them, or almost all, legal proprietors—and these were then called the freemen of England: therefore they [that is, the reformers] established it in the lowest classes of society, in those who possess no property, because these too are now called by the same name!![3]

A more radical objection to the case of those who based their argument for reform on ancient laws is found only in the Notebook and it is difficult to see why he did not include this in *The Friend*. The passage in the Notebook runs as follows:

Some delusion arises from the writers availing themselves of our just veneration & love for the Common Law of England, which is considered by each individual as the Parent & Guardian of his dearest Rights, without duly considering the great difference between Laws made to regulate the claims & Duties of Individuals, which remain for the greater part unaltered thro' all the changes of national Progression, and easily admit of explanation, enlargement, or abolition by special

---

[1] *Notebook No. 18*, f. 118v.

[2] 'Hence, wise Legislatures have found themselves under the necessity—if they would avoid perpetual change & unsettlement of the public mind—to connive at many deviations from the letter of the Law, as at so many confirmations of the spirit of it.' Ibid., f. 120.   [3] *F.*, p. 157.

Statutes—and those Laws which regulate the forms of Civil Polity, which cannot but alter according as the proportions of property and influence change in the different orders acknowledged by the state.[1]

Nowhere in the discussion in *The Friend* does Coleridge apply the distinction between individual and civil rights to establish the fact that the reformers' appeals to Common Law were inadmissible. Certainly the inclusion of this passage would have strengthened his case.

Although Wordsworth noted in 1809 that 'Coleridge was against reform', the pages of *The Friend* make it clear that he was willing to accept the necessity for reform in principle, if it could also be proved to be expedient. For such a proof he laid down three tests. It should be a practicable measure; it should be suited to existing circumstances; it should be 'necessary or at least requisite, and such as will enable the government to accomplish more perfectly the ends for which it was instituted'.[2] While it is true that his attitude hardened during the controversy over the first Reform Bill, it was not against the idea of reform that he fulminated in the Notebooks and in conversations reported in *Table Talk*, but against the inexpediency of the particular measures. As Henry Nelson Coleridge remarked in a letter to Tom Poole: 'It suits the M. Chronicle in a paragraph I saw the other day, to say that S.T.C. vituperated Parliamentary Reform: no such thing; he only abused this Reform Bill—a very different thing, I conceive.'[3]

The third test laid down by Coleridge for the expediency of a measure was whether it was such as would 'enable the government to accomplish more perfectly the ends for which it was instituted'. What are these ends? The answer he gives to this question cannot be considered as a complete definition of the function of the State, but it marks his first attempt to classify some of its functions. At the outset his readers were warned not to confuse the 'idea' of the State—to use the terminology of his later works—with its imperfect embodiment.

To examine anything wisely, two conditions are requisite: first, a distinct notion of the desirable ends, in the complete accomplishment of which would consist the perfection of such a thing, or its ideal excellence; and, secondly, a calm and kindly mode of feeling, without which we shall hardly fail either to overlook, or not to make due allowances for,

---

[1] *Notebook No. 18*, f. 119v.   [2] *F.*, p. 158.
[3] 15 June 1835, B.M. Add. MSS. 35344, f. 116v.

the circumstances which prevent these ends from being all perfectly realized in the particular thing which we are to examine.[1]

Having uttered this warning he defines what he considers are the negative and positive ends of government.[2] There is nothing noteworthy or original in the definition of the negative ends of government; these are 'protection of life, of personal freedom, of property, of reputation, and of religion, from foreign and from domestic attacks'.[3] To illustrate how well these ends were fulfilled in England in comparison with other countries Coleridge fills several pages with a series of anecdotes. These form something of an anti-climax to the broad general sweep of his 'preparatory notions' on the subject. The first anecdote takes the form of a long letter from 'an American officer of high rank', describing the anarchic conditions that he found on his arrival in Egypt in 1804.[4] From this letter, which he had originally received when he was in Malta, Coleridge drew the deduction that Britain at least enjoyed the solid benefits derived from the possession of an effective government and that she had reason to be glad to be free from any kind of interference from a foreign power. An anecdote concerning the refusal of the Maltese to volunteer in the revolutionary army during Bonaparte's brief visit to the island follows; and the series ends with two stories relating to Coleridge's residence in Germany in 1798–9. The first of these illustrates the dependence of individuals on the whims of German statesmen and the second the persecution attending any attempt made in that country to express unconventional ideas on the subject of toleration. Absurdly inadequate as they are in their context, these anecdotes and the fairly frequent references to the conditions that prevailed in other countries, emphasize the importance of Coleridge's foreign travels and make it clear that nothing made him think so well of his native country as the experience of leaving it and living abroad.[5]

[1] F., p. 159.
[2] The definition was repeated, with slight modification, in the second Lay Sermon, Lay Sermons, pp. 249–50.   [3] F., p. 160.
[4] The original letter is in the British Museum, Egerton MSS. 2800, ff. 116–18. Its author was William Eaton, who was United States Naval Agent to the Barbary States and who throughout 1804 and 1805 was actively engaged in trying to establish Ahmet Karamanli on the throne of Tripoli.
[5] The connexion between the growth of patriotism and absence in an alien land is implicit in the following sentence from the essay On the Law of Nations where he insists that love of mankind takes its origin from patriotism, which is found 'in a circle defined by human affections, the first firm sod within which becomes sacred beneath the quickening step of the returning citizen'. F., p. 189.

Although there is nothing noteworthy about Coleridge's definition of the negative ends for which the State exists, his treatment
of the positive ends is strikingly original, particularly if it is seen
in its proper historical context. These ends he holds to be four.
The first is the need 'to make the means of subsistence more easy
to each individual'.[1] The second is that the individual should be
given in addition to the basic necessities of life a share in 'the comforts and conveniences which humanize and ennoble his nature',
and that he should be able to perfect himself in his own trade or
profession through the co-operation of others, that is, through the
supply of raw materials and tools. The third end for which government exists is to hold out to every individual 'the hope of bettering
his own condition and that of his children'.[2] A later marginal
jotting in Steffens's *Caricaturen des Heiligsten* amplifies this point. It
runs: 'A peasant does not wish to be a Lord—no, nor perhaps
does he wish to be a Parson or a Doctor, but he would have the
soul of a Slave if he did not desire that there should be a *possibility*
of his children or Grand-children becoming such.'[3] Finally, the
fourth end is 'the development of those faculties which are
essential to his human nature by the knowledge of his moral and
religious duties, and the increase of his intellectual powers in as
great a degree as is compatible with the other ends of social union,
and does not involve a contradiction'.[4]

This outline of the positive ends of government is a broad and
inclusive one and can be readily used as a yardstick to measure the
relative value of any government. However, when Coleridge came
to assess the extent to which the English Government satisfied
these four necessary ends, he exhibited a degree of complacency
that suggests that he was blind to the inadequacies of early nine-
teenth-century government in England. He brought neither argument nor anecdote to support his conclusion that the first three
positive ends were 'realised under our government to a degree
unexampled in any other old and long-peopled country'.[5] Presumably the cautious qualifying phrase was added to prevent

---

[1] Ibid., p. 160.   [2] Ibid., p. 161.
[3] The comments appear in a copy in the British Museum, i. 219.
[4] *F.*, p. 161.
[5] Ibid., p. 167. Compare the complacent treatment in *The Friend* with Coleridge's
boast to Stuart: 'I flatter myself that I have been the first, who will have given a
calm, disinterested account of our Constitution as it really *is*, and *how* it is so.'
13 June 1809, *L.* ii. 550.

comparison with America and indicates a certain uneasiness in
Coleridge's mind. But it was pointless to make a comparative
judgement in this context. Government in England made no
positive attempt to satisfy these ends; it did not acknowledge
any responsibility for helping its citizens to achieve a basic subsistence level, it certainly did not concern itself with distributing
the national wealth so that all would enjoy 'the comforts that
humanize and ennoble human nature'; and it did little or nothing
to satisfy the individual's desire to better his own condition and
that of his children, particularly among the new classes of industrial workers. Their lot was singularly without hope;[1] and
yet Coleridge had recognized in the abstract the prime necessity
of keeping hope alive. 'His Maker has distinguished him [Man]
from the brute that perishes, by making hope an instinct of his
nature and an indispensable condition of his moral and intellectual
progression.'[2] The instinct of hope must never, therefore, be
allowed to die.

Why was it that Coleridge failed to use his outline sketch of the
'idea' of a constitution to reveal the deficiencies of the existing
system of government? To begin with, foreign travel had made
him excessively grateful for being an Englishman and this led him
to idealize the blessings of the English constitution. In addition
his preoccupation with principle in *The Friend*, and later in *Church
and State*, produced a convenient but utterly unhistorical confusion
of 'the idea' of an institution and its actual manifestation. He
lacked the courage to apply the principles of government that he
had discovered to the society in which he lived, and where he did
make the attempt it was done with the intention of defending the
existing system, or at best with the intention of offering moderate
not radical criticism of its shortcomings. But when this has been
taken into account it remains true that Coleridge's actual definition
of the positive ends for which government exists commands a
great deal of respect. It is the work of an idealist but not of a
dreamer. The foundation of national well-being is frankly recognized as depending on the enjoyment of the basic necessities of life
for the whole community. But because man is something more
than an animal that needs to be adequately fed, a government must
make it possible for everyone to satisfy the basic needs of his soul.

---

[1] See, for example, the chapter entitled 'The Mind of the Poor' in J. L. and B.
Hammond, *The Town Labourer*.   [2] *F.*, p. 161.

In an age in which the economic system exerted a dehumanizing effect on the sensibilities of the factory-owning class, the importance he attributed to man's satisfaction of his spiritual needs can hardly be over-emphasized.

Coleridge's belief that the Government should seek to develop the moral and intellectual lives of its citizens, his insistence that instruction was 'one of the ends of government', his definition of the best constitution as that in which 'the average sum of useful knowledge is the greatest, and the causes that awaken and encourage talent and genius, the most powerful and various';[1] all these points which he considered under the heading of the fourth end of government look forward to the most fruitful idea contained in *Church and State*, the need for the existence of a third order in the State to which he later gave the name 'clerisy'. Its function would be to guide the moral and intellectual development of the nation and to disseminate learning at a variety of levels through its graded officers. In *The Friend* Coleridge made it clear that the education that the State should encourage should not be purely secular. It should teach man 'knowledge of his moral and religious duties in addition to useful knowledge'. He drew attention to the special virtues of Andrew Bell's system, 'a system, by which in the very act of receiving knowledge, the best virtues and most useful qualities of the moral character are awakened, developed, and formed into habits'.[2] It possessed a further advantage in that it taught the individual's duties to Church and State, whereas the rival system devised by Joseph Lancaster was non-conformist in character.[3] Coleridge's references to Bell's system as 'the greatest moral steam engine'[4] and the frequency with which, according to De Quincey, he dragged his name into the conversation are absurd enough, but behind all this lies an awareness of the importance of an education that would develop moral as well as intellectual qualities and thus make each individual a good citizen in a Christian society. It is evident from everything that Coleridge wrote on politics that a belief in the ameliorating power of education, both on the individual and society, was a faith that underwent change and modification but was never destroyed.

[1] Ibid.   [2] Ibid., p. 151.
[3] Joseph Lancaster, 1778–1838, set out his ideas in *Improvements in Education*, 1803. For an interesting treatment of the rival systems see L. Stephen, *The English Utilitarians*, 1900, ii. 17–20.
[4] *Lay Sermons*, p. 45. For references to Bell in *The Friend* see pp. 60–61 and 151.

Only one essay in *The Friend* dealt with a specific administrative problem: *On the Vulgar Errors Respecting Taxes and Taxation.*[1] The vulgar errors he had in mind were those that sprang from the assumption that taxes were a product of wars and corruption and would cease with the inauguration of an era of universal brotherhood. The ultimate source of such faulty thinking was Paine's *Rights of Man.*[2] The errors were thus one further legacy of Jacobinism and as such must be discredited. He also wished to demonstrate that members of Parliament who spoke as if taxation involved the actual loss of national wealth were deliberately deceiving the people. He succeeded in proving that taxation was a necessary part of the life of a commercial nation; that a high level of taxation was usually found in a highly civilized country; and that the real criterion by which to judge whether a system of taxation were injurious or beneficial was to assess 'not the amount of the sum taken from each individual', but that 'which remains behind'.[3] But implicit in the discussion were two assumptions, the first of which was inapplicable to the England of his day and the second universally inapplicable. In the first place he assumed that the national policy of taxation ensured a fair distribution of the weight of taxation on the different classes. He would have done well to recall a passage he had written many years earlier in *The Watchman*. 'It is always to be remembered, that taxation does not carry treasure out of the country. It only takes it from the many, and gives it to the few; but this in truth impoverishes the whole, since all the active powers of a nation are paralysed, and the bulk of the poor become dependent on *bounty* instead of labour for their daily bread.'[4] Earlier still, in *The Plot Discovered*, he had asserted that since taxes were not levied in equal proportion a legislator might 'vote away the pittance of the poor'.[5] In the essay in *The Friend* Coleridge was guilty of identifying the increased pros-

---

[1] It appeared on 9 Nov. 1809 in the tenth number. *F.*, pp. 144–56.

[2] *Rights of Man*, Part the Second, chap. v.

[3] *F.*, p. 145. W. F. Kennedy suggests in *Humanist versus Economist*, The Economic Thought of Samuel Taylor Coleridge, University of California Publications in Economics, vol. xvii, 1958, pp. 26–27, that Coleridge took many of his ideas on taxation from Sir James Steuart's *An Enquiry into the Principles of Political Oeconomy*, 2 vols., 1767, including the belief that a high level of taxation was desirable and necessary in a progressive country. In general I believe that Kennedy overstresses the debt. Coleridge read Steuart in 1797. *N*. i. 308 n.

[4] A passage from the third issue of *The Watchman*, not reprinted by Sara Coleridge. *W.*, p. 83.   [5] *E.O.T.* i. 89.

perity of a single class, the commercial interest, with the condition
of the country as a whole, a confusion that he was fond of detecting in the works of the political economists. There is some justice
in Hazlitt's gibe: 'Taxes he holds to be a providential relief to the
distresses of the people.' This part of the essay was an ingenious
piece of special pleading to defend the heavy weight of taxation
that fell—much more unequally than Coleridge was prepared to
admit—on the English people as a direct result of the war against
Napoleon. The second assumption that lay behind the arguments
in the essay was that it mattered little whether the national income
derived through taxation were spent on the arts of peace or the
engines of war. 'The whole dispute', declared Coleridge, 'resolves
itself to this one question; whether our soldiers and sailors would
not be better employed in making canals for instance, or cultivat-
ing waste lands, than in fighting or in learning to fight; and the
tradesman, &c., in making grey coats instead of red or blue, and
ploughshares, &c., instead of arms.'[1] The answer he gave to this
question was that he dare not positively affirm that it would be
better, and even if it were, it was not practical to change at the
present. He was led to take up this theoretically indefensible position owing to the bitter attacks that had been made on the Government for its vast wastage of manpower and money in the disastrous
Walcheren expedition.[2] Here was an occasion when he was led to
erect invalid general principles on the basis of his partisan attitude
towards current events; and some years later he admitted in the
second *Lay Sermon* that he had exerted his best powers in *The Friend*
to present the 'fairest and most animating features' of the system
of taxation because it then appeared to be 'a duty of patriotism'
to do so.[3]

[1] *F.*, p. 155.

[2] In Apr. 1809, Austria asked Britain to grant her a subsidy and to make a military
diversion at the mouth of the Weser. A subsidy of £150,000 a month was granted,
but for political and commercial reasons it was decided to make the diversion at the
mouth of the Scheldt. The expedition, the largest that had yet sailed from Britain,
proved a complete failure. After Flushing had fallen to the French, they left the destruction of the enemy to the climate and less than half the force returned. This
senseless loss of men and materials aroused widespread indignation in England.

[3] *Lay Sermons*, p. 247. In a footnote Coleridge mentions that the essay *On Vulgar
Errors of Taxation*, which had first appeared in *The Friend*, was 'transferred almost
entire to the columns of a daily paper, of the largest circulation, and from thence, in
larger or smaller extracts, to several of our provincial journals. It was likewise reprinted in two of the American Federalist papers: and a translation appeared, I have
been told, in the Hamburg *Correspondenten*.'

The two essays on international law are also attempts to defend British policy in relation to specific events, but two major questions relating to international law are raised. Under what circumstances is a nation justified in going to war? Under what circumstances is a nation justified in infringing the neutrality of another nation? The first problem is discussed in relation to the renewal of the war with France after the Peace of Amiens, and was in origin an official memorandum prepared in Malta for Sir Alexander Ball and sent to the Foreign Office as a State paper. To use such material saved the necessity of further composition while at the same time drawing attention to the author's official career. The second problem is considered in relation to a more topical event, the seizure of the Danish Fleet at Copenhagen. Napoleon and the Tsar of Russia came to a secret agreement in the Treaty of Tilsit that if Britain did not mitigate the severity of the Orders in Council they would call on Portugal, Denmark, and Sweden to close their ports to British shipping. Canning, who heard of the secret clause, realized the threat to British shipping and took instant action. When Denmark refused to listen to argument, a land and sea attack was launched and on 8 September 1809 the Danish fleet surrendered.[1] The main purpose of Coleridge's essay was to demonstrate that the arguments that had been used to attack and defend Britain's policy on this occasion were equally unsound and to suggest lines along which this action might be defended.

In both essays Coleridge is obliged to inquire into the relationship that exists between three spheres of morality: private, national, and international. But to begin with, it was necessary to establish the fact that international relations were subject to the rule of law. 'It were absurd to suppose that individuals should be under a law of moral obligation, and yet a million of the same individuals acting collectively or through representatives should be exempt from law', he declares, 'for morality is no accident of human nature, but its essential characteristic.' On the other hand, he does not, except on one occasion, make the mistake of demanding that the same code of morals should be required from a nation in its dealings with other nations as from individuals in the sphere of private morality. In origin it is the same; in outward expression it cannot be, since the circumstances that relate to individuals and

[1] For an interesting account of this episode see Sir Charles Petrie, *George Canning*, 2nd ed., 1946, pp. 77–79.

states are never the same. Then, too, the law of nations differs considerably from the law the State prescribes for its citizens. It cannot be fixed and positive since the relations it regulates are in a state of continual flux and each dispute presents a different set of circumstances; nor has it power, as the state has, to enforce its rule.

Coleridge's defence of British policy in relation to Malta and the renewal of the war with France, depends in the main on his interpretation of treaty obligations and this in its turn depends on a subtle distinction drawn between private and international laws of contract. Britain had insisted as one of the conditions of the Peace of Amiens that Malta should remain uninfluenced by France. The treaty laid it down that the island should be handed back to the Knights of St. John; but since these had in fact ceased to exist as an effective order, to do so would have been to allow the island to pass into French hands. Coleridge recognized that an important principle was at stake. Is a nation bound by the terms of a contract when the other contracting power has deliberately practised deceit and when to carry out the terms might involve its self-destruction? His answer to this question assumes that in matters of contract the moral obligations on individuals and nations are identical. 'A treaty is a writ of mutual promise between two independent states, and the law of promise is the same to nations as to individuals. It is to be sacredly performed by each party in the sense in which it knew and permitted the other party to understand it, at the time of the contract.'[1] In order to refute the argument advanced by Lord Minto in the House of Lords in 1803, that France had a right to insist on the evacuation of Malta and that a nation must carry out the terms of a treaty in their literal sense even if this were to bring about its own destruction, Coleridge drew upon arguments that he had found in a review of *A Summary Account of Liebnitz's Memoir*, recommending to Louis XIV the conquest of Egypt,[2] and in Harrington's *Oceana*. In the former, which Coleridge came across in Malta, the reviewer justified Britain's retention of Malta on the grounds that it was morally impossible for a nation to renounce the principle of self-preservation, or to be 'an accessory to

---

[1] *F.*, p. 176.
[2] This was the review which had appeared in the *Gentleman's Magazine* and which Sir Alexander Ball promised to have translated into Italian and circulated to all officials.

her own ruin'. Tom Poole advised Coleridge to read Harrington's *Oceana* as early as 1800—'this neglected book which deserves
the study of all politicians'.[1] Notebook No. 22 shows that Coleridge read this work with care and jotted down extracts during the
composition of *The Friend*.[2] In this essay on international law he
quoted with qualified approval the following extract from *Oceana*:

A man may devote himself to death or destruction to save a nation;
but no nation will devote itself to death or destruction to save mankind. Machiavel is decried for saying, 'that no consideration is to be
had of what is just or unjust, of what is merciful or cruel, of what is
honourable or ignominious, in case it be to save a state or to preserve
liberty:' which as to the manner of expression may perhaps be crudely
spoken. But to imagine that a nation will devote itself to death or destruction any more after faith given, or an engagement thereto tending, than if there had been no engagement made or faith given, were not
piety but folly.[3]

Far from using this passage to prove that national policy cannot at
all times be 'subordinated to the laws of morality', he employs it to
develop his ideas on the moral basis of treaty obligation. Since
a treaty is a voluntary contract entered into by two states for
mutual benefit it cannot be supposed that either intends its own
destruction. If, therefore, the effect of carrying out the terms of a
treaty would in all probability have this result, then it follows that
no valid contract had originally been made. From this principle
Coleridge deduced the justice of Britain's case in making the independence of Malta the grounds for renewing the war against
France. He believed that the security of the British Empire depended on the continued independence of Malta and for Britain to
allow it to fall under French influence would be equivalent to
acquiescing in its own destruction. He concluded that no valid
contract had therefore been made by those who negotiated the
Peace of Amiens.

The essay *On the Law of Nations* is concerned with answering the
question, under what circumstances is a nation justified in infringing the neutrality of another nation? The question arose directly
from Britain's seizure of the Danish fleet in 1809. A great deal of

---

[1] Letter dated 21 Jan. 1800, Sandford, *Thomas Poole and His Friends*, ii. 4.
[2] *Notebook No. 22*, B.M. Add. MSS. 47520, ff. 18–18*v*.
[3] *F.*, p. 177. The passage was written down in the Notebook before being incorporated into the essay in *The Friend*.

the discussion is devoted to an examination of the nature of true patriotism and its relationship with the love of mankind as a whole. Coleridge denies that 'cosmopolitism is nobler than nationality, and the human race a sublimer object of love than a people'; and in a passage of great power and beauty he traces the decline of Greece as an influence on the world to the period when she lost her independence.

What were they while they remained free and independent? when Greece resembled a collection of mirrors set in a single frame, each having its own focus of patriotism, yet all capable, as at Marathon and Platea, of converging to one point and of consuming a common foe? What were they then? The fountains of light and civilization, of truth and beauty, to all mankind! they were the thinking head, the beating heart, of the whole world! They lost their independence, and with their independence their patriotism; and became the cosmopolites of antiquity.[1]

At length the time came when,

nothing remained but dastardly and cunning slaves, who avenged their own ruin and degradation by assisting to degrade and ruin their conquerors; and the golden harp of their divine language remained only as a frame on which priests and monks spun their dirty cobwebs of sophistry and superstition![2]

The example of Greece shows that 'we need no new or particular code of morals to justify us in placing and preserving our country in that relative situation which is most favourable to its independence'. Elsewhere in *The Friend* Coleridge asserts that all the greatest benefactors of mankind have in the first place been patriots. If love of mankind springs first from patriotism and if patriotism is dependent on national independence then a great country like Britain was justified in infringing the neutrality of Denmark to preserve her national heritage from imminent destruction at the hands of Napoleon.

To illustrate that Britain might rest her case on the same moral law as would have been applicable to individuals placed in a similar position he makes use of a political allegory. He tells the story of three landowners living in a patriarchal colony which had originally consisted of from twenty to thirty households, but

[1] *F.*, p. 191.   [2] Ibid., p. 192.

which had witnessed the rise of a tyrant, Misetes, who had swal-
lowed up the lands of the others with the exception of Pamphilus
and Lathrodacnus. The power of Pamphilus was equal to that of
Misetes, he was richer but not ambitious and all the other inhabitants were deeply indebted to him for whatever prosperity
they enjoyed. In the conflict between Misetes and Pamphilus,
Lathrodacnus remained neutral even though he owed his independence and prosperity to Pamphilus. The consternation of the
latter was great when he saw Lathrodacnus assembling a great
number of ferry boats, which could be of no use to him, but might
be used by Misetes to overcome the territory of Pamphilus.
Lathrodacnus called a council and agreed to submit to Misetes if
he threatened again, whereupon Pamphilus who had heard of his
decision, immediately siezed the passage boats. Lest this thinly
veiled allegory were felt to be insufficient Coleridge also put into
the mouth of Pamphilus the following reply to his accusers.

Even so, if I were out on a shooting party with a Quaker for my
companion, and saw coming on towards us an old footpad and mur-
derer, who had made known his intention of killing me wherever he
might meet me; and if my companion the Quaker would neither give
me up his gun, nor even discharge it . . . you might call me a robber for
wresting this gun from my companion, though for no other purpose
but that I might at least do for myself what he ought to have done, but
would not do either for or with me. Even so, and as plausibly, you
might exclaim, O the hypocrite Pamphilus![1]

Coleridge coyly refused to make any direct application of his
allegory to the seizure of the Danish fleet and was promptly taken
to task by a correspondent who accused him of trying to disguise
his real opinions. In his defence, which appeared in the twenty-
sixth issue of *The Friend*, he asserted that the allegory 'so far from
being a disguise, was a necessary part of the main argument, a case
in point, to prove the identity of the law of nations with the law
of conscience'.[2] But even from the outline given here it can be
seen that the allegorical form made it impossible to apply the
situation to the rule of conscience as it affects individuals. As Coleridge had asserted elsewhere in *The Friend* that political action
must always be adjusted to circumstances, it was ruinous to his
purpose to have to admit that the circumstances facing the indi-

---

[1] *F.*, p. 201.
[2] It appeared as a letter on 1 Mar. 1810. Ibid. (1809), pp. 430-2.

vidual and a nation could never be the same; and this he was forced to do. Thus it may be said that whatever interest these essays on international law may possess—and this is considerable—as essays in defence of recent British policy they fail to carry full conviction.

From this general analysis of the contents of *The Friend* it can be seen that except for the remarks on taxation, parliamentary reform, and international law, Coleridge chose to ignore contemporary political problems, or to do no more than indulge in oblique comment. As he explained in the *Prospectus* and the early numbers, he was primarily concerned with establishing principles relating to religion, philosophy, and politics. Warned by his friends that to omit the political questions of the day must limit the periodical's circulation, he remained firm. But this deliberate restriction of subject-matter at least possessed the advantage that when the papers were issued in volume form in 1812 and again in 1818, the political section had not dated as it would have done if it had been full of references to the contemporary political scene in 1809. In addition the work gained in intelligibility as a result of the re-arrangement of material that took place in the rifacimento and from the simple fact that the reader was now in possession of the complete work and consequently could have some general impression of the underlying unity of the whole.[1] The almost completely new section, *On the Grounds of Morals and Religion*, with its carefully drawn distinctions between the reason and the understanding and its soundly argued attack on Utilitarianism, did much to lay bare the fundamental philosophical ideas upon which the original essays had rested. Nevertheless the work reached only a small public. The 1812 edition, made up of reprints of the first twelve numbers, together with original copies of the remaining sixteen issues, consisted of only a few hundred copies; and it is very doubtful if the three-volume rifacimento reached many more readers. As Coleridge himself ruefully remarked, *The Friend* was a secret which he had entrusted to the public; 'and, unlike most secrets, it hath been well kept'.[2] The original periodical failed because the subjects on which Coleridge wanted to write were ill-suited to this medium of communication, while the comparative lack of success of the rifacimento of 1818 must be ascribed to an

[1] The unity is certainly an example of organic and not mechanical form.
[2] Allsop, i. 233.

insufficiently thorough revision of the original material. It was fatal to the success of this work that it retained so much of the largely fortuitous order of the original papers in the first two sections.

The style had also much to do with *The Friend*'s lack of success whether as a periodical or a printed volume. From the beginning all his friends advised him to make concessions to the tastes and limitations of the public. He recognized the wisdom of the advice but was unable to take advantage of it. As he remarked in *The Friend*:

> We insensibly imitate what we habitually admire; and an aversion to the epigrammatic unconnected periods of the fashionable Anglo-Gallican taste has too often made me willing to forget, that the stately march and difficult evolutions, which characterise the eloquence of Hooker, Bacon, Milton, and Jeremy Taylor, are, notwithstanding their intrinsic excellence, still less suited to a periodical essay.[1]

He frankly admitted to correspondents that there was 'too often an *entortillage* in the sentences and even in the thought (which nothing can justify), and, always almost, a stately piling up of *story* on *story* in one architectural period, which is not suited to a periodical essay or to essays at all'.[2] But his predilection for parenthetical clauses he stoutly defended. 'They are the *drama* of reason', he declared, 'and present the thought growing, instead of a mere *Hortus siccus*.'[3] Whether he admitted or defended the faults of his style made no difference to his practice, for a deep aversion for the fashionable epigrammatic style and an excessive admiration of the English prose writers of the seventeenth century made it impossible for him to command a truly popular style, or even to make any appreciable modifications in what had now become his habitual mode of public address. In attempting to account for the sense of disappointment that had followed the reading of the essays in *The Friend*, the sense that the reader had not been left in possession of the quantity of truth that he had expected to carry away with him during the course of his reading, an anonymous critic in the *Eclectic Review* attributed the main fault to what he called 'some kind of haze in the medium through which the spirit transmits its light'.[4] Not even the most sympathetic of Coleridge's

---

[1] *F.*, p. 9.
[2] Letter to T. Poole 9 Oct. 1809, *L.* ii. 551. 'Entortillage' occurs in a letter to his brother George of the same date, *U.L.* ii. 10.
[3] Letter to T. Poole, 28 Jan. 1810, *L.* ii. 558–9.
[4] The *Eclectic Review*, Oct. 1811, pp. 924–5.

readers would deny the truth of this. For all its rich grandeur and eloquence of expression, for all its subtlety of thought, its nice distinctions, its solemn reflections on the wisdom of antiquity, and pertinent comments on the present, the final impression that *The Friend* leaves on the receptive mind is that of a vast treasure house of intellectual riches seen through a luminous mist. The truth lies there, but it lies at a distance. A man who can get at the kernel of *The Friend*, said Southey, 'may crack peach-stones without any fear of breaking his teeth'.[1]

III. *Public Journalism Again: the 'Courier'*

There is a remarkable difference between Coleridge's essays in his own journal, *The Watchman*, and those he wrote for the national daily paper, the *Morning Post*. As soon as he entered the world of public journalism he adopted a more grave and responsible attitude towards the problems discussed and the public addressed, and this was accompanied by a corresponding change in prose style; the eccentricities and personal quirks almost completely disappeared, and he wrote with a new vigour and lucidity. The miracle was not to be repeated. No such improvement took place when he turned from his private journalism in *The Friend* to address a large national audience in the columns of the *Courier*. The same defects of disorderly arrangement, abrupt transitions from one topic to another, endless digression, promises unfulfilled, and general obscurity of expression are to be found in the newspaper articles as in *The Friend*; and the originality of thought which was the redeeming feature in his own periodical rarely enters into the essays in the *Courier*.

His connexions with the paper began at a time when he would have been more profitably employed in devoting his full powers to his own journal. On 2 October 1809 he wrote to Stuart, who had generously supplied him with paper and given Coleridge's work free publicity, to say that he was well beforehand with his work for his own paper and would like to contribute to the *Courier*.[2] He realized, he said, that 'the great sale of the *Courier* raises it above the want of literary assistance'. After making it clear that he would not be able to write in harmony with the predominant tone of the

---

[1] *Letters*, ed. M. H. Fitzgerald, 1912, p. 406.

[2] Stuart advertised the appearance of *The Friend* in the *Courier* and reprinted a certain amount of material; for example, part of Coleridge's comparison of Bonaparte and Charlemagne in Nov. 1811. See *E.O.T.* ii. 593.

paper's leading articles, he asked Stuart if he thought that Street, the editor, would accept regular contributions from one 'who had a dread and contempt of the present ministry'. The paper, he declared, 'needs a little *brightening up*'.[1] No regular engagement ensued as the result of this overture, but in December 1809 a series entitled *Letters on the Spaniards* appeared. It was not until April 1811, however, that Coleridge formed any regular connexion with the paper. It lasted six months. He became an assistant to the editor and occupied a much humbler position than he had done on the staff of the *Morning Post*, agreeing to do what was necessary to fill up spaces with odd paragraphs and poems, and occasionally to supply the leading paragraphs when Street was away on business. Some of Sara Coleridge's extracts in *Essays on His Own Times* illustrate how trivial must have been many of the tasks he was asked to perform.[2]

There is little evidence to suggest that this subservient role led to any serious compromise of principles. For example, when the Ministry insisted that Coleridge's article protesting against the reappointment of the Duke of York as Commander-in-Chief of the Army should not be published, he sought to terminate his connexion with the paper and asked Crabb Robinson to use his influence to obtain a post for him on *The Times*. Robinson speaks of his acute distress at the time.[3] Sara printed all that she could find of the original essay. Evidently she was unaware of the existence of a memorandum on the subject, which is now in the Egerton collection of manuscripts in the British Museum. One passage of this memorandum reveals clearly the importance Coleridge attributed to this episode. He wrote,

We must either declare our regrets at this event, and the reasons of our regret (which rise not merely or principally on any just and personal, but on general consequences and on the nature and spirit of our constitution) or we must forfeit our claims to consistency of public Principles—our best title to public Favor our sole title to public confidence.[4]

---

[1] *U.L.* ii. 8–10.

[2] For example, the brief paragraphs printed in *E.O.T.* iii. 802–14.

[3] *Henry Crabb Robinson on Books and their Writers*, i. 37. Robinson also gave Sara Coleridge a personal account of the episode. This is printed in a note in *E.O.T.* iii. 1027. See also A. Aspinall, *Politics and the Press*, 1949, p. 209, who gives the date of the essay as 5 July and adds an incorrect reference to *E.O.T.* Robinson gives the date as Friday, 12 July in his account to Sara. The *Courier* files in the British Museum provide no evidence for dating the cancelled essay.

[4] B.M. Egerton MSS. 2800, ff. 131–2.

Further confirmation of the importance he attributed to the principle of keeping the paper free from ministerial interference is
found in the complaint that he made to Stuart in May 1816, that
the *Courier* by losing its independence under the timid editorship
of Street, had lost the public's respect. Had the paper maintained
its independence 'the Ministry would have been far more effectu-
ally served', declared Coleridge.[1]

In spite of Hazlitt's remarks about all Coleridge's mighty poten-
tialities ending 'in swallowing doses of oblivion' and 'writing
paragraphs in the *Courier*',[2] in spite of his taunts about turning
'to the unclean side' in politics, it is clear that during Coleridge's
connexion with this paper he was not willing to acquiesce in the
suppression of truth nor prepared to use his literary talents in disseminating purely ministerial or party views. He was, however,
required to write on a number of subjects on which he had no very
strong feelings or opinions, and consequently the general level of
the writing is inferior to that in the *Morning Post*. Even on subjects
in which he was intensely interested he wrote indifferently well, as,
for example, on the subject of Catholic Emancipation. The real
cause of this inferiority was personal not political. Lamb describes his friend in the following fashion. 'Coleridge has pow-
dered his head, and looks like Bacchus, Bacchus ever sleek and
young. He is going to turn sober, but his Clock has not struck
yet; meantime he pours down goblet after goblet.'[3] Drink, drugs,
ill-health, unhappiness, these made it impossible for him to give of
his best. In fact the finest articles were those written before and
after the six months he spent as Street's assistant; namely, the
Letters on the Spaniards, written in the Lakes in December 1809,
and the *Letters to Judge Fletcher*, written in the autumn of 1814,
when staying with his friends the Morgans at Box, near Bath.

The *Letters on the Spaniards*, their author hoped, would be considered as an appendix to Wordsworth's *Convention of Cintra*, the
first part of which had appeared in the *Courier* in December 1809.
The letters have two main interests. They illustrate a practical
application to a particular cause of Coleridge's slowly evolving
theory of nationality, and they also exhibit the flexibility of his

---

[1] Letter to D. Stuart, 8 May 1816, *L.* ii. 661–2. A. Aspinall, *Politics and the Press*,
p. 371.
[2] *The Spirit of the Age*, World's Classics ed., p. 42.
[3] *The Letters of Charles and Mary Lamb*, 1905, i. 421. Quoted in *C. Life*, p. 181.

approach towards a national assembly and the value of a system of popular representation. With Wordsworth he regarded the struggle in the Peninsula as that of a whole people, sustained by a genuine national spirit, fighting against the armies of an alien invader. The Spanish cause made a special appeal to Englishmen, he declared.

It was the noble efforts of Spanish patriotism, that first restored us, without distinction of party, to our characteristic enthusiasm for *liberty*; and, presenting it in its genuine form, incapable of being confounded with its French counterfeit, enabled us once more to utter the names of our Hampdens, Sidneys, and Russels, without hazard of alarming the quiet subject, or of offending the zealous loyalist.[1]

But by the time the letters appeared English public opinion had suffered grievous disappointment and disillusion at the lack of success that had attended the struggle of the Spanish people. Coleridge's faith in the ultimate victory of the national spirit remained unshaken, however, since it was based on the belief that 'the power of the insulted FREE-WILL, steadied by the approving CONSCIENCE, and struggling against brute force and iniquitous compulsion' was invincible.[2] For historic proof he referred his readers to the struggle of the Netherlands against Philip II of Spain, and worked out in great detail and with considerable ingenuity the similarities in the situations. He laid great emphasis on the fact that one thing was absent in Spain to complete the analogy; this was the existence of some form of national assembly based on a system of popular representation which would give direction and unity to the national cause and would remain as a symbol of security and hope in a time of calamity. Nothing could be wider of the mark than H. D. Traill's assertion that in these letters the names of the 'people' of 'freedom' and 'a popular assembly had some of their old magic still'.[3] This was no late rekindling of the revolutionary fires of his youth. The very excellence of these *Letters on the Spaniards* lies in Coleridge's clear recognition of the difference between the spirit of a genuine nationalism and that of an artificial internationalism. It is this that makes it in some ways a more important contribution to the subject than Wordsworth's *Convention of Cintra*. Coleridge's writing carried within it the seeds of

[1] Letter No. 1, 7 Dec. 1809, *E.O.T.* ii. 594.
[2] Letter No. 3, 9 Dec. 1809, *E.O.T.* ii. 612.
[3] *Coleridge*, 1884, p. 136.

prophecy. In *Table Talk* is related the anecdote of how Lord
Darnley came up to Coleridge and asked him if he were mad to
suggest that the Spaniards had a chance of resisting. Two years
later, when events had begun to confirm his confidence in the
Spanish people, Coleridge reminded Lord Darnley of their conversation. ' "Who is mad now? " he asked. "Very true, very true,
Mr Coleridge," cried he: "you are right. It is very extraordinary.
It was a very happy and bold guess." ' To which Coleridge protested that 'guess' was hardly the right word.[1]

The *Letters on the Spaniards* are closely connected in thought
with the later essays in *The Friend* in which the connexion between
patriotism and internationalism is explored. The *Letters to Judge
Fletcher* in 1814 look forward in thought to the *Lay Sermons* of two
years later for they illustrate Coleridge's growing concern with
the re-emergence of Jacobinism in England.[2] At the Summer
Assizes, Mr. Justice Fletcher had delivered a long address to the
Grand Jury at Wexford in which he had attempted to analyse the
causes of the discontent among the lower classes in Ireland. He
had also suggested means by which the discontents might be
alleviated. These included the demand that absentee landlords
should spend more money on their estates and that there should be
a general reform of the magistracy of Ireland. It was a very out-
spoken address, strongly tinged with Catholic bias, and lacking in
judicial detachment. The address had been printed; and to judge
from Coleridge's references to it, had evidently been given a
fair amount of publicity. It certainly contained material which, if
quoted out of its context, might easily inflame the passions of the
lower classes in Ireland and England. Thus the circulation of this
address provided Coleridge with the opportunity that he wanted
of warning the readers of the *Courier* of the re-emergence of
Jacobinism, and of analysing its root causes.[3]

It is extraordinary how many of Coleridge's favourite ideas find
expression in these seven letters. Reminiscent of the Bristol

---

[1] Entry for 28 Apr. 1823, *T.T.*, p. 28.
[2] On the downfall of Napoleon, Cobbett wrote in the *Political Register* of 16 Apr.
1814 that it would now be possible to press for reform without being called a Jacobin.
'To revile a man as a *Jacobin* will be senseless, and will excite ridicule amongst a
people who have lost their fears. This is the great good. The bugbear is gone; the
hobgoblin is destroyed.' He failed to take Coleridge into account.
[3] Judge Fletcher's charge to the Grand Jury may be conveniently studied in the
Annual Register for 1814. Miscellanies, pp. 513-33.

lectures is the criterion used to distinguish between the patriot and
the Jacobin, namely that the patriot must always plead *for* the
poor and not *to* them.[1] Reminiscent also of this early period is his
opposition to any form of political association, particularly to any
that exacted an oath from its members. Such associations, he declared, 'prey on the noblest qualities of human nature'.[2] He was
thankful that his own short 'career of sedition' had not included
membership of such a body. To Sir George Beaumont he had
written in 1803,

... in rejecting these secret associations, often as I was urged to become
a member, now of this & now of that, I felt just as a religious young
officer may be supposed to feel, who, full of courage, dares refuse a
challenge—& considered as a Coward by those around him often shuts
his eyes, & anticipates the moment when he might leap on the wall, &
stand in the Breach, the first & the only one.[3]

Now in the *Courier* he asserted that it was an axiom in politics that
'no government can consistently tolerate any organised powers
not subordinated to itself',[4] and he inveighs against the evils of
'club government' in something of the tone later adopted in the
Lay Sermons. As in his earlier political writings, the distinguishing
mark of the Jacobins is held to be the cry of 'rights' and never that
of 'duties'. The charge that 'in order to sacrifice the *natural* STATE
to PERSONS, they must concorporate PERSONS into an *unnatural*
STATE'[5] re-echoes the substance of his attack in *The Friend*.[6] As in
the *Lay Sermons* two years later, the condition of the country is
ascribed to the predominant philosophy, and as in those works
Coleridge's solution to the problem is to look to education to
bring about the necessary moral and intellectual change. In fact he
thought sufficiently highly of one passage on the powers of a
national system of education to repeat it in the *Lay Sermons*. The
general principle 'that whatever inconvenience may have arisen

---

[1] Letter No. 1, 20 Sept. 1814, *E.O.T.* iii. 678. Cf. *Introductory Address* 1795,
E.O.T. i. 21.

[2] *E.O.T.* iii. 683.

[3] 1 Oct. 1803, *C.L.* ii. 1001. This long letter contains a most interesting and important retrospective account of his early political sympathies.

[4] *E.O.T.* iii. 684. As Crane Brinton has pointed out, Coleridge's hatred of any
imperium in imperio led him to underestimate the valuable function of corporate
bodies within the state. *Political Ideas of the English Romanticists*, 1926, p. 82.

[5] *E.O.T.* iii. 694.

[6] *F.*, pp. 116–27.

from the commonness of education, can only be removed by rendering it universal',[1] was repeated in the later work as was the distinction made between education and instruction. The *Letters to Judge Fletcher* establish beyond doubt Coleridge's right to claim that he had not changed or abandoned any of his fundamental political principles when writing for the *Courier*. But the reappearance of so many old ideas, often expressed in almost the same words as before, is symptomatic of a radical weakness, a tendency to assume that the Jacobinism at the end of the Napoleonic War was essentially the same as that which he had known at first hand in his youth, and to apply an analysis that had fitted a past set of circumstances to a completely different situation. He did, indeed, notice that the Jacobinical spirit had now sunk into the lower orders of society, but he did not sufficiently realize that the new associations had come into existence to remedy economic grievances and not primarily to force a change in the constitution or to disseminate republican ideals.[2]

Although the articles published in the *Courier* during the six months when Coleridge acted as Street's assistant are of less interest than the letters contributed as a private correspondent, they cover a wider range of subject-matter, a range that is by no means indicative of Coleridge's own interests. A large number were short paragraphs on matters of quite ephemeral interest arising from unimportant debates in Parliament, the fortunes of the English armies abroad, or from the need to keep up a running attack on the paper's chief rival, the *Morning Chronicle*. Of the remaining essays one of the most interesting is the essay on *Punishments—Scourging Females*, which expresses a bitter hatred and contempt for all forms of punishment that tended to debase human nature and satisfy sadistic impulses. It aptly concludes with the lines from *King Lear*,

> Thou rascall Beadle, hold thy bloody hand!
> Why dost thou whip that *woman*?[3]

---

[1] Letter No. 4, 2 Nov. 1814, *E.O.T.* iii. 702. Repeated in *The Statesman's Manual*, 1816. See *Lay Sermons*, pp. 43–44.

[2] The nearest Coleridge got to recognizing the economic basis of the movement was the following—'this complication and coalition of arbitrary and unchartered guilds, composed of uneducated, and too often fanatic or dissolute journeymen, for the sworn purpose of lording it over their employers'. *E.O.T.* iii. 699.

[3] *E.O.T.* iii. 766.

A number of essays of unequal merit are devoted to the controversial question of currency depreciation and three essays are devoted to the subject of Catholic Emancipation.

In the essays on currency depreciation, fundamental common sense and a philosopher's regard for the need to define one's terms enable Coleridge to expose some popular fallacies. The House of Commons had appointed a committee 'to enquire into the cause of the High Price of Gold Bullion'; and its report was laid before the House in August 1810. A spate of pamphlets ensued. The *Morning Chronicle* was fortunate in being able to call upon the services of an expert, David Ricardo, who contributed three essays demanding a return to cash payments by the banks.[1] The *Courier* entrusted the subject to Coleridge, who expressed the opposite view to that of Ricardo. Coleridge made no direct reference to the other's essays and may not have read them, as they had appeared six months before he joined the staff of the *Courier*. The word 'depreciation' had figured largely in the bullion controversy, and it was characteristic of Coleridge that his approach should have been to ask what was meant by this term, and to attempt to discover if both sides in the dispute were using the word in the same sense. He demonstrated to his own, even if not to all his readers', satisfaction that the whole question was not one of economics but of logomachy. His most important contribution to the controversy, however, was to provide a definition of money. Money, he insists, is 'whatever has a value among men according to what it *represents*, rather than to what it *is*'.[2] This definition acted as a useful weapon with which to attack Huskisson's view that gold and silver were as much money before as after they were minted and enabled him to draw an important distinction between the value of these metals as a commodity and as currency.

In the three letters on the Catholic Petition, 'the Jack-the-Giant-Killer-seven-leagued boots'[3] with which Coleridge admitted he was apt to run away from the main theme under discussion, are only too clearly evident. In the first of these letters he outlined an ambitious survey of the subject; it was to be treated under three heads: 'first, of the Catholic Question, considered as a matter of

---

[1] On 6, 18, and 24 Sept. 1810. See *The Works and Correspondence of David Ricardo*, ed. P. Sraffa, 1951, iii. 131–53.

[2] *E.O.T.* iii. 756 and repeated iii. 862.

[3] The phrase occurs in a letter to D. Stuart, 13 May 1816, *L.* ii. 664.

pure Light: 2nd, of the same, as a question of policy or practicable concession, and lastly, of the true causes of the state of Ireland, commencing with the errors during its first settlement.'[1] The first of these heads was not reached until the third letter, whose opening words help to remind us of Coleridge's continuous preoccupation with the problems of the right relationship between Church and State and the right relationship between civil and religious rights. 'Church and State—civil and religious rights—to hold these essential powers of civilized society in a due relation to each other, so as to prevent them from becoming its burthens instead of its supports; this is perhaps the most difficult problem in the whole science of politics.'[2] It was a problem, he should have realized, that could not be treated satisfactorily within the narrow limits of a newspaper essay. Undaunted by the magnitude of the task, however, Coleridge set out to consider the work of the most important writers on religious toleration. In fact the sub-title of the third letter promised the reader 'a Critique on the Systems of Toleration and Religious Rights, of Hobbes, Locke, and Warburton'.[3] However, only the views of Hobbes were examined and the essay came to an end with the characteristic Coleridgean promise, 'To be continued'. While these essays contain abundant evidence that Coleridge recognized the gravity of the problem of Catholic Emancipation and that it was really part of a larger and more fundamental constitutional problem, his own attempts to come to grips with the subject in the *Courier* were pathetically inadequate.

It is indeed odd that De Quincey should have suggested that the republication of the essays in the *Courier* would form an even finer monument to Coleridge's genius than the essays first published in the *Morning Post*.[4] It is a judgement with which it is impossible to agree. The subjects on which Coleridge wrote in the *Courier* were on the whole of less importance than those that occupied his mind in the years between 1799 and 1802, for it was a less critical period of English history. Added to which is the fact that owing to his subordinate position he rarely had the opportunity to write on the issues of greatest consequence, these being the province of Street, the editor. Coleridge took the subjects that were given him and

---

[1] 13 Sept. 1811, *E.O.T.* iii. 896.

[2] 26 Sept. 1811, *E.O.T.* iii. 925. See *Church and State*, passim, and *Table Talk*, pp. 107 and 147.

[3] *E.O.T.* iii. 925.

[4] See the passage from De Quincey quoted at the end of Chap. III, p. 80.

when health and strength permitted he did what he could to illuminate them for his readers. When he chose his own subjects, as in the case of the *Letters on the Spaniards* and the *Letters to Judge Fletcher*, he occasionally recaptured something of the fervour and verbal felicity that had characterized the essays in the *Morning Post*. But the final impression left after reading Coleridge's contributions to the *Courier* is that of a great mind working only at half pressure and totally unable to subordinate its powers to the task in hand.

CHAPTER V

POLITICS IN THE POST-NAPOLEONIC PERIOD

1. *The Lay Sermons*

IT has often been suggested that Wordsworth, Coleridge, and Southey showed little or no concern for social problems after the period of their youth. It has been said that they became insensitive to the sufferings of the poor, that they were blind to the inadequacies of the social system, and were determined to defend it at all costs. The solutions they did offer have usually been dismissed as visionary and unpractical. While it is true that in later life they were less easily moved to active sympathy with the oppressed than in their youth—and the reasons for this were personal as well as political—their actual interest in political and social problems remained unabated. Nor did they always exhibit 'a regular leaning to the side of power', as Hazlitt suggested. Even Southey, who has always fared worse than any of the other Romantics at the hands of radical critics, has been rescued from going down to posterity as a rigid unbending High Tory by the work of Professor Cobban and Professor Simmons, who have shown him to have been a zealous advocate for social, if not for political reform. The Romantics' diagnoses of social problems often appear remote and unrealistic, largely because they all recognized that the individual social sores were symptomatic of a sick society and that piecemeal social legislation, or what has been aptly called 'social engineering' by a recent writer, would prove ineffective.[1] Mere palliatives were useless; a cure must be found. Coleridge attributed the root cause of this sickness to the prevailing philosophy of the age, and his main purpose in all his later political writing was to bring about a complete moral and philosophical revolution in the governing classes of England. The two *Lay Sermons*; the republication of *The Friend* in 1818, with the addition of a whole section devoted to religion and philosophy and an attack upon the Utilitarian Philosophy; a private letter to Lord Liverpool, the Prime Minister; the two pamphlets on Sir

---

[1] See K. R. Popper, *The Open Society and its Enemies*, 2nd ed., 1952, passim.

Robert Peel's Bill to regulate the work of the children in the cotton factories; and his last work, *Church and State*; all these sought to trace the origin of the complex social problems of the day to a single cause, the state of the national moral conscience.

According to Coleridge the first *Lay Sermon* was to have been 'a small Tract on the present Distresses'. He wrote to Dr. Brabant that he had been solicited to produce such a work by the publishers, Gale and Fenner.[1] The publishers little expecting that Coleridge would take as long as he did in composing the tract or that he would include an elaborate apparatus of philosophical appendixes, announced its publication before the work was actually complete, thus giving Hazlitt the opportunity to write his malicious anticipatory review in the *Examiner*. There Hazlitt wrote: 'We can give just as good a guess at the design of this Lay-Sermon, which is not published, as *The Friend*, the Preliminary Articles in the *Courier*, *the Watchman*, *the Conciones ad Populum*, or any other courtly or popular publications of the same author.'[2] Though Hazlitt's remarks were meant to be the reverse of complimentary, in a sense what he said was profoundly true. Both in choice of subject-matter and manner of address the *Lay Sermons* contained no surprises for those who had read the author's earlier works.[3] The title Coleridge gave to the first *Lay Sermon* when it appeared in 1816 was *The Statesman's Manual: or the Bible the Best Guide to Political Skill and Foresight*. It has as a sub-title, 'A Lay Sermon, Addressed to the Higher Classes of Society'. It is a title that, as R. J. White has remarked, 'might well frighten away the uninitiated with its premonitory snuffle of snobbery'.[4] This was followed up at the end of the next year by the publication of a second *Lay Sermon*, 'Addressed to the Higher and Middle Classes on the Existing Distresses and Discontents'. He intended to write a third to be addressed to the labouring classes, whose purpose was to

[1] 21 Sept. 1816, *U.L.* ii. 180.

[2] 8 Sept. 1816. Printed in *Complete Works of William Hazlitt*, ed. P. P. Howe, vol. vii, pp. 114–18. On 29 Dec. 1816 he wrote a review of *The Statesman's Manual*, which had then been published. A letter to the editor on *Mr Coleridge's Lay Sermon*, 12 Jan. 1817, contains the germ of the later essay *My First Acquaintance with Poets*. The authorship of the review in the *Edinburgh Review* has also been ascribed to Hazlitt, *Complete Works*, vol. xvi, pp. 99–114.

[3] Connexions with the Bristol lectures have been noted by Coleridge himself, F. J. A. Hort, *Cambridge Essays*, 1856, and by H. Beeley in 'The Political Thought of Coleridge', *Coleridge: Studies by Several Hands*, ed. E. Blunden and E. L. Griggs, p. 160.

[4] *The Political Tracts of Wordsworth, Coleridge and Shelley*, 1953, p. x.

have been to 'unvizard our Incendiaries'.[1] It was advertised on the paper wrapper of *The Statesman's Manual* but never appeared.

In choosing these titles so uninviting to modern taste, Coleridge was merely carrying out the principle that he had first announced in 1795 in his lecture *On the Present War* and which he had later developed in the section of *The Friend* entitled *On the Communication of Truth and the Rightful Liberty of the Press*. In the early lecture he said that in the expression of opinion 'it is our duty to consider the character of those, to whom we address ourselves, their situations, and probable degree of knowledge'.[2] The *Lay Sermons* were intended for a relatively small public, for those who had some 'book-learnedness' and 'occasional impulses at least to philosophical thought'; and he wrote to Street that he never dreamt that they 'would be understood (except in fragments) by the general reader'.[3] Dorothy Wordsworth complained that *The Statesman's Manual* was 'ten times more obscure than the darkest parts of the Friend'.[4] He was led to adopt a slightly more popular style in the second *Lay Sermon* and some indication of the style he might have used in his address to the labouring classes is given in a Notebook jotting of about this period. 'That the Cobbetts & Hunts address you (= the lower Ranks) as beasts who have no future selves—as if by a natural necessity you must *all* remain poor & slaving. But what is the fact? How many scores might each of you point out in your neighbourhood of men raised to wealth or comfort from your own ranks.'[5] This direct approach *ad hominem* rarely occurs in the two published *Lay Sermons*. Nevertheless, it is not the innate difficulty of the style, nor the difficulty of the ideas propounded that limits their appeal, but the esoteric manner and condescending tone into which Coleridge so frequently degenerates.

What had the Bible to offer the governing classes in the way of State wisdom? To answer this question Coleridge felt obliged to define the value of history in general, to differentiate between the reading of history that sought to discover universally valid principles and that which was wholly concerned with unrelated facts and anecdotes about the great, and finally to establish the pre-eminence of sacred history.[6] The latter, which was by far the most

[1] Letter to H. J. Rose, 17 Sept. 1816, *U.L.* ii. 179. [2] *E.O.T.* i. 29–30.
[3] Letter to T. J. Street, 22 Mar. 1817, *U.L.* ii. 193.
[4] *Letters of W. and D. Wordsworth, Middle Years*, ii. 780.
[5] *Notebook No. 22*, B.M. Add. MSS. 47520, f. 61.
[6] 'I have known men, who with significant nods and pitying contempt of smiles

important task, was not satisfactorily fulfilled. In a passage like the following he establishes its theoretical pre-eminence.

In the Bible every agent appears and acts as a self-subsisting individual; each has a life of its own, and yet all are one life. The elements of necessity and free-will are reconciled in the higher power of an omnipresent Providence that predestinates the whole in the moral freedom of the integral parts. Of this the Bible never suffers us to lose sight. The root is never detached from the ground. It is God everywhere: and all creatures conform to his decrees, the righteous by performance of the law, the disobedient by the sufferance of the penalty.[1]

But his actual references to passages in the Bible are peculiarly irritating and do little to prove that it was the statesman's best manual. The following guarded reference to the 1st Book of Kings is typical.

Were it my object to touch on the present state of public affairs in this kingdom, or on the prospective measures in agitation respecting our sister island, I would direct your most serious meditations to the latter period of the reign of Solomon, and to the revolutions in the reign of Rehoboam, his successor. But I should tread on glowing embers.[2]

It is not surprising that Hazlitt singled out this passage for special ridicule in his review in the *Examiner*. When he uses the Bible to throw light on contemporary events he runs the risk of being compared with Richard Brothers or Joanna Southcott. What, for example, is one to make of the attempt to read into the passage from Isaiah, beginning 'And thou saidst, I shall be a lady for ever',[3] a prophecy of the 'true philosophy of the French Revolution more than two thousand years before it became a sad irrevocable truth of history'? Worse still, and making this passage highly ludicrous is the footnote interpreting the verse beginning: 'Therefore shall evil come upon thee, thou shalt know from whence it riseth', as a 'remembrancer' of the sudden setting-in of the frost that caused the defeat of the French at Moscow. Coleridge's practical application of the Bible to the world of politics exercised his own ingenuity in finding remote parallels without contributing anything to the understanding of the reader. For all his references

have denied all influence to the corruptions of moral and political philosophy, and with much solemnity have proceeded to solve the riddle of the French Revolution by Anecdotes.' *Lay Sermons*, p. 15.

[1] Ibid., pp. 34–35.   [2] Ibid., p. 36.
[3] Isaiah xlvii. 7 et seq.

to the audience as 'you, my friends', he is for the most part communing with himself with the pages of his Bible open before him rather than addressing a limited audience of his own choice.

In spite of his own failure to establish the right relationship with his chosen public, as in so many of his other works, Coleridge says much that is of interest about the reading public at the beginning of the nineteenth century. He stressed the debilitating effect that the emergence of a large middle-class reading public, which was eager to be entertained and instructed at small intellectual cost, had on the cultural life of the nation. Its existence he associated with the popularity of the novel and the prominence assumed by the circulating library in the lives of the middle classes.[1] Serious works went unheeded and the majority of readers remained ignorant of their own ignorance; but as Coleridge had remarked in *The Friend*, 'to attempt to make a man wiser is of necessity to remind him of his ignorance, and in the majority of instances, the pain actually felt is so much greater than the pleasure anticipated, that it is natural that men should attempt to shelter themselves from it by contempt or neglect'.[2] To counteract this cult of triviality and also the 'plebification' of knowledge that he attributed to the work of the Mechanics' Institutes and similar organizations, he thought that it was essential that the education of the governing classes should be improved. They must be taught the importance of philosophy, the proper attitude towards the value of history and the unique quality of the Bible; that it alone contained 'a science of realities'.[3]

In the Bristol lectures and in essays in *The Watchman* Coleridge had taken up the position that the reformation of society could come about only as the result of a general process of illumination and had laid special stress on the moral and political education of the lower classes. Concerning the means to be used he had had little to say, except to insist that individual effort was necessary, that a patriot must 'be personally among the poor'; and to assert that religion possessed the most efficient means of preparing the lower classes for their rights by making them aware of their correlative duties. In his later political works he retained his belief in

[1] *Lay Sermons*, pp. 40–43; *B.L.* i. 34; *U.L.* ii. 193–5. See also Q. D. Leavis, *Fiction and the Reading Public*, 1932, passim.
[2] *F.* (1837), iii. 325.   [3] *Lay Sermons*, p. 55.

the necessity for individual effort, and placed even greater stress on the power of religion, but he now sought the reformation of society through the re-education of the governing classes and not through the education of the governed. This change in emphasis sprang from his belief that all great changes in society had been brought about by the few—'what is mankind but *the few* in all ages?'[1]—and from the belief that the only effective reform was that which was willingly conceded. The history of the factory legislation, Reform Acts, and Corn Bills during the nineteenth century proves the second belief to have been ill-founded. He wished to see a new kind of social conscience developed in the minds of those who controlled the economic power of the nation and feared that if this did not take place the alternative lay between an ever-increasing oppression on the part of the rulers or a revolution on the part of the masses. The fear of the latter never seems to have been far from his mind in his last years and accounts for the note of hysteria that occurs in many of the *obiter dicta* recorded in *Table Talk*.[2] But even in the second *Lay Sermon* the analogy he drew between the structure of society and a house of cards, proves that he considered the cement of contemporary society likely to crumble at any moment.[3]

Although in the *Lay Sermons* Coleridge placed the main emphasis on the education of the governing classes, he had not abandoned altogether the idea of a national system of education. In *The Statesman's Manual* he points out two common errors in educational theory. 'The first consists in a disposition to think, that as the peace of nations has been destroyed by the diffusion of false light, it may be re-established by excluding the people from all knowledge and all prospect of amelioration.'[4] To answer this he repeats a principle that he had expressed two years earlier in the *Letters to Judge Fletcher*, that whatever inconveniences had arisen from education becoming too general could only be removed by making it universal.[5] The second error he notes in contemporary thought on education, is the belief that 'a national education will have been realised whenever the people at large

---

[1] Letter to T. J. Street, 22 Mar. 1817, *U.L.* ii. 195. See also *F.*, p. 33.

[2] For example, the fulminations against the Catholic Bill and the Reform Bill. 17 Dec. 1831, *T.T.*, p. 145.

[3] The analogy is repeated in Allsop, i. 93–94.

[4] *Lay Sermons*, p. 43.

[5] Ibid., pp. 43–44; for first use see *E.O.T.* iii. 701–2.

have been taught to read and write'.[1] Coleridge insists that the system must not have narrow secular aims; it must educe the moral as well as the intellectual powers. It was typical of an industrial society to demand only 'spinning jennies for the cheap and speedy manufacture of reading and writing',[2] and to be uninterested in full development of the human personality. On the other hand, Coleridge was equally opposed to the emphasis the Bible Societies placed on making the ignorant religious. To those who said that the task was not to remove ignorance but to make the ignorant religious, 'religion, herself, through her sacred oracles answers for me, that all effective faith pre-supposes knowledge and individual conviction'.[3] Thus with great economy Coleridge summed up the main flaws in the two contemporary approaches to the subject.

It is clear from Coleridge's early political writings that contemporary British statesmen fell far below his ideal standard; and Pitt's limitations he attributed directly to the form of education he received. All allowed expedience unrelated to principle to guide them in the formulation of national policy. On the other hand, the great statesmen of the past had habitually concerned themselves with principles and ideas, 'and every idea', asserted Coleridge, 'is living, productive, partaketh of infinity, and (as Bacon has sublimely observed) containeth an endless power of semination'.[4] An education that duly recognized the seminal power of ideas would, he believed, enable the governors of a country to read history philosophically, to collate the past and the present, and become conscious agents in the working out of God's will in history. A policy founded on ideas would also have a remarkable effect on the governed for 'at the annunciation of principles, of ideas, the soul of man awakes and starts up, as an exile in a far distant land at the unexpected sounds of his native language, when after long years of absence, and almost of oblivion, he is suddenly addressed in his own mother-tongue'.[5] Unfortunately it was the lot of most

---

[1] *Lay Sermons*, p. 44.

[2] Letter to the editor of the *Morning Chronicle*, 25 Jan. 1818, *U.L.* ii. 224.

[3] *Lay Sermons*, p. 52. The passage first appeared in *The Friend, F.*, p. 61.

[4] *Lay Sermons*, p. 25.

[5] Ibid., p. 26. Hazlitt commented on this passage in the *Edinburgh Review*: 'A few plain instincts, and a little common sense, are all that the most popular of our popular writers attribute to the people. . . . But Mr Coleridge, the mob-hating Mr Coleridge, here supposes them intuitively to perceive the cabalistical visions of German metaphysics.' *Complete Works*, vol. xvi, p. 110.

men to be possessed by ideas instead of possessing them. Hence the desperate need for wise and philosophical statesmen to give the lead. At the end of his life he cried out in despair: 'Alas I look in vain for some wise and vigorous man to sound the word Duty in the ears of this generation.'[1] The search for the ideal governor was a continuous one.

Coleridge did take one practical step in seeking to give one of the leading statesmen of the day an education in principles, but the attempt met with even less success than the *Lay Sermons* themselves. He wrote a long letter to Lord Liverpool at a time when the Prime Minister was receiving a number of private communications suggesting how the distresses of the country could be alleviated.[2] His diagnosis, in conformity with what he had written in the *Lay Sermons*, attributed the state of the country to the worship of a false philosophy. Lord Liverpool's endorsement nicely expresses his bewildered response.

From Mr. Coleridge, stating the object of his writings has been to rescue speculative philosophy from false principles of reasoning, and to place it on that basis, or give it that tendency, which would make it best suited to the interests of religion as well as of the State; at least, I believe this is Mr. Coleridge's meaning, but I cannot well understand him.[3]

Even supposing the Prime Minister had been able to understand him better, had even agreed with Coleridge's analysis of the ultimate causes of the national distress, what could he do? Very little if anything at all. It was hardly in his power to reverse the philosophy of the age by Act of Parliament. The change must come, so Coleridge frequently asserted in his writings, as the result of the influence of the 'visions of recluse genius',[4] an influence which must of necessity be slow in taking effect. But at times he was apt to make two impossible demands: that these solitary men of genius should also be great statesmen and men of action; or alternatively that the message of such recluses—and it is impossible to believe that he did not include himself among them—should find a ready welcome from minds quite unprepared, and produce a rapid effect on the thinking of an age. In his later years he made

[1] 22 Aug. 1831, *T.T.*, p. 136. Cf. *C.L.* ii. 721.
[2] Printed in full in C. M. Yonge, *Life of Lord Liverpool*, ii. 300–7.
[3] Quoted by Sir Charles Petrie, *Lord Liverpool and His Times*, 1954, p. 235.
[4] *Lay Sermons*, p. 16.

the latter all the more unlikely by employing a style that obscured rather than illuminated the essentials of his thought, and by adopting a tone of conscious moral and intellectual superiority that was bound to irritate even the most sympathetic readers.

In the second *Lay Sermon* Coleridge's characteristic strength and weakness as a critic of contemporary problems is laid bare. His strength lies always in the depth and originality of his analysis of the contemporary political scene; his weakness in his failure to prescribe any practical and effective remedies to specific problems. The work falls into three sections of very unequal value. In the first part Coleridge seeks to delineate the features of those who claim that they are able to prescribe an immediate cure for the complex distresses of the country. These are the popular demagogues and political empirics, and with the aid of a passage from Isaiah he heaps a torrent of denunciation on their heads. The middle and by far the longest section is taken up with an analysis of the ultimate causes of the present social disorders. The last section is the shortest and the weakest. Consisting of only two pages it prescribes the remedies. Certainly when the reader comes to the first of these, which is that the State should abolish the national lotteries,[1] he is very conscious of an anti-climax. The disproportion between the magnitude and complexity of the problems analysed and the proposed remedy makes it difficult to recognize that it is in strict accordance with Coleridge's idea of the negative ends of the State that it should never use its legislative powers to perpetuate positive evil. Moreover, he believed that the abolition of the annual lottery would act as a public demonstration of the moral basis on which the State rested and would thus become a moral inspiration to the people.

I am deeply convinced, that more sterling and visible benefits would be derived from this one solemn proof and pledge of moral fortitude and national faith, than from retrenchments to a tenfold greater amount. Still more, if our legislators should pledge themselves at the same time that they would hereafter take counsel for the gradual removal or

---

[1] Between 1709 and 1824 the British Government ran annual lotteries. A ticket cost £10 and the prizes were annuities. When Spencer Perceval was Prime Minister in 1806 he sought to restrict the practice. Perhaps this action partly accounts for Coleridge's exaggerated praise of him. He was Coleridge's 'Idea [of] a great and good, and most simple, great man'. *U.L.* ii. 82. In *The Friend* Coleridge refers to 'that mother-vice, the lottery'. *F.*, p. 33. Cf. early poem *To Fortune*: On buying a Ticket in the Irish Lottery. *P.W.* i. 54.

counteraction of all similar encouragements and temptations to vice and folly, that had, alas! been tolerated hitherto, as the easiest way of supplying the exchequer.[1]

But calls for moral gestures and a change of heart strike a chill and forbidding note in the ears of those who are eager for change and reform and believe that these can alone be effected through drastic and sweeping legislation. Nevertheless, at the very end of the second *Lay Sermon* Coleridge does offer one definite and practical solution to the sufferings brought about by the process of industrialization. 'Our manufacturers must consent to regulations', he declares, and a year later he wrote circulars to rally opinion behind Sir Robert Peel in his attempt to legislate on behalf of the children in the cotton mills.

The long central section of the second *Lay Sermon* refutes John Stuart Mill's contention that Coleridge wrote 'like an arrant driveller' when he wrote on political economy.[2] In fact this section shows that he had a broad grasp of fundamental economic principles and an acute insight into the special problems that arise in the transitional period between a war and a peace-time economy. The suddenness with which the Napoleonic War had come to an end made any gradual change in the economy of the country impossible, and he saw that a policy of severe retrenchment would only increase the instability of the system. But the most remarkable part of this section of the sermon is the account Coleridge gives of what we now refer to as the 'trade cycle'. With little reliable statistical information to work on and with the whole science of political economy in its infancy, Coleridge was nevertheless able to detect in the history of the previous sixty years 'periodical revolutions of credit', occurring at intervals of about twelve or thirteen years.[3] His treatment of these booms and crashes differs from that of the economists of the day, who neither inquired into their causes nor lamented their effects on the health and happiness of the people. The difference mainly arises from his special insistence that the individual must always be considered as an end in himself and never merely as an economic unit. This is seen in a

[1] *Lay Sermons*, p. 266.

[2] *Mill on Bentham and Coleridge*, ed. F. R. Leavis, 1950, p. 155. Mill is re-echoed by his most recent biographer. Coleridge's 'economics, on his few reluctant excursions into those fields were outrageously misinformed'. M. St. John Packe, *Life of John Stuart Mill*, 1954, p. 84.   [3] *Lay Sermons*, pp. 234–5.

striking passage in which he attacks the glib and comforting doctrine of the classical economists 'that in a free and trading community all things find their level'. In answer he declares indignantly:

> But persons are not things—but man does not find his level. Neither in body nor in soul does the man find his level. After a hard and calamitous season, during which the thousand wheels of some vast manufactory had remained silent as a frozen water-fall, be it that plenty has returned and that trade has once more become brisk and stirring: go, ask the overseer, and question the parish doctor, whether the workman's health and temperance with the staid and respectful manners best taught by the inward dignity of conscious self-support, have found their level again?[1]

The industrial workers were not the only ones to suffer. Coleridge related how he had seen the visible effects of lean years on the physical frames of young Dorsetshire children, 'each with its little shoulders up to its ears, and its chest pinched inward, the very habit and fixures, as it were, that had been impressed on their frames by the former ill-fed, ill-clothed, and unfuelled winters'.[2] In essence his opposition to the prevailing economic theory was similar to his opposition to the political theory of the Physiocrats; for the convenience of their theory, the hoping, suffering individual is replaced by an abstraction of their own creation, political or economic man.[3]

Coleridge attributed the economic distresses that overwhelmed the country in 1816 to the overbalance of the commercial spirit, but he makes it clear that he is not opposed to this spirit as such but only to its excessive preponderance and its incursion into the sphere of agriculture. Of the three forces in society that acted as a natural counterweight, the 'feeling of ancient birth, and the respect paid to it by the community at large', was declining; 'a genuine intellectual Philosophy with an accredited learned, and Philosophic class' did not exist; and religion, though it acted as an effective force in many ways failed in this one particular respect.

---

[1] Ibid., p. 237. For the use of the same distinction between persons and things see *F.*, p. 118; *T.T.*, p. 225; *Church and State*, pp. 15–16.

[2] Ibid.

[3] For a detailed comparison of Coleridge's economic thought with that of Malthus and Ricardo see W. F. Kennedy, *Humanist Versus Economist*. The Economic Thought of Samuel Taylor Coleridge, University of California Publications in Economics, Vol. xvii, 1958, pp. 22–29.

He believed that 'an excess in our attachment to temporal and per-sonal objects', could be counteracted only by a 'preoccupation of the intellect and the affections with permanent, universal and eternal truths'. He thought that it was impossible that the philo-sophical empiricism of the age, or a religion based on the utili-tarian ethics and gross over-simplifications of Paley, could adjust the balance, for not even the most austere of the Puritan sects, the Quakers, succeeded in counteracting and resisting the spirit of commerce. The passages that analyse the connexion between the development of a strong acquisitive instinct and the prevalence of a religious creed that made no demands on the intellect form an interesting anticipation of one school of modern history. He does not of course attribute the growth of the acquisitive instinct solely to this kind of religion. His general thesis—and no mere bald statement can do anything to suggest the subtlety of his analysis—is that the growth of a religion that proved to be acceptable to all men of common sense by utterly neglecting all the more serious questions of theology, left the 'understanding vacant and at leisure for a thorough insight into present and temporal interests'.[1]

In analysing the effect of the overbalance of the commercial spirit on all spheres of national life Coleridge was led to reflect on a number of specific contemporary problems: for example, the operation of the Poor Laws, the rapid increase in population, the effect of the paper currency and the National Debt on the economy of the country, and finally the question of whether the State had the right to use its legislative powers to control 'the self-regulating machine' of the classical economists' theory. The remarks thrown out are sufficiently original to make one wish that he had thought it worth while to develop further his ideas on each. They were developed but not in this work. For further elucidation of his views one has to turn to the remarks recorded in Allsop's *Letters, Conversations and Recollections* and in *Table Talk*, and, of course, to the jottings in the Notebooks.[2] This the contemporary reader was unable to do; and one of the main reasons why Coleridge failed to

[1] *Lay Sermons*, pp. 222–23. Sixteen years earlier in the *Morning Post* he had praised Washington's plan to endow a central university on the grounds that it would 'liberalise the too great commercial spirit' of America by centring attention on 'objects abstract and unworldly'.

[2] Allsop's records begin earlier and stop earlier than H. N. Coleridge's. In the main he covers the years 1818 to 1825, while the bulk of the entries in *Table Talk* cover the period 1825 to 1834. The later Notebooks are mainly taken up with jottings on religion and philosophy.

influence the attitude of the public on any of these problems was that his most acute observations were made in letters to friends, in notebook jottings, or in the course of conversation, and failed to find their way into his published political work. In the latter his excessive concern with the formulation of principles and his somewhat cursory, elliptical, and cautious treatment of the questions of the day obscured the essential originality and value of his approach.

In the second *Lay Sermon* Coleridge wrote that he considered it impossible to exaggerate the 'pernicious tendency and consequence'[1] of the Poor Laws. Their general effect was to make the poor even more improvident; their dependence on charity, he declared to Allsop, made them 'more and more exchange the sentiments of Englishmen for the feelings of Lazzaroni'.[2] He hated the use of the phrase 'The Poor', and in 1831 he wrote in a Notebook:

Poverty, whatever can justify the designation of 'the poor' ought to be a transitional state to which no man ought to admit himself to belong, tho' he may find himself *in* it because he is passing *thro'* it, in the effort to leave it. Poor men we must always have, till the Redemption is fulfilled, but *The Poor*, as consisting of the *same* Individuals! O this is a sore accusation against society.[3]

He regarded as particularly ominous the current phrase, 'the labouring *poor*', as if these two terms were synonymous.[4] Equally ominous was the use of the word 'operative' for the factory workers, since it clearly implied that those who used it had failed to recognize the all important distinction between persons and things.[5] According to Coleridge two classes benefited from the operation of the Poor Laws: the large landowners, who knew the 'expediency of having labour cheap, and estates let in the fewest possible portions', and the manufacturers, who needed cheap labour in order to enable them to compete with the foreign market and to enable them to remain solvent during times of depression.[6] In this *Lay Sermon* he is more concerned with the effects of the

---

[1] *Lay Sermons*, p. 256. [2] Allsop, i. 27.
[3] *Notebook No. 50*, B.M. Add. MSS. 47545, f. 45.
[4] The phrase was first noted by Coleridge in 1800 in the *Morning Post*, *E.O.T.* i. 274. See also *Lay Sermons*, p. 238.
[5] 'It is not uncommon for 100,000 *operatives* (mark this word, for words *in this sense* are things) to be out of employment at once in the cotton districts.' Allsop, op. cit. i. 135.
[6] *Lay Sermons*, pp. 257–8.

Poor Laws on agriculture than on commerce, although it is part of his main thesis that the distresses of the agricultural labourers originated from the unhealthy influence of the commercial spirit which made the landlords and farmers try to obtain, '1. the utmost produce that can be raised without injuring the estate; 2. with the least possible consumption of the produce on the estate itself; 3. at the lowest wages; and 4. with the substitution of machinery for human labour wherever the former will cost less and do the same work'.¹ The Poor Laws were, he thought, the inevitable outcome of such an attitude; and he noted, 'in agricultural districts three-fourths of the Poors' Rates are paid to healthy, robust, and (O sorrow and shame!) industrious, hard-working paupers in lieu of wages (for men cannot at once work and starve)'.² Quite apart from their dehumanizing and dispiriting effect on the agricultural labourer, great injustice arose from the unequal burden that fell on the various classes. Coleridge's opinions on this varied. In the second *Lay Sermon* he complained that the rates paid by those who were not owners of land or employers of labour were so much bounty paid to the owners of the big estates. Six years later his main complaint was that the poor rates imposed a disproportionate burden on the landed interest as a whole. The manufacturers, who gained most from the system, paid insufficient. 'The poor-rates are the consideration paid by, or on behalf of, capitalists for having labour at demand. It is the price, and nothing else. The hardship consists in the agricultural interest having to pay an undue proportion of the rates.'³ Though his account of the hardship involved varied, his fundamental objection to the system remained unchanged. He was certain that the Poor Laws exerted a demoralizing effect both on the poor and on the classes who were responsible for their continuance. When a Bill was introduced to deny poor relief at home the essential humanity of his approach found expression in the simple phrase : '*It is not bread alone, but the place where you eat it.*'⁴

Had Coleridge any practical alternative to offer? He put forward no specific plan, but it is clear from a number of passages that he thought that the Church must renew her ancient function

---

¹ *Lay Sermons*, pp. 255–6.   ² Ibid., pp. 256–7.
³ *Table Talk*, 27 Apr. 1823. T.T., p. 27. He thought that there should be a 'fixed revolving period for the equalisation of the rates'.
⁴ Allsop, op. cit. i. 66.

of acting as a mediator between the 'people and the government, the poor and the rich', thereby helping to alleviate the sufferings of the poor.[1] An entry in one of the Notebooks runs:

The injury to Religion, to the Church, to the State, & to general morality & industry, and in all these and in many other respects, to the Poor themselves, that arises from the disjunction of the Poor Laws from the Church—which yet in name they belong to? Surely, this has been strangely overlooked by the Reformers in this important subject! Reform? then look back at the original form and see how far it is applicable to the present times—This seems an important Hint.[2]

This was in some sense to return to the message of *Conciones ad Populum*, in which he had stressed the need for a religious approach to the problem of the poor. Clearly in his later life Coleridge did not anticipate that the Church should replace the State as the organization responsible for the administration of a complicated system of poor relief. He hoped that the distresses would be relieved personally by its members acting in the spirit of Christ and not in accordance with the laws formulated by the new school of political economists. A disbelief in the efficacy of private charity and a total reliance on a system of state measures was 'the essence of the new blasphemy', he declared.[3]

In the second *Lay Sermon* Coleridge glances at but does not consider fully the problems arising out of a sudden and rapid increase in population. 'By the known laws of human increase', he declared, the manufacturers had 'virtually called into existence' a new labour force.[4] His main charge against the manufacturers was that they had connived at this rapid increase in population but were utterly unwilling to accept responsibility for its maintenance in time of economic distress. In 1820 he demonstrated to Thomas Allsop that the Malthusian argument was a two-edged weapon that could be turned against the factory owner. It was all very well for the latter, brought up on good Malthusian principles, to disclaim all responsibility towards the starving labourers, saying: 'You have no claim upon me; you have your allotted part to perform in the world, so have I. In a state of nature, indeed, had I food, I should offer you a share from sympathy, from humanity; but in

---

[1] *T.T.*, p. 106, entry dated 8 Sept. 1830.
[2] *Notebook No. 24*, B.M. Add. MSS. 47522, f. 31*v*. Cf. the complaint in *Church and State*, p. 65, that the poor had been 'withdrawn from the discipline of the Church'.
[3] Allsop, i. 70.   [4] *Lay Sermons*, p. 258.

this advanced and artificial state of society, I cannot afford you relief; *you must starve.*' He must in this case be prepared for the following reply from the worker. 'You disclaim all connexion with me; I have no claims upon you? *I can then have no duties towards you,* and this pistol shall put me in possession of your wealth. You may leave a law behind you which shall hang me, but what man who saw assured starvation before him, ever feared hanging.'[1] The total effect of substituting a policy of expedience for one of principle was to destroy the moral foundation of society. Coleridge's recognition of this aspect of Malthus's theory explains the indignant tone of his marginal notes in his copy of the *Essay on the Principle of Population,* many of which were incorporated with modifications into Southey's review of the work in the *Annual Review.* In these marginal comments Coleridge succeeded in demonstrating the central weakness in the theory, as it had been first stated. He considered that Malthus was wrong to suggest that there were only two main ways in which population could be controlled and illogical to prefer the regulating force of hunger to any means of birth control.

If we believed with Mr Malthus's *warmest* partisans that man will never in general be capable of regulating the sexual appetite by the Law of Reason, and that the gratification of Lust is a thing of physical necessity equally with the gratification of Hunger—a faith which we should laugh at for its silliness if its wickedness had not pre-excited abhorrence—nothing could be more easy than to demonstrate, that some one or other of these actions, whether Abortion, or the Exposure of Children, or artificial sterility on the part of the Male, would become Virtues.[2]

His own belief in the powers of Reason and Will made him deny absolutely that there existed only a choice between famine and artificial interference in the natural process of birth. 'The whole question is this,' he declared, 'are Lust and Hunger both alike Passions of physical Necessity, and the one equally with the other independent of the Reason and the Will?' Even though the volume annotated by Coleridge was the edition in which Malthus had introduced the doctrine of moral restraint, he ignored this modification, recognizing it for what it was, an anomalous element added to make the work more acceptable.

[1] Allsop, i. 135-6.
[2] Quoted by A. Cobban in *Edmund Burke and the Revolt against the Eighteenth Century,* 1929, pp. 204-5.

Coleridge's remarks on the subject of currency and taxation in the Sermon lay him open to the charge of inconsistency. Of this he was not unaware. He sought to explain away the difference between the treatment of this topic in *The Friend* and the *Courier* and in the present work on the grounds that patriotism had demanded that he should write as he had done during the Napoleonic War.[1] In *The Friend* he had defended the National Debt by saying that it helped to establish a sense of national unity in time of war,[2] and in several essays in the *Courier* he had defended the policy of the banks in not returning to the system of cash payments; but he now considerably modified his attitude towards these two problems. He saw that in a transitional period from war to peace, the National Debt bestowed a disproportionate power on the fund-holders and that the continuance of the paper money was a symbol of artificial prosperity and concealed the critical state of the country's economy. Here at least was one issue on which Cobbett and Coleridge saw eye to eye.

Today Coleridge's views on the intervention of the State in the organization of agriculture and industry must appear cautious in the extreme, but when they are seen against the background of his age, they fall into proper perspective. His conclusions are stated simply and effectively at the end of the second *Lay Sermon*. Manufacturers must accept State regulations; the landed interest must remain free from positive state intervention but must start putting its house in order.[3] Since he had already demonstrated that the two interests were not distinctly separate and that the spirit of commerce had invaded the world of agriculture the validity of making a sharp distinction was at least questionable. He made it because he believed that the ends for which agriculture existed were identical with those for which the State existed while those of industry were not. Agriculture existed to make the means of subsistence easier, to help the individual to better his own conditions or those of his children, and to facilitate the development of his rational and moral being. This assumption that agriculture serves the same ends as the State is closely related to the idea that ownership of land is a trust, involving the discharge of specific duties towards all those who labour on one's land. Coleridge's purpose was

---

[1] *Lay Sermons*, p. 247.
[2] *F.*, p. 148. For example, 'the national debt which has wedded in indissoluble union all the interests of the state'.   [3] *Lay Sermons*, pp. 266–7.

not so much to defend the landed interest from all form of criticism or to resist any attempt by the State to introduce legislation; it
was to impress upon its members the idea that the possession of
great lands entailed the acceptance of great responsibility. He did
not, however, extend the principle that economic power carried
with it commensurate duties to the commercial interest. He seems
to have thought that what he called 'the Maxims of Trade—"an
unqualified right to do what I like with my own" ', must always
rule within this sphere.[1] The general climate of opinion of the
age made it impossible to foresee that a similar sense of responsibility might ultimately be developed in the factory owners.

Coleridge believed that the true index of the prosperity of a
nation was the state of its agriculture, and in particular the conditions enjoyed by the small tenant farmers and labourers. What he
looked for was 'a healthful, callous-handed, but high-and-warm-
hearted tenantry, twice the number of the present landless, parish-
paid labourers, and ready to march off at the first call of their
country with a Son of the House at their head'.[2] Again one is
reminded of Cobbett. Coleridge's opposition to free trade and his
hostility to the Corn Laws sprang from his recognition that the
advocates of both were guilty of treating agriculture as if it were
a mere adjunct and not the heart of the nation.[3] But he was blind
to the inevitability of change. A feudal nostalgia, which comes out
strongly in the picture of a healthy peasantry quoted above, prevented him from seeing that the whole structure of agricultural
England must of necessity undergo a radical change as a result of
the demands made upon it by the rapid process of industrialization and the accompanying growth of great cities, whose inhabitants required cheap food. To complain, as he did, that too many
people were eating the food that they had not themselves produced, was but to raise an ineffective protest against the inevitable
effects of the industrial revolution. Nevertheless his message to the
landed gentry was a timely one, for in a period in which the contrast between the enormous prosperity of the large farmers and the
poverty-stricken peasant was an affront to any standards of social
justice, he recalled the gentry to a sense of ancient duty.

---

[1] Marginal note, dated 1 Mar. 1832, on the title page of *On the Present Balance of Parties in the State* by Sir John Walsh, B.M. c. 126 h. 15 (2).

[2] *Lay Sermons*, p. 252.

[3] See entries in *Table Talk* for 3 May and 20 June 1834, *T.T.*, pp. 282–3 and 288–9.

Apart from the assertion that the manufacturers 'must consent to regulations', Coleridge has little to say about the State's responsibilities with respect to the commercial interest. His ideas on the subject were more fully expounded in the two pamphlets that he prepared and had circulated in order to arouse support for Sir Robert Peel's Bill of 1818 to limit the hours of work for children in the cotton mills. This was by no means the only occasion on which his sensibilities had been sufficiently outraged by the conditions under which large numbers of people were compelled to work to make him wish to champion their cause. In 1806 he had written in one of his Notebooks of his intention of pursuing 'steadily the plan of opening the eyes of the public to the real situation of the Needle-workers, and women in general'.[1] He added that Mary Lamb had promised to supply him with the necessary facts. Unfortunately only on very rare occasions was Coleridge brought face to face with the appalling conditions of the industrial workers. When he was, as in the case of the dockyard welders at Portsmouth, he was deeply moved. 'The poor men are pitiable slaves', he wrote to Southey. 'They all become old men in the prime of manhood.'[2] When, too, he heard of the agitation afoot to introduce factory reform for the benefit of the 'cotton children', and after he had read the report of the committee set up by Peel to investigate their conditions of work, his compassion for their pitiable state was genuine and deep and was matched by an earnest desire to do something to alleviate their suffering.[3]

The two pamphlets Coleridge wrote were *Remarks on the Objections to Sir Robert Peel's Bill*, 18 April, and *The Grounds of Sir Robert Peel's Bill Vindicated*, 24 April 1818.[4] The Bill, which was less drastic than the one that Peel had introduced in 1815, sought to prohibit children under the age of nine from working in the cotton mills and to limit the hours of work for children to $12\frac{1}{2}$ a day. On this occasion, Coleridge showed a remarkable understanding of the necessity of preparing public opinion beforehand by means of

[1] *Notebook No. 11*, B.M. Add. MSS. 47508, ff. 3–3v. and also *N. i.* 1708.
[2] 28 Mar. 1804, *U.L. i.* 318.
[3] Coleridge makes a definite reference to the *Report of the Committee on the State of Children in Manufactures*, 1816, and clearly he took his facts from this work.
[4] In 1913 Edmund Gosse issued a limited edition of the two works under the title *Two Addresses on Sir Robert Peel's Bill*. They may more conveniently be consulted in L. E. Watson, *Coleridge at Highgate*, 1925, pp. 170–87, or in R. J. White, *The Political Thought of Samuel Taylor Coleridge*, 1938. See also Wise, *Bibliography of Coleridge*, pp. 117–21.

a carefully planned scheme of propaganda. He complained that the Bill had been brought forward 'without due preparation of the public mind', and declared that the arguments in its favour should have been '*ding donged* on the public ear in paper, magazine and three penny pamphlets'.[1] He sought in some degree to remedy this defect by addressing his two pamphlets to the members of the House of Commons. They appeared during the week in which the Bill had reached a critical stage. On the 30th of April it was passed by the Commons but was subsequently rejected by the Lords. It is impossible to say what effect, if any, these works may have had on the outcome of the debate in the Commons. In the following year Coleridge referred to them as 'my inefficient yet not feeble Efforts on behalf of the poor little white slaves in the Cotton Factories', but in using the word 'inefficient' he was probably thinking of the subsequent rejection of the Bill by the Lords.[2] They deserved to be effective, for not only did they appear at exactly the right moment, but the author's grasp of the arguments used by those who were opposed to the Bill and the remorseless fashion in which he destroyed each should have exerted a powerful influence on all who were open to rational persuasion. It must have been particularly galling for Coleridge to read what wretched arguments were later advanced in the Lords to defeat this humane measure. In a letter to J. H. Green he referred to the part Lord Lauderdale had played in the debate in the Upper House. 'Whether some half-score of rich capitalists are to be prevented from suborning suicide and perpetuating infanticide and soul-murder is, forsooth, the most perplexing question which has ever called forth his *determining* faculties, accustomed as they are *well known* to have been, to grappling with difficulties.'[3] What a bitter contempt is expressed in these few lines.

Two of the main arguments brought against Peel's Bill were that the State had no right to interfere with free labour and that if it were to do so the innovation might stimulate a succession of claims on behalf of the workers for State control and protection. Coleridge takes up the position that reference to the actual practice of the legislature in the past, for example the laws to regulate the system of apprenticeship, and reference to 'the *principles* and *spirit*

[1] *U.L.* ii. 233 and 235.
[2] *Notebook No. 24*, B.M. Add. MSS. 47522, f. 42*v*.
[3] 2 May 1818, *L.* ii. 689.

of the British Constitution', establish the State's right to intervene on behalf of its citizens when their fundamental human rights are jeopardized by the selfish interests of any individuals. 'Every Canal Bill', he declared, 'proves that there is no species of property which the legislature does not possess and exercise the right of controlling and limiting, as soon as the right of individuals is shewn to be disproportionately injurious to the community.'[1] But quite apart from the question of constitutional precedents, on the subject of which he requested and probably received help from Crabb Robinson,[2] 'in what sense', demanded Coleridge, 'not utterly sophistical, can the labour of children, extorted from the want of their parents, "their poverty, but not their will, consenting" be called *free*?' In answer to the plea that reform would be best left, in so enlightened an age, to the individual manufacturers, he drew his readers' attention to the example of the Slave Trade, in connexion with the abolition of which precisely the same argument had been advanced. Yet in this case it had been found necessary to rely on something more effective than the so-called enlightened self-interest of those concerned in the trade. In his youth he too had believed that State intervention was unnecessary. Experience had brought greater wisdom. However, he continued to believe that the first essential was to rouse the conscience of the people and in his last work, *Church and State*, he enunciated the principle that 'it is only to a limited extent that laws can be wiser than the nation for which they are enacted'.[3]

It can be seen that the period from the middle of 1816 until the summer of 1818 was one in which Coleridge devoted a great deal of time and attention to political problems. The sudden surge of creative activity, which produced *Biographia Literaria* in addition to the works under consideration, sprang from a marked improvement in his health as the result of his stay with his friends the Morgans at Box and his subsequent move to Highgate, where he placed himself in the kindly hands of the Gillmans. He himself had

[1] L. E. Watson, *Coleridge at Highgate*, p. 174.

[2] He wrote: 'Can you furnish us with any other instances in which the Legislature has . . . interfered with what is ironically called "free labour"? i.e. DARED to prohibit soul murder and infanticide on the part of the rich, and self slaughter on the part of the poor.' Quoted by A. V. Dicey, *Lectures on the Relation between Law and Public Opinion*, 1948 ed., p. 224. Dicey did not know that the pamphlets actually existed.

[3] *Church and State*, p. 163. Crabb Robinson reported that in 1811 Coleridge 'spoke warmly and eloquently on the reference of laws to the formation of moral character and feeling in a people'. *Books and their Writers*, ed. E. J. Morley, i. 22.

found a safe retreat from the temptations and anxieties that had previously beset him and paralysed his creative powers, but he was conscious that the nation that had so recently triumphed over France by force of arms was in danger of being overcome by revolutionary forces in her midst. Peterloo was yet to be, but already reports of machine-breaking and of riots were pouring into the Home Office from the industrial towns in the North of England. Coleridge faced this situation in his own way. He addressed *Lay Sermons* to the upper and middle classes who were already too busy demanding repressive measures from the Government to be willing to be reminded of their own responsibilities. He offered the Prime Minister advice. He issued the rifacimento of *The Friend*. In fact he did everything except discover a way of making people listen to what he had to say, with the result that all these works, with the exception of the pamphlets on Sir Robert Peel's Bill, fell on deaf ears. One day in April 1818 he met a tinker outside a baker's shop in Highgate who summed up the national situation in the following words: 'The rich won't part with anything and the Poor have nothing to part with.' What was the real truth of the matter, Coleridge asked himself in his Notebook.

What *is* the present state? Great oppression on the part of the Rich, in their individual callings, or workday character—ex. gr. the Water Companies in London, the Bank of England, the Cotton Factors, the Corn Maximists—Great Subscription *Charities*, or Sunday Work— Bibles, &c.&c.—on the part of the Poor clubbing, debauchery,— sedition, loss of all private & all public social duty. How shall an honest man act? If he exposes the former wickedness he appears to address and is in actual danger of feeding the latter.[1]

This was the dilemma in which Coleridge found himself. His solution to the problem was deliberately to restrict the appeal of his political works to the oppressors, though he did not refer to them as such. Coleridge exaggerated in his own case the danger that his words might indirectly stir up the spirit of sedition. However, observation of the effects of the methods practised on the public by Cobbett and others led to an excessively cautious approach to this problem of addressing readers on controversial political questions. The caution is not only evident in the care he took to ensure that only the right people would read his works and that there would be no risk that criticism would either be mis-

[1] *Notebook No. 27*, B.M. Add. MSS. 47525, f. 2. The date is given as 28 Apr. 1818.

understood or misapplied; it is also evident in the hesitancy with which he tackled all the major problems of the post-war world. It was not until 1830 that Coleridge once more addressed the unheeding public on political questions. This work, *On the Constitution of the Church and State* was his last piece of political writing and proved to be the most successful and influential. It marks Coleridge's nearest approach to writing a treatise on a recognized branch of political theory, though he himself stoutly denied that it deserved to be called a treatise.

11. *On the Constitution of the Church and State*

On the Constitution of the Church and State contains Coleridge's mature thoughts on the British Constitution. In origin it arose from an attempt to formulate his objections to various Bills for Catholic Emancipation that had been placed before the House. Bills were introduced in 1813, 1821, 1825, and 1829. It was Burdett's in 1825 that led Coleridge to define his position; and an annotated volume in the British Museum indicates that a re-reading of Hooker's works at this time played an important part in the genesis of *Church and State*.[1] His friend Hookham Frere, who had been active in attempting to secure a sinecure for him, promised to lay the work before the Prime Minister, Lord Liverpool.[2] However, Frere left England before it was complete and the Prime Minister was thus saved the embarrassment of making a second attempt to elucidate Coleridge's political advice. The actual part of the treatise directly devoted to a discussion of Catholic Emancipation forms the last and smallest section, the main body of the work being taken up with a presentation of Coleridge's theory of the right relationship that should exist between Church and State.

In the Preface, which is in the form of an extract from a letter to a friend, Coleridge presented his credentials for writing on the subject of Catholic Emancipation. 'From the period of the Union with Ireland, to the present hour', he declared, 'I have neglected

---

[1] He began re-reading Hooker in 1825, but most of the notes belong to the following year. The distinctions between an Idea and a Conception and that between the functions of the Enclesiastic and those of the Ecclesistic, recorded in the margins of Hooker, found their way into *Church and State*. Hooker marginalia may most conveniently be consulted in F. Brinkley, *Coleridge on the Seventeenth Century*, Duke University Press, 1955, pp. 141–52.

[2] Coleridge's 'only Dream of Patronage' ended with Lord Liverpool's sudden illness and virtual retirement from politics in 1827. *U.L.* ii. 403–4; also *C. Life*, pp. 262–3.

no opportunity of obtaining correct information from books and from men respecting the facts that bear on the question.'[1] He also said that he had followed and carefully noted down every argument that speakers had put forward in Parliament; but the evidence of the Notebooks does little to substantiate this latter claim. Though it is probably true that he did give much thought to the subject, the actual essays on Catholic Emancipation that he wrote in the *Courier* are all disappointing, for in none of them does he come to grips with his subject. They are merely prolegomena to the main theme and the same is largely true of an interesting manuscript jotting in which he seeks to define the real question on which Parliament was required to reach a decision.

The true legislative Question may be stated thus: 1. Does there now exist aught in the average moral, intellectual, concorporative, and circumstantial condition of the Irish Population, which makes it incumbent on the Legislature of the British Empire to withhold from the Non-protestant Population of Ireland the full exercise of the Political Rights and Privileges which—supposing no such obstacle to exist, would give them collectively the share of legislative power, direct or indirect, proportional to their comparative Number, as a component part of the united Common-weal?[2]

Later in the note he insists that if the question had been discussed with exclusive reference to 'non-protestant *Irishism*, under the existing state and circumstances of the Empire collectively', the nation would have been spared a great deal of irrelevant, abstract speculation and theological dispute. As it was, it caused him acute distress to 'listen to a British Senate quarrelling, like girls, about what the Roman Catholics will or will not wish, will or will not try, to do, if the Bill passes'.[3]

It is impossible to consider *On the Constitution of the Church and State* as a work that affected in any way the cause of Catholic Emancipation, for the Bill had already passed both Houses of Parliament by the time it was published in 1830:[4] and Coleridge admits that he was tempted to suppress what he had already

---

[1] *Church and State*, p. 3. One example is seen in his acquiring the Dublin edition of W. Parnell, *An Historical Apology for Irish Catholics*, 1807, before it had been published in England. Many of the books in the British Museum containing marginalia are concerned with Catholicism.

[2] B.M. Egerton MSS. 2800, f. 109.

[3] Ibid., f. 109*v*.

[4] The Bill received the Royal Assent on 13 Apr. 1829.

written, as his objections to the earlier measures had been largely met in the various clauses of the new Bill. He gives as his reason for deciding to proceed with the publication the fact that the Bill had failed to state solemnly and formally enough the one essential safeguard that any measure for Catholic Emancipation should include. The reader naturally expects to be told immediately what this is, but he has to wait for a hundred pages or so before the safeguard is defined. Until then he has to be content with a series of cautious qualifying clauses. 'The principle, the solemn recognition of which I deem indispensable as a security, and should be willing to receive as the only security—superseding the necessity, though possibly not the expediency, of any other, but itself by no other superseded—this principle is not formally recognized.'[1] The safeguard demanded was, in fact, that the Catholic priesthood should not be allowed to benefit from what Coleridge called the Nationality, that is, the share of national wealth set aside for the National Church. Two things disqualified them: their allegiance to a foreign power; and secondly, the vow of celibacy imposed upon them by that power. The explanation of the reference to the latter disqualification, no mention of which had been made in the Bill, is to be found in Coleridge's conception of the 'clerisy', which though feudal in origin, was to consist not of celibate monks but of family men, who would establish in their own domestic lives a pattern for others to follow. Not the least of the barriers that separated Coleridge from his public was that created by a special use of language, seen here in the words 'Nationalty' and 'clerisy'. Often his attempt to achieve greater clarity and precision led to obscurity and ambiguity, and much confusion arises from the use of the words 'state' and 'church' in different senses in different parts of the work.[2]

Coleridge's discussion of the relationship between Church and State is more interesting and valuable than his comments on the problem of Catholic Emancipation. What, then, has he to say on this broader theme? He begins by warning his readers of the danger of confusing an 'idea' and a generalization. He had first worked out this distinction in relation to the State as early as 1819, in response to a sentence he had read in Heinrich Steffen's *Caricaturen des Heiligsten*, in which the German writer had said that what

---

[1] *Church and State*, p. 10.
[2] See J. Isaacs, 'Coleridge's Critical Terminology', *Essays and Studies*, xxi. 86–104.

was common to all States at all times was the Idea of a State. In several pages of his Notebook can be seen what Coleridge himself called a perfect 'exemplification of the process of seeking, groping after truth'. His own definition of an 'idea' in the Notebook jotting took the following form. 'An idea is a Form presenting and pre-supposing an ultimate end appropriately.'[1] In *Church and State* he refers the reader to the social contract as an example. It is not a generalization based on observation of many States. The social contract contains an 'idea'; this is the 'idea of the sacrosanctity of human personality'. On this analogy Coleridge bases his right to speak of the constitution as an 'idea' existing in the minds of men, but which finds only imperfect embodiment in any actual society. But as it has been pointed out, by treating the 'idea' of the social contract and the 'idea' of the constitution 'as homogeneous and passing from one to the other without any apparent awareness of their difference in kind, he managed to surround the British Con-stitution with an aura of metaphysical sanctity to which it had no claim'.[2] In the pages of *Church and State* is demonstrated one of Coleridge's worst weaknesses as a political theorist and critic of contemporary politics, his tendency to persuade himself and his readers that he was returning to first principles when he was in fact drawing certain deductions from the working of contempor-ary British institutions in the light of their historical development. The features he asserts to be the essential elements in a constitu-tion have no universal validity. A single-minded search for the essential led him to ignore the real defects of the existing system. These are conveniently dismissed as 'no necessary part of the idea'.

Coleridge's idea of a constitution rests on the assumption that in any State there must exist a balance of opposite forces. This in its turn rests on a philosophical view of the operation of opposite forces in the universe. In a long footnote he distinguishes care-fully between opposite and contrary forces. 'Opposite powers are always of the same kind, and tend to union, either by equipoise or by a common product.'[3] Sweet and sour are opposites, sweet and bitter are contraries. He holds that in all States there are two main

---

[1] *Notebook No. 3 1/2*, B.M. Add. MSS. 47499, f. 103.

[2] Anonymous reviewer of R. J. White, *The Political Thought of Samuel Taylor Cole-ridge*, in the *Times Literary Supplement*, 9 July 1938, p. 464.

[3] *Church and State*, pp. 24–25 n. The distinction had first been made in *The Friend*, F., p. 55 n.

forces. There are those working for permanence, which he identifies with the landed interest; and those working for progression, identified with the commercial interest.[1] Both depend on 'a continuing and progressive civilization'. By civilization is not meant the varnish of sophistication, but a form of culture that will establish a 'harmonious development of those qualities and faculties that characterize our humanity'. It is the function of the third estate of the realm, the National Church, to provide this necessary basis, for as Coleridge reminds his readers, 'we must be men in order to be citizens'.

In defining what duties the State has a right to expect from the National Church, Coleridge comes dangerously near to asserting that its function is simply to inculcate habits of obedience towards the State. He insists that its instructions 'should be fitted to diffuse throughout the people legality'. When, however, he speaks of its task of instilling 'civility' in the people, a consideration of the historical context might suggest that the vast majority of readers would have interpreted this as meaning the instilling of habits of 'docility'. It is surely one thing to lay down the general principle that the effect of the Christian religion on individuals is to make them more fit to become responsible members of society, acknowledging the reciprocal nature of rights and duties—and this was the position Coleridge took up in *Conciones ad Populum*—it is quite another to assign to the National Church the specific duty of teaching a code of conduct which suited the convenience of those who wielded the power of the State. It is fairly certain that Coleridge did not intend the National Church to play so subservient a role, but two deductions could be drawn from the stress he placed on the social functions of the Church: one was that made by Maurice and the Christian Socialists, who considered that the Church must take practical steps to realize the Kingdom of Heaven on earth;[2] the other, and the more frequently made deduction, was that the

---

[1] John Stuart Mill dismissed the distinction with the phrase 'plausible and seductive'. *Representative Government*, World's Classics ed., *On Liberty*, pp. 158–9. Nevertheless, the reading of *Church and State* helped him to clarify his ideas on the subject. See the whole of chap. ii of Mill's work.

[2] For F. D. Maurice's acknowledgement of his debt to Coleridge see the dedication to *The Kingdom of Christ*. Part of the dedication is quoted in B. Willey, *Nineteenth Century Studies*, 1949, p. 3. The end is quoted in L. E. Elliott-Binns, *Religion in the Victorian Era*, 2nd ed., p. 250. The influence is minimized by Professor Feiling in *Social and Political Ideas of the Age of Reaction and Reconstruction*, ed. F. J. C. Hearnshaw, p. 72.

Church was most fitly employed in maintaining habits of sobriety, industry, and obedience in the lower orders. Among contemporaries Crabb Robinson noted the ambiguity. 'He exposes himself to the charge of being desirous to appear more of a Tory than he really is, leaving an opening to back out when assailed by his Liberal friends', he declared. To the latter he could always explain that the present subordination of Church to State was no necessary part of the idea. Robinson complained that in his enthusiasm for tracing the 'idea' of a National Church Coleridge did not 'stay to enquire whether the actual Church be according to the idea'.[1]

Coleridge's conception of the purely educational and cultural role of the National Church is not open to the same objection. In describing this role he uses the word 'clerisy', but he does not insist that all who would comprise this learned class should necessarily be members of the National Church. The objects and final intention of the clerisy were:

to preserve the stores and to guard the treasures of past civilization, and thus to bind the present with the past; to perfect and add to the same, and thus to connect the present with the future; but especially to diffuse through the whole community and to every native entitled to its laws and rights that quantity and quality of knowledge which was indispensable both for the understanding of those rights, and for the performance of the duties correspondent.[2]

In the whole discussion of the system by which the forces working for permanence and progress are represented in Parliament, Coleridge moves uneasily between the 'idea' of a system of representation and its actual embodiment in the unreformed Parliament of his own day. His uneasiness on the subject is evident in his insistence that he was 'not giving an historical account of the legislative body'. To draw attention to the end for which a representative system existed was, in theory, to place his reader in a position to measure contemporary practice according to an immutable standard. In practice, Coleridge presented an account that had the disadvantage of being neither ideal nor historical and which bore little relation to existing conditions. The fatally easy transition from an account of the 'idea' of a representative system to a generalization based on British constitutional development is

---

[1] *Henry Crabb Robinson on Books and Writers*, ed. E. J. Morley, i. 400.
[2] *Church and State*, p. 47.

well illustrated in the passage in which he declared that by the very 'nature of things common to every civilised country, *at all events by the course of events in this country*',[1] the landed interest was divided into Major and Minor Barons. Considered as an attempt to formulate a picture of the 'idea' of a representative system it is a failure, since it was only applicable to a country whose constitutional development had been similar to that of England; and even when applied to the country of its origin, it provided no means of distinguishing between accidental blemishes that resulted from ordinary human fallibility and radical defects in the system.

In his treatment of the balance of constitutional forces in the two *Lay Sermons*, Coleridge had been mainly concerned with illustrating the excessive power wielded by the commercial classes and the incursion of the commercial spirit into the sphere of the landed interest. In considering the relationship of the balance of constitutional forces in relation to the existing system of representation in *Church and State*, he pointed out that the ratio of voters did not correspond to the actual division of interests within the country. In particular, he held that the large landowners, the Major Barons, had changed the original balance in their own favour at the expense of the Minor Barons and commercial interest, by buying up many of the boroughs. With a certain unwarranted degree of complacency, however, he asserted that an adequate counterbalance had developed through the operation of new forces. These he listed as being: 'Roads, canals, machinery, the press, the periodical and daily press, the might of public opinion, the consequent increasing desire of popularity among public men and functionaries of every description, and the increasing necessity of public character, as the means or condition of political influence.' This complacent attitude was the direct outcome of Coleridge's general thesis that in any nation there were always two antithetic forces at work; the force that was brought within organized and constitutional channels and what he called 'the free and permeative life and energy of the nation'.[2] The latter, he believed, was constantly being changed into the former for the good of the State, but it was impossible to define what the exact relationship should be; all one could do was to refer to the lessons of history and learn how the excess of the one or the other had led to the decay of the State. The excessive permeative energy of the democratic city-state

---

[1] Ibid., p. 28. The italics are mine. [2] Ibid., p. 90.

had led to its destruction, while, on the other hand, it was the inflexible State institutions of Venice that had brought about its decay.[1]

The practical application of the thesis that the permeative energy in a nation is always seeking to find expression through institutions was only partially worked out in relation to the contemporary scene. The central problem with which Coleridge was faced and which he never satisfactorily solved was how the new economic and social interests could be represented in Parliament without the necessity of any radical reform. In *Church and State* he deals with three ways in which the problem arose: claims made on behalf of the classes of men who had acquired education and much else besides but who had not acquired property; claims from those who had in fact newly acquired property; and the general dissatisfaction that arose from the obvious disproportion between the balance of forces in the nation and the ratio of representation in Parliament. He firmly denied the propriety of giving 'direct political power to personal force and influence, whether physical or intellectual, existing in classes or aggregates of individuals, without those fixed or tangible possessions, freehold, copyhold, or leasehold, in land, house or stock'.[2] But he nevertheless asserted that means must be found for enabling men of intellectual distinction to acquire property, for he believed that only in that way would the intellectual powers be accompanied by the necessary 'moral qualities of prudence, industry, and self-control'. The solution of this aspect of the problem obviously implies the possibility of the free circulation of property, but nowhere in his political writings does Coleridge say how this was to operate in his own society. In speaking of the 'radical fibres of a collective and registrable property, by which the citizen inheres in and belongs to the commonwealth, as a constituent part either of the Proprietage, or of the Nationalty',[3] he makes it clear that all property ultimately belongs to the State. The grant of property to an individual by the State, which is only held in trust, establishes an identity of interest between the two. The logical deduction to make from this position would seem to be that the greater the number of people able to feel this identity of interest the better for the State. But in fact Coleridge regards the main function of government as the protec-

---

[1] *Church and State*, pp. 91–92.   [2] Ibid., p. 92.
[3] Ibid., p. 93.

tion of already established property and the right of lineal inheritance.

In theory, then, the right of the individual to acquire property and therefore a share in the government of the country is accepted. What of the citizen who has acquired a sufficient theoretical property qualification but who is nevertheless debarred from enjoying the franchise under pretence of impediments that do not directly or essentially affect the character of individuals as citizens, or disqualify for the performance of civic duties?[1] To such exclusion—and presumably Coleridge mainly had in mind the various acts restricting the civic rights of Dissenters and Catholics—he was resolutely opposed. The excommunication of these classes, he held, endangered the security and impoverished the welfare of the country. Upon the third issue, the existence of a 'gross incorrespondency' between the ratio of representation and the comparative strength and importance of interests within the country, little is said. Elsewhere Coleridge made it clear that his solution to the problem of parliamentary reform was to amend the law in conformity with the direction in which actual practice had already moved, in other words, towards a system which openly admitted and gave direct expression to the idea of indirect representation. Any move towards a 'rigidly territorial plan of representation' was interpreted as converting a system based on the principle of representation of interests to one of delegation from the people; and he believed that such a delegation from their passions and wishes would prove 'a rope of sand'.[2] During the last few years of his life he insisted that he was not opposed to the principle or necessity of reform, but only to Grey's Reform Bill and the arguments advanced by its advocates. He declared that he 'could not discover a ray of principle in the government plan'.[3] In particular the basing of the franchise on such an 'unjustifiable line of political empiricism as £10 householders', seemed to be an implicit denial of the 'indissoluble blending and interfusion' of individuals in society and demonstrated the impossibility of dividing a nation into classes for the convenience of a particular system of representation. He accused those who favoured the Bill of having 'actualized for a moment a wish, a fear, a passion, but not an idea'.[4]

---

[1] Ibid., p. 94.
[2] *Table Talk*, 25 June 1831, T.T., p. 120. See also p. 143.
[3] 20 Mar. 1831, T.T., pp. 117–18.
[4] 5 Apr. 1832, T.T., p. 156.

The charge might justifiably have been directed against the accuser, whose opposition was ultimately based as much on fear of unleashing unknown powers as upon principle.

In addition to considering the composition of Parliament Coleridge was obliged to discuss the relationship between Parliament and King, since the last section of *Church and State* was an attempt to elucidate the position of the King and his responsibilities towards the National Church. To clarify this relation, he drew a distinction between two further antithetical constitutional forces, between the potential power that lies dormant and inactive until needed on some special occasion and the actual power which is always in constitutional operation, whether it be permeative in action or canalized within recognized institutions. The power which resided in the person of the King was potential in kind, he declared, and was only to be called into action on rare occasions. Wisely, in his opinion, the protection of the Church had been entrusted to the King. That it was a sacred trust was officially recognized in the Coronation Oath. Should Parliament do anything therefore to endanger the safety of the Church it became the King's duty to use his constitutional veto. It might be thought that Coleridge was here evolving a theory of the constitution to suit the circumstances arising out of the problem of Catholic Emancipation, but this was not so; all the evidence of his published political writings and of the jottings in the Notebooks proves that he had the utmost horror for any doctrine concerning the omnipotence of Parliament. Wherever he discussed the constitutional balance between Crown and Parliament he laid special emphasis on the importance of the Crown. In one Notebook jotting he refers to the King as 'the natural Magnet' of society,[1] in another he asks how it is possible to place with safety 'the revenues of this Country, its Functionaries, Armies, Fleets & Colonies in any other Man or Men',[2] and in a letter to William Sotheby in 1831 he declared that though neither Whig nor Tory he was enough of the latter to honour the King, 'as ordained of God—i.e. as no Reflection or Derivative from the (pretended) Sovereignty of the *People*, but as the lawful Representative, the consecrated Symbol of the Unity and Majesty of the *Nation*'.[3] Though these and other

---

[1] *Notebook No. 3 1/2*, B.M. Add. MSS. 47499, ff. 104-5.
[2] *Notebook No. 18*, B.M. 47515, f. 121.
[3] 3 June 1831, *U.L.* ii. 435.

passages prove that he thought the King all-important, they do not do much to establish his exact constitutional function. In one passage in a Notebook he appears to consider the function of the King in terms that would fit the actual practice of George III.[1] Discussing the machinery of government, he writes:

There must be a cabinet, with *power* in proportion—nay even that will not be enough—there must be a unit—a king—not a leaden weight —not a personification—but a *person*, whose own interests and pre-judices may at once decide where indecision would be a worse evil— a mistake—this latter point is the most delicate and most important of all.[2]

On the other hand, the chief charge that he brought against the Whigs was that they were unable to think of the function of the Crown except in terms of the man. 'The Whig habit of Thought and Feeling is to know the Man only in the King, that of the Tory to find the King in the Man'; thus he expressed the charge in a Notebook jotting.[3] He himself alternated between the extremes of viewing the King either as an indefinable constitutional force de-riving its power and wisdom from God or as a man exerting a form of personal rule through the medium of his ministers. But, whatever view he put forward at any time, it always implied the right of the King to limit the power of Parliament.

At least one of the reasons for not wishing to allow the omni-potence of Parliament was his acute awareness of the 'inherent evils of a deliberative body'. The worst of these evils was the tendency on the part of all members of Parliament to speak for immediate effect, prompted by the knowledge that power and popularity depended on success in debate, not primarily on the intrinsic value or wisdom of the policy being advocated. During the composition of *The Friend*, he recorded the follow-ing observation in a Notebook. 'The injurious effect of the House of Commons, constituted as it is, giving such an unnatural advantage to such ability, as is there displayed, that it becomes in the public feeling a kind of *maximum*, while the influences of that House are such as woefully to lower great and extra-ordinary Talents in the very few men who possess them.'[4] He

[1] See R. Pares, *King George III and the Politicians*, 1953, passim.
[2] *Notebook No. 18*, B.M. 47515, f. 19*v*.
[3] *Notebook No. 39*, B.M. Add. MSS. 47534, f. 7*v*.
[4] *Notebook No. 21*, B.M. Add. MSS. 47518, f. 26.

mentioned Burke as an example, and he noted its effect on Pitt in his justly famous character study. Nevertheless, while recognizing this defect, Coleridge believed that the debates in the House of Commons had 'educated the people of England in the science of politics more widely and fundamentally than all the works of all our writers'.[1] In *The Watchman* he included reports from previous sessions as well as from those in progress; and his own attempts at parliamentary reporting indicate that he set the very highest standards for this particular exercise of literary talent. He believed that if the policies of the political parties were to correspond with 'the three main differences compatible with the same general view of the constitution' such reporting would 'tend to enlighten the Nation at large'.[2] But the existence of a permanent Opposition Party had, he believed, produced a preponderance of evil. In accusing it of having helped to keep alive vulgar errors and of allowing itself to be dominated by 'partial views' and 'mischievous prejudices', he probably had in mind what he called elsewhere the fatal error of Fox 'in persisting, after the first three years of the French Revolution, when every shadow of freedom in France had vanished, in eulogizing the men and measures of that shallow-hearted people'.[3] But the Opposition had adopted equally partial views on the cause of the Spanish people and on the Queen's trial in 1820; and Coleridge had reprobated their conduct on both occasions. In 1823 he complained that in the recent past the Whig party 'became the absolute abettors of Bonapartean invasion of Spain'.[4] He considered the Queen's trial an 'atrocious affair',[5] sympathized with the Queen, distrusted her supporters, particularly Brougham, and recognized that the Whigs were seeking to make party capital out of the affair. He offered the editor of the *Eclectic Review* a pamphlet or essay on the subject; a rough draft of which exists in manuscript.[6] The partisan approach had deleterious effects on both Government and Opposition. 'The weightiest and soundest arguments occur to neither parties', lamented Coleridge.[7] With the passing of Grey's Reform Bill he appeared to lose all faith in Parliament and he heralded this event as marking the final and complete 'despotism of Parliament',[8] declaring that from

---

[1] *E.O.T.* ii. 337 and ii. 635.   [2] *Notebook No. 39*, B.M. 47534, f. 7*v*.
[3] *Table Talk*, 28 Apr. 1823, *T.T.*, p. 27.   [4] Ibid.   [5] Allsop, ii. 32.
[6] Allsop, i. 128–9. For rough draft see B.M. Egerton MSS. 2800, ff. 133–4.
[7] *Notebook No. 39*, B.M. Add. MSS. 47534, f. 29*v*.
[8] *Notebook No. 50*, B.M. Add. MSS. 46545, f. 9*v*. Date of entry, 22 Apr. 1831.

henceforth he had no country. 'I will never consent to be anything but an Englishman—and England is—no more!'[1]

In 1832 it was inevitable that Coleridge should have felt that he had lived and written in vain. He could not be expected to be able to foresee that his last political work, *On the Constitution of the Church and State*, would leave a permanent mark on the thought of the nineteenth century, that slowly and working in an unobtrusive fashion it would lead men to re-examine the function of the Established Church in the light of its historical development and would reawaken a sense of social responsibility in the Whig and Tory parties.[2] It was the only one of his works that achieved anything like a popular success. A second edition appeared in the same year as the first and this was followed by a third edition nine years later. Thomas Arnold complained that it was 'historically faulty', but was nevertheless profoundly influenced by the idea it presented of a Christian society.[3] In Arnold, it has been asserted, 'the Coleridgean "ideas" became a programme of action'.[4] Gladstone owed much to it in his first significant contribution to the controversies of the time, *The State in its Relation with the Church*. He described Coleridge's work as 'alike beautiful and profound'.[5] Its influence upon Maurice and the Christian Socialists has already been glanced at, but it had an equally important effect on John Stuart Mill; positive in helping him to draw up a plan for a reformed church establishment in 1831,[6] largely negative in the second chapter of *Representative Government* where he denied the validity of Coleridge's analysis of the two main constitutional forces, those working for permanence and those for progression. Such varied and distinguished attention was accorded *Church and State* for three main reasons. It contained 'seminal' ideas which were expressed with force and unusual clarity; it possessed some, though by no means all, the attributes of a technical treatise;[7] and it dealt with an

---

[1] *Notebook No. 50*, ff. 9v–10.

[2] B. Willey, *Nineteenth Century Studies*, chap. 1 and passim. Also D. C. Somervell, *English Thought in the Nineteenth Century*, 1950 ed., pp. 66–67. C. R. Sanders, *Coleridge and the Broad Church Movement*, Duke University Press, 1942, passim.

[3] A. P. Stanley, *The Life and Correspondence of Thomas Arnold*, 1881, ii. 165.

[4] B. Willey, op. cit., p. 53.

[5] J. Morley, *The Life of William Ewart Gladstone*, 1905 ed., i. 167.

[6] For influence of the 'clerisy' see letter to Sterling, 22 Oct. 1831, *Letters of J. S. Mill*, ed. H. Elliot. Karl Britton remarks that 'there was too much of Comte and too little of Coleridge'. *John Stuart Mill*, 1953, Pelican ed., p. 110.

[7] This is more true of the second and subsequent editions than the first. In the

aspect of the political life of England that was engaging the minds of all thinking men. F. D. Maurice gave it as his opinion that 'no work recently published had really exercised a more decided influence over the thoughts and feelings of men who ultimately rule the mass of mankind'.[1] And that it still possesses the power may be seen in the writings of William Temple, and in T. S. Eliot's *The Idea of a Christian Society.*

first the division of the material is very Coleridgean—Paragraph the First, Paragraph the Second—but in subsequent editions it is divided into well-arranged chapters.

[1] *Kingdom of Christ*, iii. 2. Quoted in the Preface to *Church and State* by H. N. Coleridge, 1839, p. xi.

CHAPTER VI

CONCLUSION

WE need to ask three questions before we can assess the
ultimate importance of a critic. Has what he says intrinsic
value? Is he capable of communicating his insight to
others? Does he succeed in convincing the members of the public
of the validity and importance of his critique of society so that they
will be persuaded to put his ideas into practice? As a critic of
social and political problems Coleridge succeeds in satisfying only
the first requirement. The intrinsic value of his political thought is
undeniably great. But he never fully solved the problem of communicating these intrinsically valuable ideas to others, nor did he
succeed in persuading them to apply his principles in a practical
manner to the controversies of the day. His failure in the last two
spheres can be attributed to the innate difficulty of the task he set
himself; to the literary and political conditions of his age, including the state of the Press and the character of the reading public;
and, of course, to personal causes.

Coleridge's political writings cover an extraordinarily wide range
of topics. In some form he commented on all the important issues
of foreign, colonial, and domestic policy. Such catholicity, however, necessarily meant that on many subjects he wrote with little
or no specialist knowledge and often without any great enthusiasm. This is particularly true of his writing on agricultural
problems and controversies connected with currency. But on the
major issues of the day he had something vital to say. His criticism
of British foreign policy illustrates a remarkable grasp of the subject. Here his wide reading of history, not for the facts but for the
principles illustrated, stood him in good stead and enabled him to
see Britain's position in relation to the rest of Europe and the New
World. After his early and somewhat uncritical praise of France,
which led in the Bristol lectures to a perverse desire to prove that
all the evils in the world could be attributed to England's war
with France, he recognized that the rise of Napoleon constituted
a threat to the security of Europe, and that Britain must use all her
resources to unite the other countries in common opposition to

French ambition. Coleridge unlike Pitt, who was 'waging a nine-teenth-century war on eighteenth-century methods',[1] understood the importance of both strategy and ideology. In discussing Britain's foreign policy in the Mediterranean he placed the main emphasis on questions of strategy, emphasizing the importance of Malta and Egypt; while in his writings on the Peninsular Campaign the whole emphasis was thrown on the importance of ideology. He saw that the only spirit that could oppose the tarnished ideals of the French Revolution was the spirit of national independence. The message of Burke that it was impossible 'to do anything without raising a Spirit (I mean a National Spirit) with all the energy and much of the conduct of a Party Spirit' was magnificently restated in Coleridge's writings on Spanish affairs.[2] On whatever aspect of foreign policy he touched the special regard he showed for principles distinguishes his work from his contemporaries. For example, he condemned Canning for defending the seizure of the Danish fleet on grounds of expedience. 'I never can think that statesman a great man', he declared, 'who, to defend a measure will assert—not once but repeatedly—that state-policy can not and ought not to be always regulated by morality.'[3] Mere expedience must never be allowed to guide British foreign policy.

There is reason to believe that Coleridge also devoted much time to considering Britain's colonial policy, though the space given to this aspect of politics in his published works is relatively small. The two primary documents for understanding his general attitude exist only in manuscript; these are extensive notes on Brougham's *Colonial Policy of the European Powers*, which were obviously made in preparation for a review which never appeared, and the State paper prepared for Sir Alexander Ball called *Observations on Egypt*.[4] How advanced his views were for his age may be seen in the following passage from the notes on Brougham's work. 'I am deeply convinced, that as soon as a Colony can maintain itself, the Mother Country ought to make it an equal, true and integral part of herself—and give to it all the privileges, it could enjoy as an independent state.—That we do not do so arises entirely from mistaken views on the Subject of Revenue.'[5] He was

---

[1] A. Cobban, *Edmund Burke and the Revolt against the Eighteenth Century*, p. 129.
[2] Ibid.
[3] *U.L.* i. 451. See also ii. 24, and *The Friend* essay *On the Law of Nations*.
[4] B.M. Egerton MSS. 2800, ff. 118–21.   [5] Ibid., ff. 106–8.

an enthusiastic believer in Britain's imperialistic mission. 'Coloni-zation is not only a manifest expedient for, but an imperative duty on, Great Britain. God seems to hold out his finger to us over the sea', he declared in 1833, but he insisted that it should be a national colonization, and that it should be one of hope and not of despair 'such as we have alone encouraged and affected for the last fifty years'.[1]

In his discussion of domestic issues his characteristic independ-ence and subtlety of mind are much in evidence. On most issues, however, his analysis was too complex and paradoxical to make a ready appeal. In his writings on the radical and reform movement at home, he stressed the danger involved in the rapid growth of the lower and middle-class political associations, because he feared any kind of *imperium in imperio*. Nevertheless, he was resolutely opposed to the savage repressive policy inaugurated by Pitt and imitated by his successors, though it must be admitted that he raised no voice of protest against the Six Acts of 1819. He regarded the existence of a responsible and independent Press as the greatest single safeguard for the preservation of individual freedom and he saw that it had a valuable function to perform in educating the political consciousness of the nation. But he recognized that the worst enemies of the people were those who employed this organ to mislead the people and keep them ignorant of their ignorance and was well aware of the dangers of 'a rank unweeded press'. He bitterly opposed Grey's first Reform Bill, and yet was not opposed to the idea of parliamentary reform. He regarded the new science of political economy as 'solemn humbug' and yet in his own criticism of society he showed remarkable understanding of the effect of large-scale economic changes on the social and political structure of the country. In view of these apparent inconsistencies and paradoxical attitudes it is not surprising to find that though his views on domestic problems were of great intrinsic value they were generally misunderstood. Nor is it to be wondered at that what he wrote about contemporary problems was silently ignored by the two main political parties. So complex an analysis could not be made to fit the party programme.

The most valuable ideas that Coleridge had to communicate to his contemporaries were not, in fact, such as would provide simple solutions to specific problems; they were ideas relating to a new

[1] 4 May 1833, *T.T.*, p. 216.

kind of political and social consciousness, the development of which would slowly but inevitably lead to a solution of these problems. This marks the main difference between Coleridge and, to use his own phrase, the 'catechistic Bentham'.[1] For Coleridge the structure of society was a direct reflection of man's present political consciousness and could only be changed by bringing about a revolution in the mind of man; while for Bentham the social and political world was an intricate mechanism which could be brought to perfection by adroit and calculated manipulation; and in an age in which the mechanical and inventive genius of man was swiftly and visibly transforming the physical world, it was Bentham's message that made the stronger impression. Two examples must suffice to illustrate the potential as opposed to the actual value of Coleridge's criticism. Had he ever succeeded in making his contemporaries accept 'the sacred principle' which he was never tired of alluding to, 'that a person can never become a thing, nor be treated as such without wrong', the age would have been spared much of the 'enlightened' and calculated cruelty that accompanied the rapid growth of the factory system. The second example concerns the fate of the agricultural not the industrial workers. If his message that the ownership of property was a sacred trust involving solemn duties towards one's dependants had ever reached a sufficient number of the landed gentry, the whole pattern of agricultural life in the nineteenth century might have been transformed. These two examples and those already sufficiently emphasized in earlier chapters establish the fact that Coleridge had something of vital importance to say on the social and political problems of his day.

Then why did he fail to communicate these valuable truths to those most concerned? To begin with it is important to recognize, as Coleridge himself recognized, that the nature of his criticism made the task of communication one of extreme difficulty. A Notebook jotting made in connexion with the writing of *Church and State* illustrates very clearly the relationship between the innate complexity of his thought and the problem of communication.

Alas! I have to address Men who have never distinctly or consciously referred their opinions to Principles, much less traced the several steps of the ascent; and yet in order to produce any *effect*, to

---

[1] In a note on Jacobinism, Coleridge refers to the 'bran *new style* of the catechistic Bentham'. B.M. Egerton MSS. 2800, f. 140.

make any immediate and general impression, I must state such positions only and urge only those arguments, as the Reader or Hearer will immediately see the full force of and recognize as a previous judgement of his own. In short, I dare not pretend to inform, instruct, or guide. I must not call on him to repeat for [himself] a process of reflection which I have gone thro', tho' facilitated for him by laying before him the Facts, Documents and authorities, requisite for the grounds, proofs or illustrations of the Reasoning.[1]

This passage also illustrates how essential it was for Coleridge's purpose that the reader should pass through similar processes of reflection, for as he noted many years earlier during the composition of *The Friend*, 'the shortest *way* gives one the *knowledge* best, the longest way makes one more *knowing*'.[2] It was his firm conviction that men were 'made better, not only in consequence, but by the mode and in the process, of instruction'.[3] His method of political education involved the growth and development of political consciousness. In this respect his political writings bear a close resemblance to his religious and philosophical works, where in the very process of reading the mind is stretched on a Procrustean bed until it can accommodate the ideas in their entirety. To read Coleridge's prose works with understanding is to undertake a severe mental and spiritual exercise, and like all forms of exercise it develops and strengthens the organs employed. In any age there are only a few who are prepared to make the effort. Coleridge recognized this but was undismayed. 'The public, indeed, have given no heed', he declared, 'but if only ten minds have been awakened by my Writings the intensity of the Benefit may well compensate for the narrowness of extension.'[4]

Then, quite apart from the intrinsic difficulty of the ideas propounded and Coleridge's unwillingness to simplify them so that no effort on the part of the reader was required, his failure to reach a wide public may be attributed to the strange blend of philosophy, religion, and politics that appears in all his political works. In this respect, *The Friend*, *The Statesman's Manual*, and *Church and State* are typical products of his mind; in each, one is constantly being reminded that politics is a branch of moral philosophy and that

[1] Entry dated 23 Feb. 1829. *Notebook No. 38*, B.M. Add. MSS. 47533, ff. 25–25*v*.
[2] *Notebook No. 11*, B.M. Add. MSS. 47508, f. 33*v*.
[3] F., p. 61; *Lay Sermons*, p. 52.
[4] *Notebook No. 49*, B.M. Add. MSS. 47544, f. 14*v*.

neither can be divorced from a study of man's relationship with God. Admirable in theory as this broad and inclusive treatment may be, it is little calculated to appeal to the general reader. The appeal is further diminished by the fact that the moral philosophy and religious thought to which reference is made is not that which the reader has unconsciously inherited from the past but something quite new, involving a subtle distinction between reason and understanding, and necessitating the learning of a whole hierarchy of powers and faculties ascribed to man, to each of which is assigned a definite function and appropriate sphere of activity and yet all of which are in some mysterious fashion interrelated. Mr. R. J. White has written of 'the wondrous passages . . . on the Trinity of the soul, the philosophy of nature and the omnipresence of deity',[1] in the appendixes to *The Statesman's Manual*, but how many readers in the critical year of 1817, when England seemed on the eve of a terrible revolution, would have persevered in reading these long appendixes when they had already found that the work provided no very intelligible or practical advice on how the Bible might be used as 'the best guide to political skill and foresight'. This curious mixture of religion, philosophy, and politics, and the author's non-attachment to any known system in each, severely restricted the appeal of his works; and his refusal to associate himself closely with either of the two main political parties meant that what he wrote was received with suspicion by the members of each. Coleridge was no party man; he was certainly not 'the venerable monarch of conservatism' that he has recently been called.[2] Unattached to party throughout his life, he was nevertheless unable to acquiesce in the inevitable obloquy and comparative neglect with which such independence of mind is always met. In addition an almost perverse delight in analysing the faults of the various religious sects and political parties, an over-eager search for 'the misguided men who have enlisted under the banners of liberty',[3] which is to be found in the Bristol lectures, in *The Watchman*, and

---

[1] *Political Tracts of Wordsworth, Coleridge and Shelley*, ed. R. J. White, 1953, Introduction, p. xi.

[2] M. St. J. Packe, *The Life of John Stuart Mill*, 1954, p. 84. Cf. C. R. Sander's judgement: 'He was not conservative, in the sense of excluding all that was new; or radical, in the sense of excluding all that was old; but truly liberal, in the sense of persistently searching for truth whether it were old or new and of building the new on the foundation of all the old that was worth saving.' *Coleridge and the Broad Church Movement*, Duke University Press, 1942, p. 71.   [3] *E.O.T.*, p. 11.

in the *Lay Sermons*, must have made him more enemies than friends.

A serious psychological maladjustment towards his public can be detected in all Coleridge's political writings. The very valuable introductory section of *The Friend*, in which he examined with such rare insight the relationship between the writer and the public, only helps to emphasize his own failure to establish a satisfactory relationship. Throughout his life an awareness of the probable unpopularity of his ideas and a certain sense of conscious superiority over his readers made it impossible for him to address them as intellectual equals. The consciousness that he was in possession of truths denied to others produced the characteristic note of pontification which is evident in early and late works alike. It led to the creation of an air of mystery through the use of out of the way allusions, erudite quotations, unfamiliar words, and technical terms; and to his paying a too 'willing homage to the Illustrious Obscure'.[1] It led also to the fairly frequent examples of proud self-defence against attacks that had not been and never were to be delivered. In his early life he was grossly misunderstood by his clerical High Tory relations, particularly by his brother George, and he was often driven to writing long letters to explain and justify his views. There is, in fact, a remarkable similarity between the tone adopted by Coleridge when addressing his brother on the subject of politics and the tone he customarily maintained in his later works when speaking of his Jacobinical youth. The desire to make his views appear 'respectable' had thus an interesting origin in the nature of his early family relationships.[2] In politics the defensive attitude became habitual. An additional handicap was his almost pathological fear of popularity. As long as he was sure that his words were unlikely to be fully understood he could convince himself that they contained invaluable truths. The use of a less complex style might well have attracted more readers; it would certainly have exposed him to the embarrassment of being generally understood; with what beneficial results it is perhaps idle to speculate.

[1] The phrase comes from Hazlitt's malicious anticipatory review of *The Statesman's Manual* in the *Examiner*, see *Collected Works*, ed. P. P. Howe, vol. vii, p. 116.

[2] The most characteristic of these letters is also the best known, namely the long letter of Mar. 1798 in which he announced that he had snapped his 'squeaking baby-trumpet of Sedition'. *C.L.* i. 397. But see also the letters that followed his escape from the Army.

Coleridge's lack of success in communicating his ideas to others cannot be attributed to an unwillingness to experiment with a variety of forms. He delivered political lectures, wrote political poetry, published political pamphlets, two of which were meant to appeal to the critical and well-informed circles of the House of Commons, he made two unsuccessful ventures into private journalism, he acted as a leader writer on the *Morning Post*, and he wrote a treatise on a recognized branch of political theory. There is little evidence to suggest, however, that he made or was capable of making any significant modifications in his attitude towards each new public or of adapting his style to suit the various media. The lectures delivered at Bristol, to judge from their printed form, demanded an excessive degree of thought and attention and a familiarity with the speakers unspoken assumptions utterly incompatible with public delivery. The essays in *The Watchman*, with the exception of the essay on slavery and one or two of the book-reviews, served the needs of self-expression rather than that of communication. Only in the columns of the *Morning Post* did Coleridge prove himself capable of adapting his style and manner of delivery to the subject under discussion and the character of his public. On this occasion, however, he did not have to create the relationship between himself and his readers; it already largely existed, although it must be admitted that Coleridge taught the readers of the *Morning Post* to expect more frequent references to principle and political theory than they had been accustomed to find.

In his private journalism he had to create this all important relationship. The public of *The Watchman* and *The Friend* was heterogeneous; and Coleridge's account of his canvassing tour on behalf of the first indicates that his potential readers were not necessarily men to whom he found himself bound by bonds of mutual sympathy. The existence of a sympathetic relationship was essential for the full flowering of his genius. His best poetry was written during the period of intimacy with the Wordsworths at Nether Stowey, his most creative comments on politics, philosophy, religion, and literature were uttered spontaneously in convivial and congenial company; and when all the sources of human affection seemed denied, he retreated into the pages of his sole confidants, his Notebooks. Almost the only reason for founding a small private journal is the knowledge on the part of the editor that there exists a small public with tastes and interests in common whom he is capable of pleasing and is eager to serve, and with whom he is confident of establishing an intimate and sympathetic relationship. It is, one must admit, notoriously the resort of cranks. Although Coleridge recognized that he must appeal to the few, and in the case of the *Lay Sermons* clearly indicated the public he had in mind, he lacked the gifts necessary to build up an atmosphere of mutual confidence, nor did he possess the literary tact necessary to consolidate the ranks of the elect. He adopted the ambivalent position of proudly claiming to be a prophetic voice crying in the wilderness while at the same time angrily reproving the public for not heeding his message.

In Coleridge's failure to find a practical solution to the problem of communication lies the main explanation for his failure to fulfil the third requirement of a critic, that his writings should produce an immediate effect on the minds and behaviour of his readers. It is not the whole explanation. Certainly this failure limited the number of his readers, but if his writing had possessed the power of effecting a radical change in the thinking and conduct of a mere handful of public men and of moulding them into the 'abstract Idea' of a wise statesman, his words would have exerted an incalculable influence on the whole nation. Here we come to a most serious defect in Coleridge's equipment as a political critic; he failed to recognize the importance of political and legislative action. Consequently he wrote little that was immediately applicable to the contemporary scene. Though he was right to insist that all great practical changes in society are ultimately the product of a change of heart, he assumed unjustifiably that once a reader accepted the truth of any of the general principles enunciated, he would be capable of seeing its relevance to the complex problems of the day and would be capable of doing what Coleridge confessed in his wiser moments was a most important and delicate task, that of discovering appropriate means for the achievement of the already agreed and defined end. In *The Friend* he admitted that it was 'the character of the mass of mankind to seek for the attainment of their necessary ends by any means rather than the appointed ones'.[1] His own excessive caution in applying principles to specific cases and his unwillingness to follow out their implications very far should have acted as sufficient reminder of the

[1] *F.*, p. 33.

difficulty involved. It was unreasonable of Coleridge to expect his readers to be capable of doing what he himself shirked. To preach a brand of political evangelism and yet to fail to prescribe any rule of conduct or mode of action was equivalent to inculcating faith at the expense of good works. This is not wholly true of the Bristol lectures where at least the simple message 'Go, preach the GOSPEL to the poor' prescribed the form of action.[1] But how much more difficult it was for the readers of *The Friend* or the *Lay Sermons* to decide how to translate into action the new sense of social responsibility that these works might have aroused in their minds. An anonymous reviewer accused Coleridge of not having clinched his argument in *A Moral and Political Lecture*.[2] The same objection might be brought against much of his political writing. The argument is left in the air; the reader is aware of having been lifted to some lofty pinnacle from which he has surveyed, sometimes with blinding clarity, a vast tract of metaphysical and political speculation; but he longs to be set down on solid earth and to be provided with some practical advice on how to improve the world in which he lives. The 'smack of Hamlet',[3] which Coleridge acknowledged in his own character can be detected in his political writings. 'Constantly occupied with the world within, and abstracted from the world without', he fails to give the proper importance to any form of political action, personal, corporative, or legislative.[4]

There are, in fact, remarkable similarities between Coleridge's political and literary criticism. To begin with, almost the same variety of means were used to communicate his literary as his political views, but it must be admitted that he succeeded better in disseminating his literary ideas. Nevertheless, even here, his main influence on his contemporaries was through the spoken, not the written word; through public lectures, and chiefly through his conversation with Lamb, Hazlitt, De Quincey, and Wordsworth. In his written literary criticism and in his public lectures on Shakespeare and other writers, the same defensive attitude towards his public is to be found as when he addressed his readers on politics. In both cases it arose mainly from the knowledge that his canons

---

[1] *E.O.T.* i. 22. [2] *Critical Review*, Apr. 1795, vol. xiii, p. 455.
[3] 24 June 1827, *T.T.*, p. 47.
[4] *Literary Remains of Samuel Taylor Coleridge*, ed. H. N. Coleridge, 1836–9, 4 vols., ii. 205.

of criticism were not those of his age, that they depended on the acceptance of philosophical ideas that were little understood, and that their originality was suspect. The elaborate philosophical apparatus that is used to support the definition of Imagination in *Biographia Literaria* might be compared with the equally elaborate philosophical appendixes in *The Statesman's Manual*. Both are equally forbidding and both to the uninitiated savour of a species of metaphysical legerdemain. Love of digression is common to both forms of criticism. Of his lecture on *Romeo and Juliet* Crabb Robinson remarked that it was delivered 'in the character of the Nurse'; the same might be said of some of his political utterances. Characteristic of both literary and political criticism is the long-delayed approach to the subject. The promise to define the Imagination in chapter iv of *Biographia Literaria* is not fulfilled until the thirteenth chapter and then only partially, while in *Church and State* the necessary security for any kind of Catholic Emancipation, which is referred to obliquely at the beginning, is not satisfactorily explained until the end. There is the same frequent reference to the author's life, the same allusions to little-known writers, the same air of mystery, the same esoteric use of language. But whereas Coleridge's linguistic innovations made an invaluable contribution to the vocabulary of technical literary terms, his contributions to the language of political theory were far less important.[1] No one has followed Coleridge in using the terms *Propriety* and *Nationalty* to differentiate between property which is privately held and that which is set aside for the nation, to be enjoyed by the National Church. Only the word *clerisy* has achieved any currency outside the critical works dealing specifically with Coleridge. Nevertheless, his semantic sense served him well in other ways in his political writings; it helped on many occasions to demonstrate the paucity of his opponents' arguments and to show that many questions were fundamentally questions of terminology and logomachy. It is unfortunate that in his own search for precision he should so often have created ambiguity and not clarity.

The literary and political criticism spring from a single source, the desire to demonstrate the god-like faculties with which man is

---

[1] For his contribution to literary criticism see J. Isaacs, 'Coleridge's Critical Terminology', *Essays and Studies*, xxi. 86–104. Julius Hare valued highly Coleridge's enrichment of the vocabulary of philosophy. *Guesses at Truth*, by Two Brothers, 1871 ed., pp. 235–6.

endowed, to illustrate the wholeness of human experience and to formulate the laws which constitute our being as moral agents, sensitive and artistic souls and as citizens of a State. He wished to show ' "Quid sumus, et quidnam victuri gignimur"—What our faculties are & what they are capable of becoming'.[1] A parallel description of the right subordination of the human faculties is found in each sphere of criticism and for understanding a great deal of the political thought a thorough grasp of the Coleridgean process of desynonymising is necessary. The two most important examples of this process which are found in both literary and political works are the distinctions made between Reason and Understanding, and between Genius and Talent. The first became his most effective weapon for defeating the Rights of Man School of political thought. The second, however successful it may have proved in his literary criticism, showed itself to be less valuable in the sphere of politics, since it provided no criterion for measuring the good as opposed to the great. It is clear from all this that the worlds of literature and politics interpenetrate in Coleridge's works. Perhaps the most striking example of this is the connexion Coleridge establishes between Napoleon and Milton's Satan, both being seen as creatures who glory in the proud assertion of the self-sufficient human will.[2]

As a political critic Coleridge's psychological insight served him better than the natural speculative cast of his mind. Speculation all too easily became an end in itself, a fatal flaw in the armoury of a critic of society. His profound understanding of individual and group psychology which is everywhere in evidence in his works has, more than any other single quality, guaranteed their survival and constitutes their chief claim to attention today. This rare insight into the human mind and patterns of social behaviour, the 'System of our Nature' as he called it in an unpublished sermon in 1799,[3] enabled him to reject convincingly all political systems that either ignored 'the facts of the mind' or were built on a false psychology of man. It also enabled him to sketch the outline of a constitution which would satisfy the individual citizen's basic physical and spiritual needs. 'Fear, hope, and memory', he realized,

[1] Letter to George Coleridge, c. 10 Mar. 1798, C.L. i. 397.
[2] 'Notes on Milton, Remains of Lecture III of the Course of 1818.' *Lectures and Notes on Shakespere*, 1897, p. 524.
[3] *The original of a discourse Written for whom I neither know or care* . . ., 6 Oct. 1799. B.M. Add. MSS. 35343, f. 40.

'are the three great agents, both in the binding of a people to a government, and in the rousing of them to a revolution.'[1] The most important of these is hope. Since hope is an instinct of our nature and 'a natural instinct constitutes a right, as far as its gratification is compatible with the equal rights of others', he asserts that the State must hold out some promise to the citizen of bettering his condition or those of his children.[2] It must also do all within its powers to humanize and ennoble its citizens. Whatever tended to debase the nobility of human nature, whether it was slavery, the employment of young children in the cotton mills, or the acceptance on the part of the commercial classes of Malthusian economic doctrine, became an object of bitter attack. 'A Slave is a Person perverted into a Thing; Slavery, therefore, is not so properly a deviation from Justice, as an absolute subversion of all morality',[3] he noted, and longed to release all those who had fallen into the clutches of the nightmare Life-in-Death. Psychological insight, too, led him to distinguish sharply between political and all other forms of consciousness and to prescribe a different code of morality for the relation of the citizen to the State from that for the individual and his own conscience. A no less important product of his wide empirical study of human nature was his analysis of the characters of the leading politicians of the day. Although these studies may be deficient in historical objectivity, they possess a degree of animation and universal appeal that is rarely found in political journalism. The 'subtle-souled psychologist' is much in evidence.

Coleridge's works are not much read today except in extract. This is not because they are unreadable but largely because they are inaccessible. Much political wisdom is hidden away within them and they contain passages of excellent prose, but it must be admitted that they are not easy works to read as a whole. Nevertheless the contention that 'no writer of comparable gifts has expressed himself in so pitiable a style', is untenable.[4] It is a very personal style; it is also a very uneven one; and, as Humphry House remarked, he often manages 'to be clumsy and illuminating in the same

---

[1] *M.P.*, 2 Oct. 1802, *E.O.T.* ii. 511.   [2] *Church and State*, pp. 75–76.
[3] Egerton MSS. 2800, f. 111.
[4] Judgement entered by the anonymous reviewer in the *Times Literary Supplement* of R. J. White, *The Political Thought of Samuel Taylor Coleridge*. The review, 'Coleridge on Politics . . . A Frightened Philosopher', is an important contribution to the subject. *T.L.S.* 9 July 1938, p. 464.

sentence'.[1] But it is not for their literary style that we turn to works of political criticism. All those who are seeking political wisdom will find that the thought has dated remarkably little with the passage of time. The explanation for this may be found in Coleridge's own words. 'Whatever may have been the specific theme of my communications, and whether they related to criticism, politics, or religion, still principles, their subordination, their connexion, and their application, in all the divisions of our tastes, duties, rules of conduct and schemes of belief, have constituted my chapter of contents.'[2] While an excessive concern with the formulation of principles undoubtedly accounts for the comparative neglect with which his political works were treated by his contemporaries, it has saved them from complete neglect in subsequent ages. His political writings not only provide an illuminating critical commentary on the problems of his age; but they also contain imperishable political wisdom.

[1] H. House, *Coleridge, The Clark Lectures, 1951–2*, 1953, p. 23.
[2] *Lay Sermons*, p. 134.

THE AUTHORSHIP OF CERTAIN ARTICLES IN THE *MORNING POST*

WHEN Sara Coleridge made her collection of her father's miscellaneous political writings, *Essays on His Own Times*, she had in her possession a number of signed newspaper cuttings and access to an incomplete file of the *Morning Post*. A cautious editor, she divided the articles according to their source and printed all those for which no signed cuttings existed under the heading, 'Contributions to the *Morning Post*, judged chiefly from internal evidence, to be probably Mr. Coleridge's'. The authorship of this latter group has not been questioned; and it now seems that for a variety of causes, she failed to include other articles which, on the basis of internal and external evidence, might equally well be described as 'probably Mr. Coleridge's'. In an article in the *P.M.L.A.* Mrs. Glickfield drew the conclusion that Coleridge had probably begun contributing prose articles earlier than had been previously thought, and that six articles, five of them political, might now be added to the Coleridge canon.[1] To these I would add a further two items: a paragraph in the *Morning Post* for 22 January 1800 in the form of a 'Note by the Editor' answering a letter that had commented on one of Coleridge's essays on Ireland; and a long and important essay, 'Mr. Addington's Administration', which appeared on 22 March 1802. Dr. D. V. Erdman has added two further pieces, both on George Washington, and has published transcripts in the *Bulletin of the New York Public Library*.[2] For the convenience of the reader, I have printed all nine political pieces recently attributed to Coleridge in Appendix C and have provided a provisional check-list of Coleridge's prose contributions to the *Morning Post* in Appendix B.

The evidence for attributing the essays, 'On Peace', 6 November 1799, and the 'Advice to the Friends of Freedom', 12 December 1799, is extremely strong. The most important piece of external evidence is contained in a letter from Coleridge to Southey on 24 December 1799, in which he writes: 'For Stewart I write often his leading Paragraphs, on Secession, Peace, Essay on the new French Constitution, Advice to Friends of Freedom, Critiques on Sir W. Anderson's nose, Ode to Georgiana, D. of D. (horribly misprinted) christmas Carol, &c &c—'[3]

---

[1] 'Coleridge's Prose Contributions to the *Morning Post*', *P.M.L.A.* lxix, No. 3, June 1954, pp. 681–5.
[2] 'Coleridge on George Washington: Newly Discovered Essays of 1800', *B.N.Y.P.L.*, vol. lxi, no. 2, pp. 81–97.   [3] *C.L.* i. 552.

Here Coleridge specifically mentions writing the two essays in question. In addition, the Coleridge essay of 8 January 1800 contains a reference back to 'a long article On Peace', the remarks in which were claimed to have been prophetic. Sara knew of the existence of this essay 'On Peace' and quotes from it in a note at the end of the third volume of *Essays on His Own Times*,[1] but she does not attribute the authorship to her father, presumably because she assumed that he did not begin writing for the *Morning Post* until he received Stuart's offer and had arrived in London on 27 November 1799. But there is no reason why he should not have sent the article to Stuart before receiving any definite offer; and the degree of interest aroused by the article 'On Peace' may in fact have led Stuart to recognize Coleridge's potential powers as a political commentator for the first time and thus may have been instrumental in persuading him to employ him.[2]

The evidence for attributing the other articles is less conclusive. Mrs. Glickfield assigns the essay for 6 January 1800, also 'On Peace', to Coleridge on the grounds that Sara was misled by the date 6 January, which appeared on her cuttings of the official letters from Bonaparte, Talleyrand, and Grenville. They should have been dated 7 January. Sara probably assumed that as her cuttings were for 6 January no essay for this date would be found in her file of the *Morning Post*. Certainly the general theme of the essay of 6 January falls into place in the series on the subject of Bonaparte's 'Overtures for Peace'. It contains a characteristic defence of the author's prolixity; a proud assertion of his independence, together with a passage on 'the spirit of property', which is in complete harmony with Coleridge's views expressed in other articles on France.

The next item in chronological order, a brief editorial comment on the subject of Ireland, was discovered by the present writer in the process of working through the files of the *Morning Post*. On 22 January 1800 a letter to the editor, dated 15 January, singled out for special praise Coleridge's series of articles on the new French Constitution, the series on the Overtures for Peace, and the 'Advice to the Friends of Freedom'. The correspondent declared that he had found in these articles 'the abstract principles by which they ought to be appreciated and judged, canvassed with singular acuteness, developed with sound judgment, with enlightened and liberal philosophy, and discussed in correct, classical, and elegant language'. Explaining that the letter was not for publication—could it have been by Coleridge himself?—he went on to object to the phrase 'a wild and barbarous people' that had appeared in Coleridge's article on Ireland on 15 January 1800. Assum-

---

[1] *E.O.T.* i. 218 and iii. 1007–8.

[2] 'It provoked replies from two of the treasury journals to which someone, probably Stuart, replied briefly in the *Post* on 8 November.' Glickfield, op. cit., p. 682.

ing that the letter was genuine and not by Coleridge, what would have been more natural than for Stuart to hand over the composition of an editorial note to the author of the essay that had given offence? Three pieces of internal evidence suggest that Coleridge wrote the 'Note by the Editor'. Four lines on the effect of poverty and ignorance on man's nature are quoted from his poem, *The Dungeon*.[1] The use of the Latin tag *Adhuc sub lite est* at the end is characteristic and is used later in *The Friend*;[2] and the reference to reason as a ventriloquist, an unusual simile, is paralled by a much later reference to truth as a ventriloquist. Compare the sentence from the editorial note: 'If we could dissever from the idea the ludicrous association, we would personify REASON a ventriloquist; it is of inferior importance into what uncouth vessel she throws her voice, provided only that it is audible,' with the following from a letter written on 13 December 1819: '. . . from whatever dirty corner or straw moppet the ventriloquist Truth causes her words to proceed, I not only listen, but must bear witness that it is Truth talking.'[3] Belonging to the same year are two articles on George Washington in which Coleridge's interest in America found expression, the first a character study and eulogy on 27 January 1800, and the second a long essay on 25 March inspired by the publication of Washington's will. Dr. Erdman, in the article already referred to, has produced conclusive internal and external evidence for attributing both to Coleridge.

The other essays that may be assigned to him belong to a later period of his connexion with the *Morning Post*. For the two short periods of time spent in London during the winter of 1801–2, when he again wrote for Stuart, Sara prints only two articles. At the end of one of these, 'Reported Changes', 3 December 1801, a footnote was appended announcing: 'To-morrow, if possible, the subject will be continued, and the argument concluded, in an article on the Report that Mr Grey is to succeed Lord Hobart, as Secretary of State. In this article will be disclosed important facts.'[4] Sara Coleridge noted that the article did not appear. But, as Mrs. Glickfield has pointed out, an article doing precisely what had been promised appeared on 11 December 1801. She does not mention any internal evidence; this is in fact strong. The general tone and argument is much the same as in the article of 3 December, and phrases from the earlier article are taken up in the later one. For example, on 3 December, in making the point that if Fox remained in secession the way seemed open for a coalition, Coleridge wrote: 'It *seems* smooth, but it is treacherous and insecure, and, as it appear to us, leads by labyrinthine windings to the very den of the monster, from which we all wish to escape.' In the opening paragraph on 11 December is found the following: 'If they did coalesce without

---

[1] *The Dungeon*, ll. 6–9.   [2] *F.*, p. 30.   [3] Allsop, i. 20.   [4] *E.O.T.* ii. 477.

compelling any retraction, they would return by a maze to the den of the monster, from which they wished to escape.' Again the article of 3 December had issued a warning that grounds might again be fabricated for justifying an interference in existing civil liberties. 'They have a PRECEDENT', it was declared. On 11 December the writer distinguished between revolutionary and long-established governments, and pointed out that while in the former, measures are judged according to their immediate consequences, in the latter, 'it is the EXAMPLE, the PRECEDENT, which constitutes the importance, and determines the character of public measures, equally of private actions'. Such examples of repeated idea and phrase certainly suggest common authorship. In addition, the article includes a characteristic Coleridgean quotation, 'Heu! retulit praedas, non palman, victor ab hoste', and an anecdote relating Dr. Bentley's favourite remark to freshmen, which was the kind of story that would come more naturally to Coleridge, a Cambridge man, than to Stuart who had not been at either of the ancient English universities. A further article on 'The Reported Changes' appeared on 23 February 1802. It contained a reference back to the article of 11 December, 'we thought it our duty (now two months ago) to warn the opposition of the snare laid for them by the new circumstances of the times'. It ends with a Latin quotation and a promise to analyse the 'character and proceedings of the Minister' in the next day's issue.

Mrs. Glickfield notes that this was one of Coleridge's characteristic unfulfilled promises; but, in fact, an article entitled 'Mr. Addington's Administration' appeared on 22 March 1802. While it is true that Coleridge was at Keswick when the article was published, it contains nothing that could not have been written at the end of February before he left London. It could also have been written away from London, as so many of his newspaper essays were and sent to Stuart by post. The whole character study of Addington turns on Coleridge's favourite distinction between genius and talent; and the contrast made between Addington, the 'man of small talent' and Bonaparte, 'the greatest genius in the world, who is as restless, ambitious and artful, as he is superior in ability', resembles closely the contrast made between Pitt and Bonaparte in an earlier series of articles. The conventional ship of State image, introduced in the article of 23 February is once again taken up in this later article and developed with Coleridgean ingenuity. I think that there can be little doubt that this important essay on Addington and his Ministry was written by Coleridge.[1]

Near the end of her note Mrs. Glickfield draws attention to certain aspects of Sara Coleridge's work as an editor. She notes minor editorial

---

[1] For a fuller discussion of the evidence see my note 'Coleridge on Addington's Administration' in *M.L.R.* liv, 1959, pp. 69–72.

revision in the republication of the series of articles entitled 'Comparison of the Present State of France with that under Julius and Augustus Caesar', and also the difference between the ending of the last essay in this 'Comparison' as it appeared in the *Morning Post* and as it was reprinted in *Essays on His Own Times*. She also points out that damage to a sheet in Sara's file of the *Morning Post* made it necessary to supply by conjecture some of the missing words in the second letter 'To Mr. Fox', including the phrase 'upstart Corsican'.[1] Reference to a complete file reveals that the word was 'low born'. In noting this, however, Mrs. Glickfield failed to point out that the poet had already used the phrase 'upstart Corsican' in the first letter 'To Mr. Fox', and so the credit for coining this much quoted phrase must still be Coleridge's.[2]

[1] *E.O.T.* ii. 584.
[2] 'Did you utter one word of alarm at the atrocious ambition of the First Consul? One sentiment of pity or indignation at the iron despotism, under which this *upstart Corsican* had reduced forty millions of your fellow creatures.' Italics are mine. Ibid. ii. 566.

PROVISIONAL CHECK-LIST OF POLITICAL ARTICLES CONTRIBUTED TO THE *MORNING POST* BY COLERIDGE

NOTE

THIS provisional check-list serves a number of purposes. It indicates the total number of political articles in the *Morning Post* that have so far been attributed to Coleridge, by whom they have been attributed, their titles, or subject-matter where no titles exist, and their dates. The arrangement in one chronological sequence, with page reference to the three volumes of *Essays on His Own Times*, enables the reader to overcome the inconvenience of Sara Coleridge's arrangement of the essays in two separate chronological series. The articles can now be more easily read in their original order. Owing to the imperfect file from which she worked, Sara was unable to assign a definite date to a number of Coleridge's contributions. I have made good this deficiency and arranged the articles accordingly. Until Dr. Erdman's work is complete and a new edition of the *Morning Post* essays is available, this check-list should prove a useful supplement to the table of contents in the first two volumes of *Essays on His Own Times*.

ABBREVIATIONS AND SYMBOLS

*	Articles not assigned to a definite date by Sara Coleridge.
[ ]	Titles added in brackets to indicate the subject-matter of a piece without a title.
S.C.	Articles printed by Sara from signed newspaper cuttings.
S.C.?	Articles judged by Sara on internal grounds to be by Coleridge.
G.	Articles attributed to Coleridge by Mrs. Glickfield.
E.	Articles attributed to Coleridge by Dr. D. V. Erdman.
C.	Articles attributed to Coleridge by the present writer.

CHECK-LIST

Date	Title	Authority	E.O.T.	Appendix C
6 Nov. 1799	On Peace	G.		189
7 Dec. 1799	[French Constitution]	S.C.?	ii.330	
12 Dec. 1799	Advice to the Friends of Freedom	G.		193
24 Dec. 1799	[Fox's Secession]	S.C.?	ii. 338	

Date	Title	Authority	E.O.T.	Appendix C
26 Dec. 1799	[French Constitution]	S.C.	i. 179	
27 Dec. 1799	[French Constitution]	S.C.?	ii. 342	
31 Dec. 1799	On the French Constitution	S.C.	i. 183	
1 Jan. 1800	[Foreign Intelligence: Austria's defeat]	S.C.	i. 189	
2 Jan. 1800	[Peace Proposals]	S.C.	i. 193	
3 Jan. 1800	[Peace Proposals and French Constitution]	S.C.?	ii. 348	
4 Jan. 1800	[Peace Proposals]	S.C.	i. 199	
6 Jan. 1800	[Peace Proposals]	G.		195
7 Jan. 1800	[Lord Grenville's Note]	S.C.	i. 212	
8 Jan. 1800	On the late Negotiation	S.C.	i. 218	
10 Jan. 1800	[Foreign Intelligence]	S.C.	i. 227	
10 Jan. 1800	To the Editor of the *M.P.*	S.C.	i. 231	
10 Jan. 1800	Talleyrand . . . to Lord Grenville. [Metrical Letter]	S.C.	i. 233	
13 Jan. 1800	[Benjamin Constant]	S.C.?	ii. 253	
14 Jan. 1800	P[olitical Parties in France]	S.C.	i. 238	
15 Jan. 1800	[Irish Union]	S.C.?	ii. 357	
21 Jan. 1800	[2nd French Note]	S.C.	i. 242	
22 Jan. 1800	Note by the Editor	C.		198
22 Jan. 1800	*Lord Grenville's Note	S.C.	i. 261	
23 Jan. 1800	[Peace Proposals]	S.C.	i. 248	
25 Jan. 1800	The Overtures for Peace	S.C.	i. 253	
27 Jan. 1800	*[Irish Debates]	S.C.	i. 266	
27 Jan. 1800	[General Washington]	E.		
28 Jan. 1800	The Sovereignty of the People	S.C.?	ii. 363	199
30 Jan. 1800	[Peace Proposals]	S.C.?	ii. 361	
1 Feb. 1800	On the Late Debate	S.C.	i. 268	
3 Feb. 1800	Intercepted Correspondence	S.C.	i. 275	
6 Feb. 1800	Analysis or Skeleton of the Debate in the House of Commons, 3 Feb.	S.C.	i. 285	
6 Feb. 1800	[Reflections on the Debate]	S.C.?	ii. 367	
12 Feb. 1800	[Secession of Austria and Russia]	S.C.?	ii. 371	
17 Feb. 1800	A Second Essay on the Intercepted Correspondence	S.C.?	ii. 374	
18 Feb. 1800	[Report of Pitt's Speech of 17 Feb.]	S.C.	ii. 293	
22 Feb. 1800	[Peace with France]	S.C.	ii. 306	
26 Feb. 1800	[Income Tax]	S.C.	ii. 310	
27 Feb. 1800	[Prussia]	S.C.?	ii. 381	
11 March 1800	Bonaparte, in his relations to France	S.C.	ii. 313	

Date	Title	Authority	E.O.T.	Appendix C
13 March 1800	Bonaparte, in his relations to England	S.C.?	ii. 384	
15 March 1800	[Foreign Intelligence]	S.C.?	ii. 388	
17 March 1800	[France and Egypt]	S.C.?	ii. 391	
19 March 1800	[Character of Pitt]	S.C.	ii. 319	
25 March 1800	General Washington	E.		201
27 March 1800	Review of a Pamphlet by Arthur Young	S.C.	ii. 395	
21 April 1800	[Popularity of Bonaparte in France]	S.C.?	ii. 403	
6 August 1800	[War not a Crusade]	S.C.?	ii. 409	
3 Oct. 1800	Monopolists and Farmers	S.C.?	ii. 413	
6 Oct. 1800	Of farmers . . . introduction by Coleridge	S.C.?	ii. 438	
14 Oct. 1800	Letter to the Editor	S.C.?	ii. 451	
27 Nov. 1801	[Reported Changes]	S.C.?	ii. 456	
3 Dec. 1801	The Reported Changes	S.C.?	ii. 464	
11 Dec. 1801	The Reported Changes	G.		204
23 Feb. 1802	[Reported Changes]	G.		211
22 March 1802	Mr. Addington's Administration	C.		213
21 Sept. 1802	Comparison of the present state of France with that of Rome . . .	S.C.?	ii. 478	
25 Sept. 1802	Comparison No. 11	S.C.?	ii. 489	
2 Oct. 1802	Comparison No. 111	S.C.?	ii. 505	
5 Oct. 1802	Affairs of France	S.C.?	ii. 515	
9 Oct. 1802	[Monarchy in France]	S.C.?	ii. 522	
12 Oct. 1802	*On the Circumstances that . . . favour the return of the Bourbons	S.C.?	ii. 532	
14 Oct. 1802	Letter to the Editor	S.C.?	ii. 587	
21 Oct. 1802	*Once a Jacobin always a Jacobin	S.C.?	ii. 542	
4 Nov. 1802	To Mr. Fox	S.C.?	ii. 552	
9 Nov. 1802	Letter 11. To Mr. Fox	S.C.?	ii. 572	

ARTICLES NOT INCLUDED IN *ESSAYS ON HIS OWN TIMES*

Morning Post, 6 November 1799

ON PEACE

The report of a negotiation for peace is still circulated, without, as we think, the slightest foundation; and one of the principal Government Prints has had the candour and boldness to deny the fact, and reprobate the rumour. It would serve the purpose of Ministers, to keep up the drooping spirits of the country, by hopes of a speedy peace, at a moment when a crowd of calamities shew the people that the restoration of Monarchy in France, the real object of the war, is unattainable; it would be helping to keep them in power to delude the nation by hopes of peace at this time, by converting our misfortunes in Holland, and the reverses in Switzerland, into reasons for believing that an end will now be put to the war. While Ministers can excite hopes of peace with the Republic from our failures, and hopes of peace with a Monarchy from our victories, they will lull the people into a false security, and prevent every popular exertion which misfortune might stimulate, to discard from His MAJESTY's Councils men who have eternal war against the French Republic in their hearts, and with whom a peace, honourable to this country, never will be made by the Directory. We have seen, upon repeated occasions, with what pains Ministers have laboured to impress the public mind with an opinion that they were willing to make peace; they brought forward quibbling resolutions, that they would treat as soon as France was "able to maintain the accustomed relations of peace and amity with other Powers;" when such subterfuges would no longer answer the purpose, when the Government of France was less eligible than when those resolutions were passed, they sent Lord MALMESBURY to Paris, and again they sent him to Lisle, to sooth the public feeling. Whether or not Ministers were sincere in these overtures, has been a question; but it must be owned, that they made advances, particularly at Lisle, which might be stigmatised as mean and humiliating. France, on the contrary, betrayed the most shameless ambition, and treated our offers with a degree of insolence and contempt; so unreasonable was she in her demands, and so arrogant in her conduct, that the whole blame of the failure of those negotiations justly fell upon her, and Ministers received the unanimous, the zealous support of Great Britain in the prosecution of the war. But whether Ministers were sorry for the failure of this negotiation may also be a question, particularly, since their late exultation in that event. It may be a question, Whether they were not so liberal in their offers at Lisle from a knowledge, that, offer what they would, all would be rejected, and that the more liberal their offers, the rejection of them would rouse this country the more? This may have been the motive for their conduct; but we give them full credit for their sincerity, and we applaud the efforts they made for peace in the last negotiation. We cannot point out one step more which they should have taken: they went as far, we will not say farther, than the honour of the nation would permit.

But when we recollect the shifts to which Ministers resorted four years ago to persuade the country they would make peace when a fit time occurred; when we recollect also, that at that time peace was the great object of the French Government, then conducted by the men since sent to Cayenne; when we see that our Ministers never offered to negotiate till France was in the height of her triumphs, intoxicated with glory, and likely to reject reasonable terms; and when we now hear a proud burst of exultation (drawn forth by a transitory success, of which Ministers have been the dupes) at the failure of the negotiation at Lisle; upon a review of these, and every other circumstance since the commencement of the French Revolution, we feel a strong conviction, that one unaltered, and unalterable, spirit of hatred of that event and its consequences, past, present, and to come, has never ceased to animate and direct the British Cabinet; and that it never can make a sincere peace with the French Republic, even tho' it should sign a treaty, and observe the stipulations; should it even do this, it would only be to pacify and amuse the people, that it might watch a favourable opportunity of again plunging them into a war, for the restoration of French Monarchy. This is the language of the partizans of Ministers; they assert the French and English Constitutions (by the latter, they mean Mr. Pitt's Administration) cannot exist together. The assertion is true. Mr. Pitt never will conclude peace in the hour of success, for then he is duped, and he dupes the country with hopes of marching to Paris; and in the hour of failure, if he makes peace, it must be disgraceful. France will exact from one who has rendered himself so obnoxious, harder terms than she would from others. This she will naturally do according to Mr. Pitt's own reasoning, and very just reasoning it is; that the more you are bent on my ruin, the more must I disable you. This is Mr. Pitt's argument for reducing France to her antient limits; this will be the argument of France for making hard and disgraceful terms with Mr. Pitt. But the more hard and disgraceful they are, the more perhaps they may ultimately please him. Since he has rejoiced in the failure of the negotiations at Lisle, why may he not hereafter rejoice, that the terms of a peace actually signed were so disgraceful, as to make the English people pant for the renewal of the war? To make peace with honour and safety, those who make it must be at peace in mind. How disgraceful would it be for this country, represented as it is by its Administration, to make peace, by the agency of the present Ministers? In a free Government, it is supposed, that the people approve of their servants, in fact, that the actions of the servants become the actions of the people, unless those servants are dismissed. We may therefore suppose the French Government regard Mr. PITT's actions as the actions of the people of Great Britain. In what light then will they view the people of Britain, after being the uniform and inveterate enemies of the French Revolution; after exulting in the failure of the negotiations at Lisle; after every act which can manifest an implacable hatred, and an unalterable desire to destroy them; after all this, will not the French Government view the English nation, as meanly and perfidiously making peace only because it is defeated, and unable to continue the contest with a hope of success; as signing a treaty, not with a sincere desire of being at peace with the French Republic, but in hopes of being able at another time to attack it with better fortune? The impression upon France will be, that the peace is hollow and insincere, and therefore she will exact the harder and the more degrading conditions. Ministers have declared in Parliament, that in making peace with a Monarchy, they could safely accede to a larger cession of territory to France than if they were making peace with a Republic. Will not the Directory use the same reasoning, and insist upon harder terms from Mr. PITT, who is their pledged enemy, than from Mr. Fox, who has uniformly disavowed any right to model, or interfere about the form of the French Government? It has hitherto been the good fortune of England, that the way to a sincere and honourable peace has been prepared by a change of Ministers. New men have come into office, who had constantly condemned the war; and the enemy thus seeing that the country was sincerely desirous of peace, received overtures with kindness, and settled the terms with the temper of friends; the best conditions have been obtained, and a sincere spirit of peace has reconciled both parties. Even in countries where freedom is unknown, a change of Ministers commonly precedes so great a change of measures. In France, at present, this great step has been taken; the men who rejected our overtures at Lisle have been disgraced; and those who have succeeded would probably make peace with any others than the sworn enemies of every thing that constitutes the present French Government.

It then remains with the people of England to decide whether they will have Mr. PITT and a war, varied, perhaps, by a hollow and short-lived peace, or Mr. Fox and a peace as secure as any that ever was concluded, and on conditions as honourable and advantageous as circumstances may entitle us to expect. For if such could not be obtained, Mr. Fox must continue the war, though with a very different view. He would only contend for fair and honourable terms of peace, and not, like Mr. PITT, have the restoration of the French Monarchy as his real object. A war conducted on such motives would far sooner terminate than one for the restoration of the Throne, and it could not fail of uniting every subject in its support.

But the great question which weighs on some weak minds is, whether or not Mr. Fox would favour changes at home, leading to the calamities which have afflicted France? Every artifice, and the most indefatigable industry have been exerted by Ministers and their friends to impress the affirmative on the public mind.—Their success has exceeded every calculation of reason, and this is the true secret of their power; it is this that has secured them in office, and excluded their opponents. The very chance of witnessing in this country the scenes that have occurred in France, naturally and justly makes the people shrink from whatever brings with it that chance. But let us investigate without prejudice, what are the facts upon which such gross calumnies of Mr. Fox have been founded. Mr. Fox denied our right of interfering in the internal affairs of France, and scouted the idea of our being able to restore Monarchy. Has not Mr. PITT yielded to Mr. Fox's opinion by his negotiations at Lisle and Paris? For advising to prevent this war by negotiation, Mr. Fox was stigmatized as the advocate, the hired advocate of the Convention. Has not Mr. PITT negotiated, and imprisoned GILBERT WAKEFIELD, for doubting his sincerity? Mr. Fox has been consistent in approving a Parliamentary Reform, first agitated with spirit by Mr. PITT and his present supporters; but even of this question it is known that Mr. Fox has never been a forward advocate, nor has he approved extreme theories, such as Universal Suffrage. Mr. Fox has opposed the Two Bills, as they were called—bills of which we must say no more, than that Ministers dared not carry them through an approving Parliament in their original state, and of which Ministers themselves have acknowledged the true character, by leaving them a dead letter on the statute book. Mr. Fox has opposed the suspension of the Habeas Corpus; one of the greatest privileges of Englishmen, the chief prop of our constitution, the bulwark of our liberties. We might enumerate every act of which Mr. Fox has been the opposer; such as sending money abroad without the consent of Parliament, tripling the assessed taxes, &c. and easily prove—nay the feelings of the country would *now* acknowledge the wisdom of his advice. And the country will at last feel and acknowledge, that leaving France to settle her own Government is not allowing her to new model that of England; and that defending the most valuable branches is not destroying our Constitution. These truths the public will at last believe, tho' conviction should be dearly purchased.

It will at last be discovered who are the men who really aim at the destruction of our constitution; and however Loan Jobbers may boast, as they did four years ago, that Mr. PITT had a treaty of peace in his pocket, as if he alone could make peace or war when he pleased! it will be found that no peace can be concluded by the present Administration. They may negotiate or menace, they may stoop to the enemy to preserve their places, and traduce the best friends of this country; but still there will be no peace while they are in power. The public must be taught to look their situation in the face; they feel the calamities of war; they know the remedy.

Morning Post, 12 December 1799

ADVICE TO THE FRIENDS OF FREEDOM

That *the Gentlemen in the confidence of Government* should consider it as part of their occupation to abuse, with equal virulence, each successive ruling faction in France, is more natural than politic. For if the French Rulers have been indeed dishonest and ignorant, robbers, assassins, and blunderers, there still remains a justifiable hope, that this feculence, which has boiled up on the surface of the revolutionary cauldron, may at last be wholly scummed off; that experience must have trained, and that some fortunate moment will bring into action a corps of wise and virtuous Statesmen; and that the evils which individual mismanagement has occasioned, individual talent may remove. But if the Leaders in France have been already as wise and virtuous as can be expected of men; if their measures, domestic and foreign, have risen out of necessity and the mere nature of the case, then it were to be feared that the case itself is untenable, and that that system which involves such necessity is unfit for France, unfit for human nature. Thus, in proportion as we diminished our disapprobation of the Leaders, we should increase our aversion from the Republic. We are not however surprised, that the hirelings of the Ministry do that which they can do most readily; personal invective is an easy trade; and they have been long apprenticed to it. These Gentlemen have long ago worn out, in all sober men, the power of being *surprised* at *their* blunders. All that they afford us is now and then an occasion of amusement.

But it makes, we confess, a different and most melancholy impression on our minds, that men, *who believe themselves* the friends of freedom, should be so duped by the heat of the game as to play into their adversaries' hands; and that while the culprits in France are industriously criminating each other, the professed lovers of liberty in England should be employing every trick of sophistry in exculpating them all; incessant manufacturers of excuses for men, who have scarcely the impudence to attempt a definite excuse for themselves. What a **rare**

O

fluidity must a man's PRINCIPLES possess, that can be emptied so rapidly from one mould into another, and assume, with such equal facility, the shape of each! We recognize three distinct classes of these tenacious, though versatile apologists. The first is composed of men who endeavour to make bad practices sit easy on them by the adoption of bad principles. *Humists* in opinion, debauchees in conduct, they have lost all power of sympathising with whatever exists in society, and mistake for philosophy, and a love of freedom, that restlessness of mind and body which results from lewd habits and embarrassed circumstances. These men find, from each successive explosion in France, a stimulus so necessary and so pleasurable, that each in its turn is first palliated and finally justified. Their modes of justification are, indeed, laughably inconsistent with each other; but this forms no objection with men who love *fashions* in philosophy, and would deem it a proof of intellectual poverty to appear thrice together in the same habiliments. Of the comparative number of this first class we can form no opinion; a very few are much too many. In the second class we place those who, having dwelt with unfeigned benevolence on the mass of evils in society, associate with all who profess to heal them, feelings so ardent, that they do not suffer themselves to distinguish between physicians and empirics. They look upon the present Ministry not only as too completely occupied in the anxieties of self-defence, to be interested concerning the permanent well being of their fellow-subjects; but even as prosecuting a direct system of hostility against the hopes and comforts of the middle-ranks, and the amelioration, knowledge, and social affections of the lower classes.

As tending to this end, and not from any interested motives, they justly survey with abhorrence the taxes on incomes, the jealous provision against popular discussion; but, above all, the heavy imposts on paper, newspapers, and letters. To France, some of these men are attached by their love of the Sciences, which more eminently flourish there, and which appear more decisively connected with the immediate good of mankind; while others, who have long amused themselves with shaping out, in their own imaginations, better states of society, are seduced to an obstinacy of hope that they will be realized in France, only because they see no chance of their being realized elsewhere. The third class is far the most numerous, and comprises all who apologise for the French in direct and habitual opposition to the Minister; all who, with little extravagance, and as little greatness of mind, are in the habits of personal dislike of Mr. Pitt and his party; who, fixing their feelings on men rather than measures, have made an ejection of the present Members from the Administration an object and a passion, and who will always find some excuse, even for the enemies of mankind, provided they happen at the same time to profess themselves the enemies of

Mr. Pitt.—Passion makes men blind; and these men, by the alarm which their intemperate zeal, unfixed principles, and Gallican phraseology excite, form around the Minister a more effective phalanx of defence, than all his body-guard of Loan-jobbers, Contractors, Placemen and Pensioners, in and out of Parliament. But these are times in which those who love freedom should use all imaginable caution to love it wisely. There exists a large number of men, in every sense of the word respectable, who remain attached to the present Ministry only from fear of worse men. How shall they be induced to sympathise with our principles, unless they can be convinced that those principles impel us to sympathise with them in their abhorrence of men and measures, whose iniquity consists in their militation against all principles? Good men should now close in their ranks. Too much of extravagant hope, too much of rash intolerance, have disgraced all parties: and facts, well adapted to discipline us all, have burst forth, even to superfluity. 'Twere surely wiser and better to sink at once voluntarily into the resignation of despair, than to tantalize ourselves with hopes which have no firmer foundations than Robespierre's, Tallien's, and Barras's.

Morning Post, 6 January 1800

[PEACE PROPOSALS]

The Paris Papers to the 31st ult. have given us a list of the exiles permitted to re-enter the territories of the Republic. Their particular places of abode are specified, and each is to be placed under the superintendance of the Minister of Police in the Commune marked out for him. The choice of the Commune has been chiefly determined by its nearness to the families and business of the person appointed to reside in it. We have likewise copied from these journals an official list of the three hundred Legislators. Both these lists prove one point; that the new Government is using every possible means to make itself considered as the centre of union for all parties. Men of talents and character have been chosen, almost wholly without reference to their former opinions. This measure involves a most politic and judicious species of self-adulation; for it tells the people of facts, which carry with them no ordinary appearance both of fearlessness and humanity, that the necessity and propriety of the new order of things are so palpable, that no wise and honest man can refuse his assent to them. In the mean time the parties themselves, who have been thus chosen or recalled, will probably be prevented by personal delicacy and gratitude, from immediate hostility against the Constitution, while they really exert themselves in the cause of the Republic: nor is it indeed impossible that, menaced as France is at present, many sincere lovers of Freedom may perceive, in

the usurpation of the modern PISISTRATUS, such *temporary* advantages as
reconcile them to a temporary submission. Other measures have been
adopted, favourable to morals and civil Liberty. The free use of religious worship, and of the places dedicated to it on other days than the
Decade, is permitted by a consular decree; and, instead of the oaths
formerly exacted, a simple *promise* is required of fidelity to the Constitution. Of the French Armies nothing occurs particularly noticeable, except that the Army of Italy is reinforced by twenty thousand men from
Switzerland. General MOREAU has arrived at the Army of the Rhine,
the right wing of which had entered into winter quarters.

No mention is made in these Journals of the letter sent by BUONA-
PARTE to His MAJESTY;—but those who have seen it, say that it is respectful and temperate. We continue to give it as our decided opinion,
that the French Government is *sincere* in its wishes for peace; and that
Ministers believe as we do, and for this very reason avoid negotiation.
We once stated our conviction, that the French Government had no
hope, that the English Cabinet would accede to pacific overtures, when
Austria had rejected them. That conviction remains. However low we
may estimate the integrity of BUONAPARTE and his faction, we think too
well of their *discernment* to believe otherwise. But this in nowise im-
peaches the *sincerity* of their offers. To make offers without *expectation*
that they *will* be accepted, does not constitute insincerity, provided a
real *wish* exists that these offers *may* be accepted. Ministers were accused
of criminal insincerity in the negotiations at Lisle, not because they had
no *expectations* that their offers *would* be acceded to, but because it
was believed they had no *wish* they *should* be successful.—It is most
assuredly not inconsistent with the strictest honour to make proposals,
of which we really wish the acceptance, although our reason at the
same time forces us to fear that what we wish will not take place. But
where the wishes and the expectations coincide, and both are directed
against the acceptance of our own proposals, this is indeed insincerity.
With this Ministers were charged: with this we do not think BUONA-
PARTE chargeable.

We have been explicit, perhaps prolix, in our explanation. But he who
is the creature of no party, who acts and feels for himself, unbiassed by
any, *he* will be, of all others, most subject to malicious or ignorant
charges of inconsistency. While he criminates one Government, he is
supposed to be tacitly praising its enemy: as if, of two balls, we could
not call one black without implying whiteness in the other. We detest
equally Jacobinism and usurpation in the French, and the principles of
despotism preached by their opponents—we look with equal horror on
those who murder a lawful Constitution, and those who, under pretence of medicine, administer poison to it. We deem it among the most
fatal errors in some friends of freedom in England, that they have

thought it necessary to a consistent opposition to Ministers, that they should *slur over* the follies or wickedness of France. We think otherwise. TRUTH is *our* policy. We despise the absurdities and dread the fanaticism of France; believing, however, at the same time, that but for the war against France they would have died in their infancy. To the war carried on under the pretence of extirpating them, we attribute their unnatural longevity, and whole powers of propagation. They are now at the last gasp: and without the reanimating aid of invasions and terror will die without hope of resurrection. It may be well and modest in the Journals that receive *mandates* from masters, to talk of opposition prints as having received instructions from their employers. We acknowledge no master; and have no other employer but the Public. To that employer we will remain faithful, careless concerning the calumnies and misrepresentations of the ill-meaning and the unmeaning, whoever they be, whether the hirelings or the opponents of the Minister.

In the service of the Public we persevere in putting the Ministers the deeply interesting question: Under what pretext do you persist in wasting the blood and treasures of your Country? Peace is evidently the wish, as it is undeniably the interest, of the New Government. The ambition of France, a just subject of apprehension, is checked: her principles, at which we were idly alarmed, are exploded. The continuation of the war with her will necessarily awaken either the one or the other. We deny, that a Peace concluded with the present Government would imply an admission on our side of its original legality. That all the despots in Europe are not equally *righteous*, is no reason why we should not be at peace with them all. We admit, that an honourable Treaty concluded with BUONAPARTE would tend to confirm his power, and that by this and his subsequent moderation it may continue, till the revival of commerce and manufactures in France calls into active power the spirit of property, and consequently brings with it a Government modified accordingly. But we affirm, that war will not only confirm his power still more than peace, but that it will have a tendency to *justify* it; it will render moderation less necessary; and *should* his Government be overthrown, the analogy of all the past justifies us in affirming, that it will introduce some other usurpation equally violent, on principles infinitely more pernicious. Supposing for a moment, that Royalty could be restored—what reason have we for affirming its permanency? Will not the principles of Jacobinism remain? Can the faction of the Royalists boast more talent, more activity, more energy than the Republicans? Will it not disturb the present state of property infinitely more than the usurpation of BUONAPARTE? And by the very act of disturbing property, will it not necessarily bring Jacobinism once more into play? And will not Royalty therefore, if restored, perish, like a bubble, by the very agitation that produced it?

Morning Post, 22 January 1800

NOTE BY THE EDITOR

In our paper of Wednesday we used the words "a wild and barbarous people, brutalised by the oppression of centuries," as descriptive of the lower classes of the Irish.—We find by the above spirited and well-written letter, which was not intended for insertion, but which our Readers will thank us for publishing, that this phrase has been mis-understood. The word "barbarous" was meant to be perfectly synoni-mous with "uncivilised;" and this defect of civilisation, with its accompanying evils, attributed as a crime to the successive administra-tions of that much injured country, and adduced as an apology for *their* conduct, "into whose souls the iron had entered." *Apology*! We fear that this is a cold and inapplicable phrase. The extravagancies of one, whose eyes have been burnt out by his gaoler, demand a deep and indignant condolance, not apology. It is the doom awarded *against* a bad Government by the eternal wisdom, that even the horrors com-mitted against it must be enumerated among its own crimes. What it does is not more its guilt than what it suffers; it is wounded by the re-bounding of its own weapon. We peruse the accounts of the ferocious vindictiveness of savage tribes with terror, rather than moral disappro-bation. They have been instructed by none, and none have had the power of instructing them. It is far otherwise with the ferocities which may have been perpetrated by the poor sufferers in Ireland. These have, indeed, excited our moral sense to a painful excess of feeling, not against that which they are, but against those who, causing them to be what they are, have cut them off from that great and enlightened char-acter, of which, indeed, their very ferocities are at once the proof and the perversion.

> "Each pore and nat'ral outlet shrivell'd up
> "By ignorance and parching poverty,
> "Their energies roll back upon their heart,
> "And stagnate and corrupt!"—

The Irish national character we have ever contemplated with a melancholy pleasure, as a compound of strength and vivacity; an amal-gama of the qualities of the two rival nations, England and France. Ireland itself is placed in the most enlightened part of the world, the sister of, perhaps, the most enlightened kingdom in it. It has had the same gracious line of Kings with ourselves. What indignation, then, must not every good mind feel against that parricidal faction, which has contrived, as it were, to mock a miracle of God, and make a *Goshen* of darkness in a land surrounded by dawning or noon-day light! The opposition of such a faction to the measure of the Union, we cannot but consider as a species of presumptive argument in its favour, if there be no weightier arguments on the contrary side. But iniquitous as this faction has evinced itself to be, yet still their actions shall not prejudice our minds against their reasoning. TRUTH is of too divine and spiritual an essence to be susceptible of commixture with the foulness of its accidental vehicle. Light is light to us, though it be flung from the torch of a fury! If we could dissever from the idea the ludicrous association, we would personify REASON a ventriloquist; it is of inferior importance into what uncouth vessel she throws her voice, provided only that it is audible.

If it were *possible* (but we are convinced it is not) that Ireland could make and maintain itself an independent nation, uninfluenced by France, and retaining for England that feeling of compatriotism, which the use of the same language ought in nature to communicate—if this were possible, we should be ready to admit, that though the same blood flows in the extremities as in the heart, yet that in the extremities it necessarily flows more languidly! But we appear to ourselves to see a necessity that Ireland should remain connected with this country; and this being taken as a postulate, we do not perceive how, in the present state of feeling and opinion among the majority in Ireland, such an independent legislature can be given to it, as will be able and inclined to take off the oppressive laws of exclusion from the people, without presenting cause of alarm to this country. If the Members from Ireland are to form a part only of an Imperial Legislature, the rights of suffrage, and every concomitant privilege, may then be safely conceded, and indefinitely extended. Still, however, we are not blind to the evils of a national minority; but here we seem to have only a choice of evils. These opinions we venture *in transitu*; and not without great self-distrust. *Adhuc sub lite est.*

Morning Post, 27 January 1800

[GENERAL WASHINGTON]

The officers and sailors of the American ships in the port of London, yesterday paid a just respect to the memory of their deceased friend General Washington, by attending at St. John's Church, Wapping, in naval mourning. We dare not record his death without attempting to pronounce his panegyric. This mournful office is both our duty and our inclination; but we confess, that we feel our powers oppressed into sluggishness by the sense of its difficulty. To build up goodly phrases into rhetorical periods, and attach to the name of Washington all splendid generalities of praise, were indeed an easy task. But such vague declamation, at all times an unworthy offering to the memory of the departed, is peculiarly unappropriate to the sober and definite greatness of *his* character. Tranquil and firm he moved with one pace in one path, and neither vaulted or tottered. He possessed from his earliest years that prophetic consciousness of his future being, which both makes and marks the few great men of the world, who combine a deep sense of internal power, with imaginations capable of bodying forth lofty undertakings. His feelings, constitutionally profound and vehement (and which, if uncounteracted by the majesty of his views, would have been wild and ferocious), gave him a perpetual energy; while the necessity of counteracting and curbing these feelings gradually disciplined his soul to that austere self-command, which informed and moulded the whole man, his actions, his countenance, his every gesture. Thus, sympathising inwardly with man, as an ideal, not with men as companions, he perfected in himself that character, which all are compelled to feel, though few are capable of analysing, the character of a commanding genius. His successes, therefore, great in themselves, and sublime in the effects that followed them, were still greater, still more sublime, from the means, by which they were attained. It may be affirmed, with truth, that if fortune and felicity of accident were to resume from his successes all which *they* had contributed, more would remain to him than perhaps to any man equally celebrated: his successes were but the outward and visible language of that which had pre-existed in his mind. But this character and these praises others have approached or attained, who, great in the detail of their conduct for the purposes of personal ambition, had subdued and fettered their feebler passions, only to become more entirely the slaves of a darker and more pernicious influence.—In Washington this principle and habit of self-subjugation never degenerated into a *mere* instrument; it possessed itself of his whole nature; he ripened his intellectual into moral greatness, intensely energetic yet perseveringly innocent, his hope, the happiness of mankind, and God, and his own conscience, his end! Hence among a people eminently querulous and already impregnated with the germs of discordant parties, he directed the executive power firmly and unostentatiously. He had no vain conceit of being himself all; and did those things only which he only could do. And finally he retired, his Country half-reluctant, yet proud in the testimony which her Constitution and liberty received from his retirement. He became entirely the husband and master of his family; and the lines which Santeuil composed for the statue of the great Condé in the gardens of Chantilly were yet more applicable to the father and hero of the American Republic.

> Quem modo pallebant fugitivis fluctibus amnes
> Terribilem bello, nunc docta per otia princeps
> *Pacis amans* laetos dat in hostis ludere fontes.

Washington thought, felt, and acted in and for his age and Country; the same temperance presided over his opinions as his actions. He sympathised with the moral and religious feelings of the great mass of his fellow-citizens, and was that sincerely, which others assuming politically, have betrayed hypocrisy, when they meant to have exhibited condescending greatness. He neither rushed before his age and country, nor yet attempted to under-act himself; his actions, from the least to the greatest, he inspired with one high and sacred charm, by being always in earnest! Posterity will adjudge to him the title of GREAT, with more sound and heart-felt suffrage, because he appeared no greater!

Morning Post, 25 March 1800

GENERAL WASHINGTON

We would fain believe that the whole of General Washington's Will has been perused by no man without some portion of that calm and pleasureable elevation which uniformly leaves us better and wiser beings. It would have been deeply interesting, considered only as the last deliberate act of a life so beneficial to the human race; but independently of this sublime association, it is in itself an affecting and most instructive composition. Like all the former manifestations of his character, it gives proof that a true and solid greatness may exist, and make itself felt, without any admixture of wildness, without any obtrusive appeals to the imagination: it gives proof, consolatory and inspiring proof, how many virtues, too often deemed incompatible with each other, a thinking and upright mind may unite in itself. It were scarcely too much to affirm of this Will, that all the main elements of public and private morals, of civil and domestic wisdom, are conveyed in it either directly or by implication. It is, indeed, no less than an abstract of his opinions and feelings, as a PATRIOT, FRIEND, and RELATION, and all arising naturally and unostentatiously out of the final disposal of a fortune not more honourably earned than beneficently employed. Appertaining to his character, as the American PATRIOT, more exclusively than the other pages of the Will, is the plan and endowment of a CENTRAL UNIVERSITY. The motives which impelled the General to this bequest, he has stated with such beauty and precision, as scarcely leave any thing for the philosopher or the eulogist to add. We can only subjoin to the advantages so ably enumerated, that such an institution must be eminently serviceable to America, as having a direct tendency to soften and liberalise the too great commercial spirit of that country, in as far as it will connect the pleasures and ambitions of its wealthy citizens, in the most impressible period of life, with objects abstract and unworldly; and that while by friendships and literary emulations it may remove local jealousies, it will tend to decorate the American character with an ornament hitherto wanting in it, viz. genuine local attachments, unconnected with pecuniary interests.

Of a mixed nature, partly belonging to the patriot, and partly to the master of a family, is the humane, earnest, and solemn wish concerning the emancipation of the slaves on his estate. It explains, with infinite delicacy and manly sensibility, the true cause of his not having emancipated them in his life time; and should operate as a caution against those petty libellers, who interpret the whole of a character by a part, instead of interpreting a part by the whole. We feel ourselves at a loss which most to admire in this interesting paragraph, the deep and weighty feeling of the general principle of universal liberty; or the wise veneration of those fixed laws in society, without which that universal liberty must forever remain impossible, and which, therefore, must be obeyed even in those cases, where they *suspend* the action of that general principle; or, lastly, the affectionate attention to the particular feelings of the slaves themselves, with the ample provision for the aged and infirm. Washington was no "architect of ruin!"

In the bequests to his friends, the composition evidences the peculiar delicacy and correctness of his mind. The high value which he attached to his old friend, Dr. Franklin's legacy of the gold-headed cane, by bequeathing it, and it alone, to his brother, Charles Washington; the spyglasses, left, with the modest parenthesis, "because they will be useful to them where they live;" yet not without stamping the value on those precious relics, as having been useful to himself in the deliverance of his country; the wisdom of remitting the box to Lord Buchan, with the gentle implication of the impracticability and impropriety of performing the conditions, with which the box had been originally accompanied; that reverence for the primary designation of a gift, implied in the words "agreeably to the original design of the Goldsmiths' Company of Edinburgh," and which words were besides necessary, in order to prevent the interpretation, that he had remitted it from inability to find any man in his own country equally deserving of it with the Earl; the bequest of the Bible, and of the swords, the first without annotation, the last with the solemnity of a christian hero; all and each of these we have dwelt upon, as evidences of a mind strong and healthful, yet with a fineness and rapidity of the associating power, seldom found even in those who derive sensibility from nervous disease. The gratitude, the deep and immortal gratitude, displayed in the declaration of the motives of his bequest to his nephew, Bushrod Washington, is of a still higher class of excellence; and the virtue is individualised, and has a new interest given it, by his attention to the very letter of an old promise, no longer in force. The accuracy with which the estates are marked out will aid the distant posterity of the present Americans, in their reverential pilgrimages to the seat of their great PATER PATRIAE. The attachment which he has shewn to all his relations; the provisions he has made for them all; and the attentions to honourable causes of local preferment in these provisions; are circumstances highly noticeable. Highly noticeable too is the disjunction of this family attachment from that desire of the aggrandisement of some one branch of the family, so commonly adherent to it. He has weakened by evidence the best and almost the only argument for primogeniture, *in new countries*. One fact strikes us particularly in the perusal of this Will.—Of all Washington's numerous relations, not one appears as a placeman or beneficiary of the government—not one appears to have received any thing from their kinsman as President and Influencer of the United States, yet all have evidences of the zeal and affection of the President, as their kinsman. *It is not so everywhere.* There is something in the arrangement of the will, beyond any example, which we recollect, instructive and judicious, he commences with a positive or perfect duty, the payment of duties, then goes immediately to the most respectful and affectionate attention to his wife, which becomes more intellectual, more moral, from the circumstance, which he after notices, of his having remained without issue; he proceeds to his concerns as master of his family, and provides for the emancipation of his slaves; and having finished his most immediate and *most* sacred offices, viz. the domestic duties, he rises, *then*, and *not till then*, into the PATRIOT; and founds a central University. After his own family comes his country, and then his relations by consanguinity not of his own family—after these his friends; and all those whom fellow-ship in arms, or old acquaintance had endeared to him; and last of all, he proceeds to the circumstantial disposal of his estate. Throughout the whole, there reigns a *humanness* of feeling, a complete union of himself with the mass of his fellow-citizens, so as even to avoid references to any public characters in that country; and above all, an ardent wish for improvement, combined with reverential observance, and affectionate awe for present and existing customs and feelings. But WASHINGTON was too great a man to court singularity. The dwarf, that steps aside from the crowd, and walks by himself, may gain the whole crowd to turn and stare at him—Washington could attract their admiration, while he moved on with them, and in the midst of them.[1]

[1] Cf. Coleridge's later treatment of Washington in the *Courier*, 21 Dec. 1809, *E.O.T.* ii. 644–5. 'If when a Washington, having purchased the *independence* of his country by far-sighted patience and enduring courage as a warrior, and then established and watched over her *freedom* with the wisdom of parental love, unmoved by the entreaties of his fellow-citizens, lest by yielding to them he should form a precedent injurious to their posterity, retires to the unambitious duties of private life, and disclaiming all titles but those given by domestic love and reverence, bows at length his dear and venerable head to the emancipating angel, and restores his spirit to that great Being, whose goodness he had both

Morning Post, 11 December 1801

THE REPORTED CHANGES

We affirmed that the Members of the Old Opposition could not honourably coalesce with the present Ministry, without having previously compelled them to such retractions as it were idle to suppose the present Ministry inclined to make; and that if they did coalesce without compelling any retraction, they would return by a maze to the den of the monster, from which they wished to escape. We are confident that we have fully evinced the truth of the former part of the assertion; the latter remains to be proved, or, at least, made probable. To prove this, let us suppose for a moment that the Opposition join Mr. Addington, and suffer the obnoxious laws and measures of this and the late Ministry to pass into precedents. Hereby they cannot but strip themselves of all that influence which is derived from the affections of the people, and the independent friends of our laws and constitution. They give up their great freehold estate in the public opinion, and become tenants at will under the favour of the Court. At the same time, by uniting themselves with Ministers, without extorting any censure of the war, they bring themselves forward, and *volunteer* the ill-fame in which the inglorious, perhaps dangerous, conditions of the peace will probably involve the authors of it. At present the Opposition may say, with truth, "Our support of the peace was wise and necessary; and that it was so, is the bitterest satire on the commencers and conductors of the war, who rejected, with insult, the enemy's proposal, in the hour of her danger and humiliation, and chose the moment of her fullest triumph to make the same proposals themselves." But when they shall have united themselves in the Ministry, and have shared the *good things* of the State with their old opponents, this plea will have become too indecent, if not to be made, yet certainly to be listened to. They will have the cry of all parties against them.

In the meantime, it is not to be supposed but that they will endeavour to re-establish themselves in the affections of the public by some avowed efforts in favour of a free and liberal Government; it is not to be believed but that the feelings of personal honour, as well as of an old attachment, will incline them to make a struggle to unite Mr. Fox with them in the Ministry; and should the pacification and the conditions of it become universally unpopular, no doubt they will attempt to throw

adored and imitated—if for such a man we collect all terms of honour and affection, and fondly involve his name in phrases expressive of his virtues, must we remain mute, and stifle the feelings which the *contrast* to all this must needs awaken in us? and even though this contrast should furnish a humiliating proof, that the slaves of iniquitous ambition can carry guilt to a height which dwarfs the best virtues of the best and most heroic of men in the comparison?'

off the odium, by bidding the shame of the peace rest on the authors of the war.—All these are sure cards in the hands of the faction of the Alarmists, and the friends of the Court. Their attempts at popularity, and the measures tending to it, will offend and alarm the inner Cabinet; their attachment to Mr. Fox will certainly tend to reconcile the King to Mr. Pitt, by compelling him to a *comparison of dislikes*; and the attempt to *shift* the ignominy of the peace to the proper shoulders, cannot fail to create dissentions, and open hostilities in the Ministry itself.—Nor is it improbable that the Opposition Members may be at variance among themselves, in consequence of these personal jealousies and heart-burnings, which the division of honours and places seldom fails to create in the formation of every new Ministry. Thus, then, divided in itself, suspected by the Sovereign, and unpopular with the people, this heterogeneous Ministry will yield but a feeble resistance to a party strong in its own members, united by hope and a deeply rankling hatred of all free measures, openly[1] favoured by the Court, and probably supported by a greater part of the commercial and colonial interests of the country. We fear that there can be little doubt of the ultimate success of this party, and, if they succeed, no doubt at all, that they will return to power with all the strength of a complete victory, and with a strong opinion of the public in favour of their consistency, while their old opponents, ejected and hopeless, are disliked by the one party for their former professions of free principles, regarded by another party as apostates from those principles, and disowned by all parties but that which their personal influence may create.

Indeed, we have little doubt that the really powerful and effective part of the present Ministry are connected heart and hand with the party of Lord Grenville and Mr. Windham, and that they stretch out their arms to their old opponents to *strangle*, and not to *embrace*. Nay, we suspect that they wish to dupe the Opposition into this disgraceful coalition before the dissolution of Parliament, and that the first session of the new Parliament will be the death-bed of this short-lived Ministry. We are induced to this suspicion by no vague speculations, but by positive facts, which appear to us to admit of no other interpretation. First, it is well known that Mr. Addington keeps aloof from all election

---

[1] One may generally penetrate the self-estimation of a Party, and its real hopes, by the reeds it leans upon, or the twigs at which it catches. The reception that Mr. Windham met with from his Royal Master at the last levee, is the momentary consolation of the Opposers of Government, and the enemies to the peace. His Majesty certainly shewed the most marked condescension for this great Statesman whom he detained a-part, in secret and apparently in very serious conference for a full half hour, during which, from the frequent obeisances and personal manners of Mr. Windham, it was conjectured that he was making acknowledgments for some expressions of approbation, or other testimony of the King's confidence and good will, and at least a favourable interpretation of his late conduct in Parliament.—(*Times.*)

concerns; and that the interest of the Crown will not be exerted in favour of the men of moderate principles. It is, indeed, pretty well understood that the Ex-Ministers will manage the next election, nearly as if they were still in office. Secondly, the man whom they have singled out as the first to be brought over, and the particular office which has been pitched upon for him, are equally suspicious. The confidential paper of Government, on Saturday se'nnight, said, "Lord Hobart, it is reported, goes out to India, to succeed Marquis Wellesley as Governor-General. His successor, as Secretary of State, has been mentioned to be one of those who have hithertofore been distinguished on the Opposition bench of the House of Commons." Another paper affirmed that the Member of the Opposition is Mr. Grey. The report was circulated before it appeared in the papers; in stating it, therefore, we are in no danger of being accused as the authors of it.

It is an obvious piece of policy in the Ministers to gain over a man of high honour, constant integrity, and great personal weight; a man deeply rooted in the esteem of his country. All this, and more than all this, they found in Mr. Grey; and they have pitched upon, perhaps, almost the only office, the acceptance of which would bring in its train such deserved odium, as even his high character could not bear up against; and with this design they must assuredly have selected it, if it be true, that the place destined for Mr. Grey is the same which is now held by Lord Hobart. (Nay, if[1] it be false, we shall almost believe that the creatures of the late and present Ministers have purposely circulated the story, as well knowing that the very report would leave a scar behind it.) For that office exists in contradiction to Mr. Burke's Bill, and to that system of economy in Government, which Mr. Grey, in concert with all the Old Opposition, uniformly and strenuously recommended. When a third Secretary of State was created in the person of Mr. Dundas, Opposition complained of it as a direct violation of a bill adopted by Parliament in an awful crisis, and with circumstances of more than usual solemnity. The Ministers overruled the objection, on the ground of the absolute necessity of the office; and whether it were or were not *necessary*, yet it cannot be denied that during the war it was

---

[1] One of the Daily Papers promises a very interesting Dissertation on the Report of Mr. GREY's becoming Secretary of State in the room of Lord HOBART. In the first place, the report was never in existence among any well-informed persons; and it is not paying any great compliment to the Hon. Gentleman to appoint him to an office which there is reason to suppose will be abolished at the Peace. A dissertation on such a subject must be very interesting.—(*Times.*)

Though *The Times* of yesterday contradicts the report which we stated long ago, that Mr. Grey and Mr. Tierney were likely to hold official situations, the report is not the less prevalent, even amongst the best informed in the higher circles, and the contradiction in question is only another proof of the ignorance of the Paper alluded to.—(*True Briton.*)

an important and active employment. But Peace is concluded, and the office continues. Another pretence, of course, must be found for its continuance, and Lord Hobart is called *the Secretary of State for the Colonies*.[1] The business of the colonies has hitherto been transacted (even during the busy and anxious years of the war) by the Secretary of State for the Home Department, the office now filled by Lord Pelham, and no other true reasons can be given for this alteration; than that the pure, the patriotic Mr. Addington feels the convenience of extensive patronage as forcibly as any of his predecessors, and takes as shameless measures to effect it. Between thirty and forty thousand pounds per annum of the public money are expended to keep up, or rather to create, an unnecessary establishment; and the first unfavourable impression on the mind of the people, which in these cases is deemed the chief evil, this is to be transferred to Mr. Grey; and thus, a twofold end effected— an extension of patronage will be secured, which Ministers want much; and the character of a powerful and popular patriot tarnished, which, if we mistake not, they want still more. We flatter ourselves that we have proved that no Member of the Opposition can unite with the present Ministers, their principles remaining unretracted, without a desertion of his own; but to deliver up these principles into the hands of a faction for a price, and that price an illegal, or at best an unconstitutional office—

"Who would not scoff, is such a man there be?
"Who but must weep if ATTICUS is he?

Were we for a moment even to drop all considerations of public virtue and public interest, and consider it merely as an every day bargain between trading statesmen, we should still blush to see a man, whom it has become a habit with us to honour, wear a boot, which even Lord Hobart finds to small for him, and is to seek elsewhere the patronage, and consequent means of providing for his friends and family, which have, it seems, been all *forestalled* at Whitehall. And most true it is, that the Duke of Portland, before he resigned, had *"picked the bone clean."* Nothing seems to have escaped his penetrating glances. A very lucrative sinecure place in Jamaica, now held by Mr. Wyndham,

---

[1] The very day on which *The Times* sneered at this Paper for promising this article (imagining, as every honest man would imagine, that Lord Hobart's office would be abolished at the peace); it inserted the following paragraph, which for the *first time* publicly noticed Lord Hobart's *new title*. The paragraph manifestly came from authority:—"We have authority to state, that it was on the presentation of Lord Hobart, as Secretary of State for the department of War AND COLONIES, and not of Sir James Turner, as erroneously reported in the papers of yesterday, that Mr. Mackenzie, the Gentleman who first penetrated through Canada to the Frozen and Pacific Oceans, had the honour of presenting to His Majesty, at the Levee on Wednesday, the Book he is about to publish on that interesting subject."

and given to him in reversion by the late Lord Egremont, his father, when Secretary of State, the Duke of Portland has secured, by reversion, to his grandson, an infant scarcely a year old. Another sinecure, held by Lord Ducie, Marshal of Barbadoes, the Duke of Portland has secured in reversion for an *Eleve* of his, a Mr. Carter, possessed of 3000£. per annum, independent fortune. What other sinecures and reversions the Duke has secured for his family and supporters, we are not as yet particularly acquainted; but we have good reason to believe, that his Noble successors, the Lords Pelham and Hobart, looked blank on each other, when they found that his Grace had not only left the stream of patronage low, but had actually turned the *course* of it into his own grounds.

But, it may be objected, it is with Mr. Addington, and not with the Duke of Portland; that Mr. Grey is solicited to coalesce, with Mr. Addington,

> —"Whose pure soul is
> "A pattern to all Ministers living with him,
> "And all that shall succeed."

And is Mr. Addington then really this disinterested man, whose actions disarm all suspicion, and *leave no room for opposition*? No sooner is he seated at the helm, than (with that Lynx-eyed perception of the before unsuspected virtues and talents of their own relations, which new Ministers are always blest with by virtue of their office) he discovers, that his wife's sister's husband, Mr. Adams, is very fit for a Lord of the Treasury: and a Lord of the Treasury he makes him! With an eye no less microscopically powerful he detects in Mr. Bragg, his sister's husband, a similar fitness for Treasurer of the Navy (a place worth 4000l. a year), and a Privy Counsellor: and of course, it stands with reason, that his brother, Hely Addington, that his own brother *must be* the fittest man in the kingdom to be Secretary of the Treasury. This latter instance is an additional proof, that humility and true prudence are inherent in the very blood of the Addingtons. Hely, once a Lord of the Treasury, sate at the board as the Secretary's master; but he descends from dignity to wealth, from their Lordships definite salaries to a Secretary's numberless perquisites. Mr. Hely Addington is a true Bat!. In the gentle owl-light of preferment, when it was neither light nor dark with the family, he soared aloft, as a bird; but now that the family greatness has risen, like the morning sun, he resigns the privilege of wings, becomes a true snug mouse, and feeds upon the *cheese-parings*, and *candle-ends*. *Prob pudor*! And these are the men with whom Mr. Grey is to be joined in office! What is even the Duke of Portland's conduct compared with this? He only predestined the honours and rewards of the State to an infant, who, for aught we know to the contrary, may turn out hereafter to be as prudent, gentle, and temperate a Statesman as Mr. Wyndham, the present possessor of the office, to whom his father, Lord Egremont, had in the same way secured it in reversion! to an infant, who may even turn out as *wise* a Statesman as his own grandpapa, and, in the event of scarcity, write as *wise* letters to the Lord Lieutenant of the county of Oxford! But Messrs. Bragg, Adams, and Hely Addington—alas! alas! they are full-grown realities and it would be a violation of all Christian faith, hope and charity, not to presume somewhat better of the infant. Old Dr. Bentley was accustomed to pass by all the Seniors, &c. of his College unnoticed; but always and most respectfully touched his cap to the *Freshmen.* "The young ones (said the Doctor) *may* come to something; but the others, I *know* what they are."

We would fain believe that it is impossible that a man like Mr. Grey (no trading Statesman, no mere man of business, but one who has ever addressed his country in the high and commanding tone of genuine English principles) that such a man should coalesce with a Party, whose principles and whose measures he has repeatedly and loudly affirmed to be the assailers of the Constitution of his country, and the Liberties of all mankind, who have retracted no one of these principles, and who, in the very outset and maiden blush of their Ministry, betray all the rapacity and selfishness, not to say the corruption, of their predecessors! He will not, we are assured, join himself in any Ministry, from which Mr. Pitt is not excluded; the only result of which will be, that Mr. Pitt will, of course, return, a somewhat humbler man, to the Alarmists and Friends of the Court, who will gladly receive him as their *General* in the political campaign, if he only will yield a more direct obedience to the decisions of the *inner War Council*. Thus with a Leader, who has certainly the opinion of the monied men in his favour, as a Financier, and with sure friends and agents in the Ministry itself, the Alarmists wait securely for the moment, when the ambition, or bad faith, or prosperity of the enemy shall have spread dissatisfaction among the people, or any attempt at measures in consistency with their former professions on the part of the proselytes to the new Ministry shall have disgusted or alarmed the Court; the word is given; Lord Hawkesbury and Mr. Addington resign, and fall back into their former ranks, or ascend into dignified inaction, the remaining Ministers are displaced, and all things return to their former position, except the character of the Opposition. They, alas! are gone forever. It was thought convenient to make a Peace; the least important and least ostensible part of the Old Faction are brought forward on the front of the stage to conclude it; and the character of it is to be shared by the Opposition. They have full confidence that this peace will not be permanent, at all events that it will become unpopular; and they have made the feint of yielding to the

Opposition, that they may throw them off their guard, and out of their ranks, while they making a circular movement, fall upon them in the rear, in the moment of their greatest disorder.

No man can wish to play into his enemy's hand; and when he believes his enemy to be the enemy of his country, no good man ought to wish it. And it is on this ground chiefly that we wish to rest our argument; and this, we would fain believe, will be the most powerful with the patriot, whose name we have thought it our duty to bring forward.——
In revolutionary governments, (and, in a less degree, in governments purely despotic) measures must be judged by their immediate consequences, for they create no precedents. It is far otherwise with us. With us the stability of our laws and constitution is every thing. We derive one inestimable advantage from this, namely, that our politics and our morals are built on the same foundation: it is EXAMPLE, the PRECEDENT, which constitutes the importance, and determines the character of public measures, equally as of private actions. It requires nothing but a good heart to perceive how favourably this must act on the dispositions and understanding of a free nation, which habitually interests itself in the proceedings of its government; how it tends to make us what by foreigners we are believed, and, we hope deservedly believed to be, at once a calculating and an honest people. The Ministers, who made light work with the Habeas Corpus act, the Bill of Rights, and the laws which forbid the sending of money out of the kingdom without the consent of Parliament, have both attacked the morals of the nation, and weakened the foundations of our internal peace. By innovating on those laws, which were made to protect the subject against the government, they prepare the way for innovations in those laws, which make the government sacred in the eyes of the subject. On these high grounds the Opposition have appeared to us to act, on all important occasions, through the whole of the war—at least, in all the questions relating immediately to *English* politics. They form, not only their justification, but their well-merited panegyric, if they complete the work they have begun; but their sentence of condemnation, and the bitterest satire on them, if they themselves unravel *in the dark* the web, which they had half-woven in the day-light. For now is the time that must decide whether the acts of the late and the present Ministry are to be recorded as precedents, or as warnings :—whether those who have hitherto shewn themselves the skilful and honest physicians of the state, shall degenerate into quacks, administering the "poppy and mandragora" of oblivion and unnatural reconciliation, at the moment, when the knife and the cautery alone can prevent the foam of a mad faction from being taken up into the blood, and carried into the very heart of the Constitution. The Opposition must either continue to criminate the Ministers as a pernicious faction, or plead guilty

to the charge, which these Ministers have so repeatedly urged against them, that they are themselves one. If, unhappily, they satisfy themselves with the bargaining for the permanent exclusion of one or two obnoxious individuals, and without further advantages, consider stepping into their places, as gaining a victory, it will be a victory in which

Heu! retulit praedas, non palmam, victor ab hoste.

That the present Ministry are desirous that this reconciliation should take place, we cannot doubt: for they will gain a support, which they stand in need of. But, we doubt, still less, if possible, that the faction of the Alarmists; that the Earl of Liverpool, Mr. Windham, and Lord Grenville, look on to such an event, with at least equal pleasure. For the support, which the Opposition will afford to the present Ministers, will, from various causes, be both transitory and incomplete; but the *tarnish* on their characters will be complete and permanent—and, any after Opposition which the party may wish to institute, will be regarded by the people, as little more than the snarling at a bone between dogs, who had just before been hunting in couples.— *"Fellows of mere outside and bark."*

Morning Post, 23 February 1802

[REPORTED CHANGES]

It is now known, that the negotiation between the present Ministers, and certain Members of the Opposition, is at an end. Mr. Fox's speech at the Whig Club gave it the finishing blow. We doubt not that this great statesman declared all that he himself knew; but the public would be greatly deluded, if they should infer from that speech that no negotiation ever had been on foot. It is an undeniable fact, that certain gentlemen of high character, the known friends of the Members, whose names were given in almost all the public prints, did speak openly of a Coalition, as a probable event. It is undeniable, that efforts were made to form such a coalition, and much activity and stratagem used by more than one or two men of distinguished talents and high reputation on either side. From a knowledge of these proceedings, and still more from what we observed of the general tone of public feeling, we thought it our duty (now two months ago) to warn the Opposition of the snare laid for them by the new circumstances of the times. Men are never so strongly tempted to abandon consistency of principle, as when the opposite expectations, which opposite principles had led the two hostile parties to form, are both equally disappointed. To this state of general feeling, this seeming crash and break-up of all parties, was added the incautious gratitude of certain of the Opposition to Mr. ADDINGTON, as a peace-maker; and a further bond of union seemed to be

formed by the new opposition of Lord GRENVILLE, and the high Anti-
Jacobins. It was a pardonable mistake to think him their friend, whom
they perceived to have a common enemy. We rejoice that no evil (at
least no serious or remediable evil) has arisen from the peril in which
the friends of the country were placed. But we were justified by facts as
well as by probable reasons, in the warning which we gave. Nay, we
may even appeal to the late speeches, both of Mr. SHERIDAN and Mr.
Fox, for the truth of our assertion, that there were grounds for *fearing*
a *schism* in that body of men, which by its great talents and consequent
influence on public opinion, if not by the number of its votes, has often
restrained the Ministers from acts of oppression; and though it could
not prevent powers from being incautiously delegated to them, has yet
compelled them to be cautious in the exercise of those powers—a body
of men, who strove to save the country from a ruinous war, in the first
place, and who would have afterwards procured for it an honourable
peace, if its advice had been taken while Britain was capable of making
an impression on the enemy. However, the negotiation, of whatever
kind it may have been, and in whatever causes it may have originated,
is now at an end. Mr. Fox's speech informs us indeed, that none of the
leaders of Opposition ever listened to the overtures which the Ministers
were making; while, on the other hand, the friends of the Ministers
assert, that the negotiations broke off on Mr. ADDINGTON's part. There
is one way of reconciling the apparent contradiction in these assertions;
and this way is probably the truth. We may suppose, that overtures
were made by Ministers to one or more Gentlemen of high honour and
character, and that such terms were insisted upon by them as the conditions of their acceptance, as would have rendered the coalition strictly
honourable on their part, though it would have called for such retractions from the present Ministers as they neither would make if they
were able to do, nor could make, if they were willing, retaining their
official situations.—That the parties never could coalesce with honour
every man of common sense foresaw: or if there were any one of the
persons immediately concerned who did not perceive it; this is only a
new proof how much the wishes may sophisticate the understanding.
The state of parties remains at present the same as at the resignation of
Mr. PITT. The party of Mr. WINDHAM and Lord GRENVILLE opposing
the peace with consistent principle, the old Opposition supporting it
with consistent principle, and the Ministers persevering in it in contradiction to all their former principles, and without reference to any
new distinct principle. Simply they needed it, as the means of their
power.—Nothing was more easy than to make such a peace. A general
compliance with the enemy's demands formed the whole of the recipe.
But it was necessary to their popularity, nay, even, to their existence as
a distinct party, that they should obtain a peace from the enemy; and

they may be almost said to have taken out a patent for their ministry from the FIRST CONSUL. How long this state of parties will continue will depend in a great measure on the plans of BONAPARTE—on how long he may find it wise to abstain from measures which this country cannot look to and remain quiet. Whenever his forbearance ceases, the most probable event is that Mr. PITT will once again be called to the head of affairs, and new disputes will reunite his party (we can scarcely look on Mr. ADDINGTON in any other light), and that of the high Anti-Jacobins. But grant that happier omen may soon arise! It is, however, of no small consequence that the public should thoroughly understand the character of the present Minister, lest false expectations should confer on him a false popularity, and prolong the Premiership of a man who might, no doubt, guide the vessel of the state in the regular trade-wind of a long established peace, but who has surely neither the talents, nor the experience, nor the decision of character requisite for a steersman in a sea, where a calm is only the uncertain pause of the tempest. We propose, therefore, to-morrow, to analyse both the character and the proceedings of the Minister; and to his encomiasts, who may imagine that we detract from his merits, we wish to recommend the speech of the Roman Philosopher, concerning his pupil—*Melius de Nerone sentio quam tu: cantare enim tu illum dignum putas, ego autem tacere.*

Morning Post, 22 March 1802

MR. ADDINGTON'S ADMINISTRATION

We easily forget, or forgive, or perhaps overlook, the faults and errors of men of small talent. The existence of such faults does not alarm our fears, and the detection of them does not gratify our envy. It is on this ground (for we would not willingly have recourse to the supposition of any assumed and *convenient* blindness) that we must explain a circumstance which surprises us not a little, namely, that the Administration of Mr. ADDINGTON has been pronounced hitherto unobjectionable by men who nevertheless declare aloud their hostility to the measures of his predecessors. What language Mr. ADDINGTON may have held in private, what hopes he may have encouraged, what plans he may have disclosed, we know not—neither do we pretend to determine whether he has disclosed the same views to Mr. PITT and Mr. TIERNEY, or whether, previously to closing the brazen Temple of *Janus*, he has thought fit to pay his devotions to the two-faced God. However this may be, yet private conversations must be made to weigh more than either experience or theory will justify, if they can counterbalance the whole of the Minister's public and parliamentary acts. His Administration has been declared unobjectionable by men, who yet can find no words too harsh for the measures of Mr. PITT and the faction of the GRENVILLES. Now, one of the very first acts of his Administration was the Bill of Indemnity, by which he openly identified himself with his predecessors, in all the measures which had most provoked the hostility of the friends of freedom, and made it public, that he dissented from them in that point only to which the friends of freedom were naturally the most inclined to yield their assent. But, was this the only objectionable measure?—Objectionable in the strongest sense of the phrase, it surely was; and we challenge the admirers of our history to point to any measure of Government since the Revolution, by which the spirit of our Constitution and Laws has been equally violated, or the common moral feelings more grievously insulted.—The Court Party are not so easily satisfied, it seems, as some of the old supporters of free principles appeared *inclined* to be. The Court Party seem to have taken for their maxim the words of the jay—

> There is a difference in fact
> 'Twixt a promise and an act.

They demanded *acts* from the Minister, and what they demanded he willingly gave. When Mr. ADDINGTON came into power, it was necessary that the war should be supported. For such support he could look only to his predecessors in office, the GRENVILLES, and the high Antijacobins. He seemed to have courted these by the attempt to exceed in violence all that had been most obnoxious in their administration. He continued the martial law in Ireland under circumstances more severe; he suspended the Habeas Corpus Act in England, as if from no other motive, than to shew the people of England what a trifle he deemed the suspension of the Habeas Corpus Act to be; and while he made a solemn apotheosis of all the crimes and blunders of his predecessors, by the Bill of Indemnity, he stigmatised even with a wantonness of insult the members of the Opposition, by excluding them all from the Committee of Secrecy, as unfit to be entrusted with the welfare of their country. The former Ministers, even in the very heat and tumult of the contest, had always allowed on such Committees one or two members of the Opposition, and some independent members of parliament; Mr. ADDINGTON, who had just before passed all the illegal acts of the former Ministers, into law and precedent, by composing a committee appointed to examine into the real state of Treason and Sedition in these kingdoms, entirely of placemen and fanatical partizans. These were the steps of the *accommodation ladder*, all, no doubt, pre-adjusted, before Mr. ADDINGTON was suffered to climb up into office by means of it. But when he gained the height, it was clear that he could retain it only by making a peace with France. We must, therefore, suppose, that those of the old Opposition, who have been able to see nothing objectionable hitherto in Mr. ADDINGTON's Administration, date that administration from this event; or that their gratitude to the Minister, as a Pacificator, has been so intense and intoxicating, as to have made them not only forgive, but even forget, all his preceding measures. Mr. ADDINGTON, on his part, now assailed by a division of his former friends, and blest by the same spirit of forgiving and forgetting, stretches out his arms to the Opposition, and makes dazzling overtures to men, whom a few months before he had stigmatised by a public act that, interpreted in its utmost, would go nigh to throw a suspicion on the first and fairest characters of the country, as the favourers of revolution. Their intellect, their talents, their experience, were all undoubted. And what then, but unsound principle, could be adduced, to stamp such men unfit to be entrusted with the suppression of Treason! But now the preliminaries of peace are signed—a peace, with which every one, but the GRENVILLES and BURKITES were delighted, with the *terms* of which every one, but the Ministers themselves, were disgusted or humbled!

This peace was signed and must be supported. His old political connections, the GRENVILLES, were its bitter enemies. To the Opposition Mr. ADDINGTON was obliged to look for aid. Something more however than the mere signing of preliminaries was necessary to unite in support of his general Administration, men to whose principles it had been hitherto in every other respect hostile. The unconstitutional measures and personal insults of last spring had raised a wall of separation between them and the new Minister, which he could not overleap. To effect an union, he was obliged to show a disposition to undermine, and, like PYRAMUS, to breathe his amorous wishes through it. Accordingly insinuations were made, and half promises held out, of the adoption of a system consonant with the feelings and principles of Opposition. He was to suffer the Habeas Corpus Suspension, the Treason and Sedition Acts, to expire.—The Government of Ireland was to be tempered with mildness and moderation. Our establishments were to be reduced—all selfish jobbing was to be discountenanced—and a rigid economy to be observed in the public expenditure. As Mr. ADDINGTON ran before the wishes of the GRENVILLES to obtain their support during the war, so now he promised to run before the wishes of the Opposition after the Peace. He had no principles but a love of power, no feeling but a sense of weakness. Conscious debility always endeavours to supply the want of strength by address and cunning. Mr. ADDINGTON was all things unto all men, in hopes that all men would be of one mind and temper to him.—Great plausibility and affected candour were called in to his aid, and he contrived to be at the same time on good terms with Mr. PITT and Mr. TIERNEY, while he was adored by the English Jacobins.— These appearances were flattering but they were delusive. Events have deadened the spirit of all parties, but the calm of disappointment must not be mistaken for the calm of content. Whenever the Definitive Treaty shall be signed, parties will form, and if Mr. ADDINGTON does not provide against that period, he will find the appearances that led him to suppose he was supported by both sides denoted that he was supported by neither. Had he pursued a true system of conciliation, he would not in any instance have gone the full length of either the one side or the other; but by outrunning the *unconstitutional* career of the GRENVILLES in so many instances, he has rendered it impossible for him to shew any countenance to the Opposition without exciting the disgust of the one party and the suspicion of both. It is not by alternately vibrating between Jacobins and Royalists, that BONAPARTE conciliates the affections of these parties in France, but by accommodating himself to both to a certain extent. This is acting on a solid foundation, and with a view to a permanent effect. The system of Mr. ADDINGTON is the very reverse. It is a temporising, fugacious policy, that loses all its power and effect the moment it comes to be exposed. It is a system of dissimulation, and as it has been already seen through, it must have consequently excited suspicions in both parties, however prudent they may have found it to conceal their sentiments. To some of the Members of Opposition he may hold out that he enters into their views, but dare not, by an immediate and practical avowal of them, break with Mr. PITT, lest he should be left in a minority. To Mr. PITT he may hold out that he only sooths the Opposition, with a view to public quiet, while he considers himself a mere *locum tenens*, until favourable circumstances shall arise for his return to power. These plausible pretexts, and the daily hope of the Definitive Treaty, will secure his Administration from the attack of either party pending the Negotiation. As events shall afterwards arise, he may expect to fall in with the one side or the other; and while he may congratulate himself on the certainty, under any change, of a peerage and a pension, with the office of Speaker in the House of Lords, he may cherish the hidden hope that changes will be difficult and that the mutual jealousy of contending parties will enable him to preserve his power. If he can retain the premiership, his success is complete. If he cannot, he still succeeds in the degree, as he will retire with profit, and the reputation, which a want of enemies leaves to the feeble and inoffensive in power. It is more easy to discover the chance upon which he calculates with a view to personal interest, than to reconcile his proceedings with any fixed principles of national policy, or any solid system of Government.

We have already hinted our opinions of the abilities of Mr. ADDINGTON. They are beneath mediocrity. Long used to a situation of parade and specious appearance, a daily witness of the homage paid to eloquence, he seems to have considered them the only essential qualifications. In the two former, habit has come successfully in aid of nature. No Minister can be more pompous and shewy. In his cultivation of eloquence, he has not been equally fortunate. An imposing manner, and some facility in applying common place observations constitute the extent of his oratorical attainments. In his style of speaking; nay, in his very tone and manner, as well as in his conduct, he labours to imitate Mr. PITT. He sets out with an air of openness and candour; but he makes so many reservations, so many conditions in his progress, that his proposition, which was at first laid down as positive and precise, becomes at the end equivocal and indefinite. There is difference, however, between him and his model in this particular. Mr. PITT puzzles his audience by his ingenuity, Mr. ADDINGTON by his confusion. The one renders himself unintelligible by his sophistry; the other is not understood, because that which is not clearly conceived, can never be clearly and definitely expressed. He never displays dexterity in debate, expansion or vigour of mind, a strong discriminating power, originality of thought, or richness of fancy. His intellect is too short-sighted to see beyond the point immediately before him, and hence, in a case of complexity, it is mere chance if one part of his argument does not contradict the other. He is easily thrown into confusion, and he betrays a total want of ability to rally. He cannot repair an error, or cover a retreat. Whenever he is defeated, the defeat is most decisive. There is scarcely a public occasion in which his powers have been brought into action, that does not furnish proof of these remarks. Two must be particularly in remembrance. One last Spring, when he gave up Mr. ABBOT on the Irish Martial Law Bill. The other, his late contest with Mr. ROBSON, on the subject of the bill for 19£ 10 protested at the Sick and Hurt Office, exposed still more the small wares of which his mind is composed. The ignorance which he betrayed of the practice of public offices was no impeachment of his understanding, though highly disreputable to him as a minister. But the manner in which he took up the subject disclosed the state of his intellect. He inferred national insolvency (and contended for it) from a practice that has ever existed without injury to the public credit. No sooner was he convicted of one error than he denied some other fact, till at last, beaten from every position, he was obliged to blink the question by moving the order of the day on Mr. ROBSON's motion, giving that gentleman a complete triumph over him. This affair in itself is a matter of no importance; but as a taste of Mr. ADDINGTON's abilities, it is decisive. In the city there is but one opinion.

The country is deeply interested in understanding the character and views of its chief Ministers at this moment. Whether in war or peace, we shall have to struggle with a rival nation, at present the most powerful in Europe, guided by the greatest genius in the world, who is as restless, ambitious, and artful, as he is superior in ability. We shall have to struggle also with numerous financial and commercial embarrassments. This is, perhaps, the most critical aera in our history, and will require the most skilful talents to carry us through it. That Mr. ADDINGTON is equal to the task, standing as he does, without system or principles to guide his conduct, embracing to-day what he rejected yesterday, confounded by the least difficulty, a Tory one hour, a Whig the next, changing with every new breeze; that he is fit to guide the helm no man of sense will believe. No Statesman can rely on him, and happy is it for England that the defenders of our constitutional liberties have not joined his administration. Paradoxical as it may seem, happy is it also for England, that his talents are of such a very inferior class. Had he less vanity, he would have been more reserved, and have studiously avoided those prominent situations which have so frequently exposed the extent of his powers. Had he possessed a little judgment, he would not have so frequently committed himself on points in which victory was nothing, and defeat was fatal to his fame. Had he been a dextrous debater, he might have preserved himself, even with all his deficiencies, safe and untouched in the sort of warfare in which he has hitherto been engaged, and against the sort of assailants whom he has had hitherto to encounter.

Thus we should be now upon a dangerous sea with the double disadvantage of a bad pilot, and that pilot possessed of our utmost confidence. With an implicit reliance upon his skill, we should perhaps know nothing of our danger until our ruin became inevitable. Thanks to the vanity, the precipitancy, the indiscretion of Mr. ADDINGTON, we have not these complicated disadvantages to encounter. After the decisive proofs which he has given of his weakness, proofs on which the meanest capacity can decide; the public neither has, or can have, confidence in his talents. They must, therefore look to themselves; and, whatever may be its danger, whenever the vigilance of a nation is thus aroused, it will always find the means to work its own salvation.

SELECT BIBLIOGRAPHY

MANUSCRIPT MATERIAL

A. *Notebooks*

Notebooks Nos. 1–50, British Museum, Add. MSS. 47496–47545.
Gutch Memorandum Book, British Museum, Add. MSS. 27901.
Notebooks Nos. 56, 59, 60–63, and 65, Victoria College Library, Toronto.

B. *Other Manuscript Material*

Egerton MSS. 2800 and 2801.
Add. MSS. 34046, on which *Letters from the Lake Poets*, 1895, was based.
Add. MSS. 35343–5, on which *Thomas Poole and His Friends*, 1888, 2 vols., was based.
Pinney Papers, Racedown, for a letter from Azariah Pinney to Wordsworth, 26 Nov. 1795.

C. *Marginalia*

The following are all in the British Museum. Press mark is given for each.

ANON. *Notes on the Reform Bill by a Barrister*, 1831. C.126.h.15 (3).
FITZGIBBON, J. *The Speech of . . . John Lord Baron Fitzgibbon*, delivered in the House of Peers, 13 March 1793. C.45.f.18(4).
GODWIN, W. *Thoughts Occasioned by Dr Parr's Spital Sermon*, 1801. C.45.f.18(3).
HARTLEY, D. *Observations on Man*, 3 vols., 1791. C.126.i.2.
HOOKER, R. *Works*, 1682, Ashley 5175.
MALTHUS, T. R. *An Essay on the Principles of Population*, 1803. C.44.g.2.
PARK, J. J. *Conservative Reform*: or a Letter addressed to Sir Wm. Betham, 1832. C.126.h.15(4).
PARNELL, W. *An Historical Apology for Irish Catholics*, 1807, Dublin. 9508C.25.
STEFFENS, H. *Caricaturen des Heiligsten*, 2 vols., 1819–21, C.43.b.14.
WALSH, J. *On the Present Balance of the Parties in the State*, 1832. C.126.h.15(2).
—— *Popular Opinions on Parliamentary Reform*, 1831. C.126.h.15.
WHITE, J. B. *Practical and Internal Evidence against Catholicism*, with occasional strictures on Mr. Butler's Book of the Roman Catholic Church, 1825. C.43.b.19.

PRINTED MATERIAL

Works which appear in the List of Abbreviations at the beginning of this book are not included. Place of publication is London except where otherwise stated. Press marks refer to British Museum.

A. *Coleridge's Political Works*

A Moral and Political Lecture. Delivered at Bristol, Bristol, 1795. C.71.d.2. Harvard Library copy, 19476.305.2, contains MS. notes in Coleridge's hand.

Conciones ad Populum: Or Addresses to the People, Bristol, 1795. C.58.b.31.

The Plot Discovered: Or an Address to the People Against Ministerial Treason, Bristol, 1795. C.55.b.18.

An Answer To 'A Letter to Edward Long Fox. M.D.', Bristol, 1795. Ashley 2840(1).

The Statesman's Manual: or the Bible the Best Guide to Political Skill and Foresight. A Lay Sermon, Addressed to the Higher Classes of Society, 1816. Ashley 2850 and 2851 contain marginalia.

'Blessed are ye that sow beside all Waters.' A Lay Sermon, Addressed to the Higher and Middle Classes, on the existing Distresses and Discontents, 1817. 1026.k.4.(1).

Remarks on the Objections which have been Urged Against the Principle of Sir Robert Peel's Bill, 18 April 1818. Ashley 2861, contains marginalia.

The Grounds of Sir Robert Peel's Bill Vindicated, 24 April 1818. Ashley 2862.

On the Constitution of the Church and State, according to the Idea of Each. 1st and 2nd ed. 1830.

B. *Biographical and Critical, and Selections*

AYNARD, J. *La Vie d'un poète: Coleridge*, Paris, 1907.

BEELEY, H. 'The Political Thought of Coleridge', in *Coleridge: Studies by Several Hands*, ed. E. Blunden and E. L. Griggs, 1934.

BONNARD, G. 'The Invasion of Switzerland and English Public Opinion', in *English Studies*, xxii, 1940, pp. 1–26.

CESTRE, C. *La Révolution française et les poètes anglais, 1789–1909*, Dijon, 1906.

CHAMBERS, E. K. *Samuel Taylor Coleridge. A Biographical Study*, Oxford, 1938.

COBURN, K. *Inquiring Spirit; a new presentation of Coleridge from his published and unpublished prose writings*, 1951.

COLERIDGE, E. H. *Anima Poetae from the unpublished notebooks of Samuel Taylor Coleridge*, 1895.

—— 'Fragmentary and Unpublished Life of Coleridge', in *Coleridge: Studies by Several Hands*.

COLERIDGE, H. N. *The Literary Remains of Samuel Taylor Coleridge*, 1836–9, 4 vols.

COTTLE, J. *Early Recollections, chiefly relating to the late Samuel Taylor Coleridge*, 1837, 2 vols.

—— *Reminiscences of Samuel Taylor Coleridge and Robert Southey*, 1847.

EAGLESTON, E. A. 'Wordsworth, Coleridge and the Spy', in *Coleridge; Studies by Several Hands*.

ERDMAN, D. V. 'Coleridge on George Washington, Newly Discovered Essays of 1800', *Bulletin of the New York Public Library*, vol. lxi, No. 2, pp. 81–97.

EUGENIA, Sister. 'Coleridge's Scheme of Pantisocracy and American Travel', *P.M.L.A.* Dec. 1930, pp. 1069–84.

GILLMAN, J. *The Life of Samuel Taylor Coleridge*, 1838.

GRAHAM, W. 'Politics of the Greater Romantics' in *P.M.L.A.* xxxvi, 1921, pp. 60–78.

HANSON, L. *The Life of S. T. Coleridge. The Early Years*, 1938.

HOUSE, H. *Coleridge. The Clark Lectures 1951–2*, 1953.

ISAACS, J. 'Coleridge's Critical Terminology', in *Essays and Studies*, xxi, 1935, pp. 86–104.

JOHNSON, S. F. 'Coleridge "The Watchman"; Decline and Fall', in *R.E.S.* Apr. 1953, pp. 47–48.

KENNEDY, W. F. *Humanist Versus Economist*: The Economic Thought of Samuel Taylor Coleridge, University of California Publications in Economics, vol. xvii, 1958.

MACGILLIVRAY, J. R. 'The Pantisocratic Scheme and its Immediate Background', in *Studies in English by Members of the University College of Toronto*, 1931.

MILL, J. 'Coleridge', 1840, conveniently reprinted with an introduction by F. R. Leavis in *Mill on Bentham and Coleridge*, 1950.

MUIRHEAD, J. H. *Coleridge as Philosopher*, 1930.

SANDERS, C. R. *Coleridge and the Broad Church Movement*, Duke University Press, 1942.

STUART, D. 'Anecdotes of the Poet Coleridge and his Newspaper Writings', in the *Gentleman's Magazine*, May, June, July and Aug. 1838.

TRAILL, H. D. *Coleridge*, 1884.

WATSON, L. E. *Coleridge at Highgate*, 1925.

WHALLEY, G. 'The Bristol Borrowings of Southey and Coleridge', in *The Library*, Sept. 1949, pp. 114–31.

—— 'Coleridge and Southey at Bristol', in *R.E.S.* Oct. 1950, pp. 324–40.

WHITE, R. J. *The Political Thought of Samuel Taylor Coleridge*. A Selection, 1938.

—— *Political Tracts of Wordsworth, Coleridge and Shelley*, Cambridge, 1953.

C. *Background*

I have found the following particularly useful:

ASPINALL, A. *Politics and the Press, c. 1780–1850*, 1949.

BRINTON, C. *The Political Ideas of the English Romanticists*, Oxford, 1926.

BROWN, P. A. *The French Revolution in English History*, 1918.

COBBAN, A. *Edmund Burke and the Revolt against the Eighteenth Century*. A Study of the Political and Social Thinking of Wordsworth, Coleridge, and Southey. 1929.

HINDLE, W. *The Morning Post, 1772–1837*, 1937.

ROSE, J. H. *William Pitt and National Revival*, 1911.

—— *William Pitt and the Great War, 1791–1806*, 1911.

WEARMOUTH, R. F. *Methodism and the Common People of the Eighteenth Century*, 1945.

WICKWAR, W. H. *The Struggle for the Freedom of the Press, 1819–1832*, 1928.

PRINTED IN GREAT BRITAIN
AT THE UNIVERSITY PRESS, OXFORD
BY VIVIAN RIDLER
PRINTER TO THE UNIVERSITY